Crisis of Fear

Secession in South Carolina

Steven A. Channing

SIMON AND SCHUSTER

NEW YORK

To my parents

Preface

Few events in American history have excited as much debate, or have been the subject of as much skilled examination as the causes of the Civil War. Explanations, both studied and polemical, accompanied the roar of the first cannon balls. The general tone and tendency of this historiography has been to look beyond the apparent issue of slavery in a search for more "fundamental" political, economic, social or intellectual causes. My own desire to take on a problem which had been written about so often and so well arose out of a dissatisfaction with the multiplication of equally abstract and plausible interpretations. Moreover, the premise of many of these explanations seemed to be to repudiate the beliefs articulated by actual participants in favor of theories which placed those tragic figures in the grip of great invisible social forces.

The present study originated in manuscript research into the race attitudes and anxieties of South Carolina whites in the period 1836 to 1866. It soon became clear that despite the mass of historical literature dealing with the secession of the Southern states, the relationship between the inescapable problem of race relations and the political decision of secession seemed to have been either ignored or inadequately demonstrated. Merely to say that the lower South withdrew from the Union to defend slavery explains little. Why slavery was believed to be threatened, why a different structure of race relations than enslavement of the blacks was inconceivable to most whites, what the fears and passions were which were mighty enough to drive a people to revolution—these underlying questions have not received sufficient attention from historians. Using South Carolina as a model, it is hoped that this book will help to begin answering these questions.

I am grateful to have had the opportunity of completing the initial research and writing of this study as a doctoral dissertation at the University of North Carolina at Chapel Hill. Of the many who helped me there my thanks go above all to Joel Williamson, who tolerated my ramblings and remained always a gentle, kind, and persuasive director of the research project; I am fortunate to call him friend. I am grateful to Fletcher M. Green, who contributed perhaps more than he realized to my personal confidence and my interest in Southern history; and to Isaac Copeland, Director of the Southern Historical Collection, who very kindly provided a valuable reading of the manuscript. A friend and inspiring teacher also is Hans L. Trefousse of Brooklyn College, who first revealed to me the joys and pains of historical writing. Here in Lexington it has been my good fortune to have had the counsel of Matthew Hodgson. Finally, my everlasting gratitude goes to Thomas P. Govan, a great teacher and critic, for helping me at the beginning and the end of a long apprenticeship.

The primary sources for this study are the manuscript collections of private correspondence surviving from the antebellum years. The profession is boundlessly indebted to the historians and archivists who have patiently built up these collections over the past generation. Without their work this reexamination of a much studied subject would have been impossible. I am especially grateful to Dr. Copeland, Dr. Carolyn A. Wallace and Miss Anna Brooke Allan of the Southern Historical Collection of the University of North Carolina Library; Dr. Mattie Russell of the Manuscripts Division, Duke University Library; Mr. E. L. Inabinett and Mrs. Clara Mae Jacobs of the South Caroliniana Library, the

University of South Carolina; and Mrs. Granville T. Pryor of the South Carolina Historical Society. Although space does not permit a complete listing here, I also wish to extend my sense of appreciation and admiration to the able directors and staffs of the other archives and libraries which provided material used in this book.

It gives me pleasure to acknowledge the financial assistance received in the course of writing and revising the manuscript. From the University of North Carolina at Chapel Hill, a Waddell Fellowship for dissertation research. From the University of Kentucky, a summer research fellowship, and funds for travel and typing. And from the Society of American Historians, the Allan Nevins Prize. Although the last was not intended as direct assistance for research it provided invaluable financial and emotional aid in the last months of revision. For typing assistance I am indebted to Mrs. Harriet Gordon and Mrs. Andrea Colten. In any discussion of financial and emotional support there is, first and last, my dear wife Rhoda.

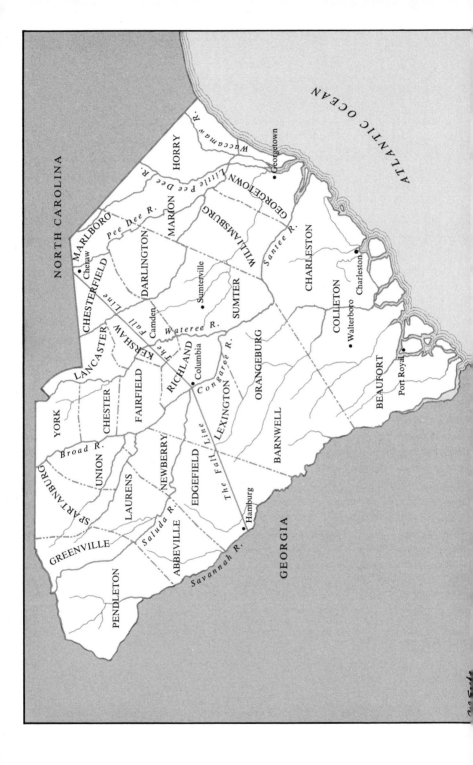

Contents

List of Abbreviations

Ala.Arc   Alabama State Department of Archives and History
DU   Duke University Library, Manuscripts Division
LC   Library of Congress, Manuscripts Division
NYHS   New York Historical Society
NCArc   North Carolina Department of Archives and History
PaHS   The Historical Society of Pennsylvania
SCArc   South Carolina Department of Archives and History
SCHS   South Carolina Historical Society
USC   South Caroliniana Library, the University of South Carolina
SHC   Southern Historical Collection, the University of North Carolina at Chapel Hill.
UChic   The University of Chicago Library, Manuscripts Division
VaHS   The Historical Society of Virginia

The danger of a conflict between the white and the black inhabitants of the Southern states of the Union (a danger which, however remote it may be, is inevitable) perpetually haunts the imagination of the Americans, like a painful dream. The inhabitants of the North make it a common topic of conversation, although directly they have nothing to fear from it . . . . In the Southern states the subject is not discussed; the planter does not allude to the future in conversing with his friends; he seeks to conceal them from himself. But there is something more alarming in the tacit forebodings of the South than in the clamorous fears of the North.

—ALEXIS DE TOCQUEVILLE, 1835

PART ONE

CHAPTER ONE

The Fear

1860

The northbound express left Charleston on Wednesday, January 11, and did not reach Richmond until six o'clock Thursday night. The air grew crisp as the cars rattled up the flat coast into hill country, grayish green under the midwinter sun. Christopher Memminger sat pale and stiff in his seat, his daughter beside him. He labored over his speech and occasionally gazed out at the passing farms and villages; by mid-morning the countryside moving past his window had become like the politics of his state, ever changing, yet always the same. The newspapers said he was closing an historic circle. Benjamin Watkins Leigh had come from Virginia a generation before to help calm the Nullification spirit, and now Memminger was paying the debt. But he knew better. It was South Carolina for action then and now. Memminger also knew that some had objected to sending him on this mission. He had battled against the Negro seamen exclusion acts. He had opposed the furious cries for the expulsion of free Negroes and Northern schoolteachers. Worse, he had resisted separate state secession only seven years before. Still, his fairminded devotion to the state had carried him to a position of leadership in the state House of Representatives. Today he was carrying the hopes and fears of South Carolina to the leaders of Virginia.

The sun had long since set when his train rolled into Union Station. There would be brass bands and candle-lit processions, speeches, rallies and the splendor of a Richmond ball during Memminger's stay in the handsome old capital. But the soft words of his hosts would end when he rose before a hushed Assembly to plead for concerted action against the North. South Carolinians had seen this moment coming for two generations. They had seen the shape of the sectional crisis even before 1800, when the Northern states abandoned slavery and the first efforts were made to encourage Federal proscriptions against the increasingly peculiar institution of the South. Now the vision had become reality. Security for slavery in the Union was gone, "and either there must be new terms established or a Southern Confederacy is our only hope of safety."[1] These were Memminger's words to Virginia, Memminger, once the calm, once the realistic Unionist. His troubled journey was over, and a nation's was only beginning.

— 1 —

The raid itself had been doomed from the start. Three months before Memminger began his ride, John Brown had entered northern Virginia with a handful of followers. Within hours he had captured the Federal arsenal at Harpers Ferry and offered uncertain sanctuary to the slaves surrounding the town. But hours passed and no slaves came. Two days later, by the morning of October 18, 1859, Brown lay captured and bleeding. His dream of igniting a slave insurrection was crushed, but he had set in motion a chain of events which was to lead to that precious goal he had pursued with such frenzy, the destruction of slavery.

At once, exaggerated reports of the raid flashed across the nation. The first excited dispatches from Baltimore claimed that Harpers Ferry had been seized by six to eight hundred "insurgents." South Carolina newspapers were immediately glutted with stories from Virginia to feed the obvious hunger for details. They told of clashes in the frozen woods around the village, of

[1] C. G. Memminger to W. P. Miles, December 27, 1859, William Porcher Miles Papers, SHC.

18

THE FEAR

the treachery of assailants black and white, and of the wonderful
loyalty of the slaves. There were reams of declamatory articles
about Brown and his bloody exploits in Kansas; and there were
detailed lists of weapons taken from the little group.[2] The most
terrible of these weapons, more for the fearful image they evoked
than for their potential utility, was a large number of cast-iron
pikes. Many of these pikes were taken by Virginia secessionist Edmund Ruffin, who enthusiastically began dispatching them
throughout the Southern states with the label "*Sample of the fa-
vors designed for us by our Northern brethren.*" One of the pikes
was sent to South Carolina Governor William Gist, and another
to the editor of the Charleston *Courier,* and both were prominently displayed.[3] Letters to John Brown from Frederick Douglass and Gerrit Smith were printed in the Charleston newspapers,
and these only confirmed the immediate assumption that the attack was in fact the latest and most awful scheme of the abolitionists. South Carolina slaveholders read a widely quoted letter
from the antislavery leader Smith which denied that appeals to
morality and Holy Writ would ever destroy slavery. And Carolinians read the transcript of an interview held with Brown just
after his capture. "I don't think the people of the South will ever
consider the subject of slavery in its true light," Brown had
calmly declared, "till some other argument is resorted to than
moral suasion." Caught up in their own frustrations, Northern
abolitionists seemed ready to sanction violence.[4]

At first it was widely feared that the raid at Harpers Ferry was
only the opening stroke in some grand abolitionist plot. These

[2] Charleston *Daily Courier* and Charleston *Mercury,* October 18, 1859.
[3] Edmund Ruffin MS Diary, LC, November 9 and 10, and December 16,
1859; *Courier,* October 18, 1859.
[4] Gerrit Smith's letter was printed in the New York *Herald,* October 18,
1859, and John Brown's interview after his capture was printed in *ibid.,*
October 21, 1859; both items were soon copied by the South Carolina
newspapers examined. The raid was clearly identified with Northern "fanaticism" on slavery. See, for example, Floride Calhoun to Ann F. Clemson,
November 13, 1859, Thomas Green Clemson Papers, Clemson University Library. The support given by leading abolitionists to the attack on Harpers
Ferry is discussed by C. Vann Woodward, "John Brown's Private War," in
The Burden of Southern History (New York, 1960), pp. 41–68.

anxieties gained substance when newspapers began printing descriptions of John Brown's personal maps of the Southern states. Like others, the map of South Carolina contained numerous strange crosses, indicating, as the dispatch darkly suggested, "the points of attack and the course of the insurrectionary movement." With census figures written on the map, the people of South Carolina appeared to be convinced that the abolitionists had planned attacks upon those areas where the slave population exceeded the white (most of the counties of the state).[5] Given this imagined scope, it was not surprising to see radicals North and South seize upon the raid to confirm their opposite persuasions. Carolinians read of antislavery meetings in New York City where white and black mingled to hear Nat Turner and John Brown praised, while in Charleston the organ of the foremost Southern nationalist, Robert Barnwell Rhett, was drawing frightening parallels to that same massacre in Southhampton County nearly thirty years before. The Charleston *Mercury* went to the length of printing excerpts from the Newport (Virginia) *Herald* of 1831 which described "Old Nat's" attack in gory detail. Those who would manipulate the tender chords of public sentiment had been given the perfect issue.[6]

But there was no need for artificial stimulation of the public mind. The spasm of fear which swept across South Carolina in the days and weeks after Harpers Ferry was not willfully created by extremists. With unconscious insight John Brown had struck at the deepest and most intimate anxieties of the white South. The fear and rage he had aroused were at the heart of the secession movement.

And yet it was part of the constant cycle of realism and self-deception that this truth was alternately admitted and denied.

---

[5] *Courier*, October 24, 1859, quoting the Baltimore *Exchange*. Descriptions of the map taken from Brown appeared in most of the South Carolina newspapers consulted. Months later, Baptist minister Iveson Brookes advised the editor of the New York *Chronicle* that Brown's map showing "numerous localities where there exists great disproportion in the population of the whites & blacks" must have been obtained by abolitionist "emissaries" traveling through the South. Iveson Brookes to "Brother Church," March 7, 1860, Iveson L. Brookes Papers, USC. See also Hermann Von Holst, *John Brown*, edited by Frank Preston Stearns (Boston, 1889), p. 125.
[6] *Courier*, November 1, 1859; *Mercury*, October 25, 1859.

Carolinians had lived with their slave problem for so long that some had grown insensitive, and denied that Brown's abortive assault held any special warning. It had always been this way. The black insurrection on Santo Domingo in the 1790's had at once aroused the deepest fears, while cementing the social commitment to retain slavery. During those years from 1803 to 1807, when the state opened its shores to the foreign slave trade in the first flush of the cotton boom, there were those who apprehensively called for an end to the influx of fresh "barbarians"; the trade remained open, but care was taken to exclude those recalcitrant Negroes from the West Indies. When the town of Camden was excited by a slave insurrection conspiracy trial in 1816, some residents swore they would leave a "country that we cannot go to bed in safety." But few appeared to heed their own warning. Beginning with the immensely frightening Denmark Vesey insurrection incident in 1822 the next decade saw slave unrest in South Carolina reach a violent peak, and in 1831 Nat Turner himself apparently inspired a planned uprising by the slaves of Union District. Yet the reaction of the state was to strengthen the bonds of slavery and the penalties for insubordination on the one hand, while elaborating the public lie of slave contentment on the other. Incidents of slave unrest had become so common in the state by the 1830's that James Henry Hammond, a future governor and senator, could naturally use the image of a community aroused by fear of insurrection as a way to exemplify a state in turmoil. "The Government [of France]," he wrote while on a trip to Europe, "is constantly in such a state of alarm as when our negroes are supposed to be rising—Every day some persons are arrested." Still men came forward to deny that the blacks were capable of conspiring, and that there was any fear of such misbehavior.[7]

[7] "Recommendations to the Legislature," April 1805, Kershaw County Grand Jury MS Papers, USC; R[achel] Blanding to Miss Hannah Lewis, July 4 and 25, 1816, William Blanding Papers, USC; Rossanah P. Rogers to "Dear Brothers," October 29, 1831, William W. Renwick Papers, DU; James H. Hammond to Francis W. Pickens, September 6, 1836, James H. Hammond Papers, DU. For an excellent discussion of the racial upheavals of the 1820's, see William W. Freehling, *Prelude to Civil War: The Nullification Controversy in South Carolina, 1816-1836* (New York, 1966), pp. 49–86.

With the success of efforts to strengthen the police control of slaves and to create a rigid public orthodoxy on the "great question," attempted insurrections and rumors of slave plots declined in the generation before secession. But the people of South Carolina were not without constant reminders that they lived in an enemy camp. Cases of arson linked to disaffected slaves were common references in private correspondence and newspapers. More striking was the constant recurrence of murderous attacks on overseers and masters by supposedly contented bondsmen; and these blacks were often dealt with in summary fashion. In 1824, Amos Kendall, then an editor in Kentucky, reported the murder of an overseer on a plantation outside of Cheraw, in northern Chesterfield District (County), South Carolina. "The negro was immediately taken, condemned, hanged, and his head cut off, his body burnt, and his head stuck up on a pole and carried about as a terror to other slaves!"[8] Such fearful examples continued unabated, and it was unnecessary for the slaves to commit any overt act of violence to inspire fear. With the population of many tidewater parishes (subdivisions of counties in the low country) reaching eighty or ninety percent slave, the mere physical presence of these familiar, and yet strangely frightening people was itself a source of anxiety.[9] Still men came forward to criticize the reaction of their fellow Carolinians to John Brown's attack, because it falsely suggested that South Carolina whites were "really afraid."[10] To the end of the Civil War, public and private correspondence contained heated denials of insecurity

[8] (Frankfort) *Argus of Western America*, June 20, 1824.
[9] Typical references to the fear of arson appear in M. C. M. Hammond to James H. Hammond, June 14, 1845, James H. Hammond Papers, USC; John Edwin Fripp MS Plantation Diary, SHC, May 26, 1858. References to the fear of slave murder and insurrection may be seen in William Elliott to Emily Elliott, February 3, 1859, Elliott-Gonzales Papers, SHC; Joseph R. Miller to "Father," August 10, 1838, John Fox Papers, DU; James Louis Petigru to Hugh Swinton Legaré, January 9, 1839, James Louis Petigru Papers, USC; Wade Hampton to Richard Singleton, August 14, 1842, Richard Singleton Papers, DU; David Thomson to "Dear Cousin," August 29, 1854, David Thomson Papers, USC; Mary Bates to Mrs. Charles Dana, Jr., January 8, 1839, Mary Bates Papers, USC; William P. Hill MS Diary, SHC, April 9, 1847.
[10] [Frederick Adolphus Porcher], "Matters and Things in General," *Russell's Magazine*, VI (February 1860), 443.

and expressions of confidence in the fidelity of the slaves. Refusing to see, and being unable to see, how often reality belied this confidence was only one of the contradictions inherent in the race thought of Southern whites.

Thus, when John Brown called out to the slaves to join him in a fight for their freedom, he evoked as well the anxiety which permeated the attitude of whites toward the Negro. The niece of James Louis Petigru spoke for many Carolinians when she wrote her husband about the raid. From "Badwell," her plantation home in Abbeville, she asked whether he had seen a description of Brown's terrible maps. She noted that Abbeville itself was marked, and all those other places across the state where the slaves were to rise. What a mournful prospect. "From your silence I suppose . . . you thought I would be frightened nearly out of my life. I only feel, God have mercy on us. Such revelations make one wonder how insecure is our situation & fear for the Future." To be sure, life went on in South Carolina after October 1859. Ships sailed out from Charleston with their rich cargoes of cotton and rice, and the endless round of sowing and harvesting turned its slow cycle from hilly farms to lush plantations. But the atmosphere was different. John Brown had plunged a knife deep into the psyche of Southern whites, and life would never be quite the same again.[11]

— 2 —

Even as a truer picture of events at Harpers Ferry emerged, Carolina newspapers began to record arrests all over the South of men believed to be agents of Brown. Any strange event or character having the remotest connection with Virginia took on a more ominous look in the unbalanced accounts of Southern newspapers. A man arrested in North Carolina who confessed to a

[11] Jane Caroline Pettigrew to Charles Pettigrew, October 30, 1859, Pettigrew Family Papers, SHC. The psychological impact of the raid cannot be overstated. One depressed soul, Dr. Henry Bacot, was literally deranged by the excitement. "He imagined that some huge conspiracy was about being organized for the destruction of the Southern States of the Union." Draft of letter by Dr. Henry W. DeSaussure, June 20, 1860, Bacot-Huger Papers, SCHS.

killing in Virginia was at once supposed to be "connected in some way with the Harpers Ferry affair." Under the vivid heading "Kansas Work at the South," the Savannah *Republican* interpreted a series of destructive fires in Talbot County, Georgia, as proof that detachments of John Brown's mythical army had passed through. For evidence they pointed to the "X" scrawled across Talbot on the captured map of Georgia. From Montgomery, Alabama, came the disconcerting sound of voices demanding the lynching of an "unsound" stranger allegedly caught bearing a letter from "Old Ossawattamie" himself. And from Tennessee, South Carolinians read the tale of a free Negro barber chased through the streets of Knoxville by a mob chanting *"Fred. Douglass is in town . . . . Just run down the hill! Catch him! catch him! Shoot him! shoot him!"*[12]

South Carolina, which had long exemplified all the precipitate passion in Southern behavior, was not exempt from this latest witch hunt. On October 25 Richard Yeadon, editor of the staid Charleston *Daily Courier,* led off the outcry with dire warnings of unnamed "emissaries" already at the devil's work in those communities marked on the now infamous map of the state. As will be seen, it is as difficult now as it likely was for contemporaries to judge critically how real the abolitionist threat was to control of the slaves. But as the news of the assault on Virginia seeped into the rural districts, the public voice, previously muddled by debates over tangential issues, grew firmer, clearer, and more strident. Whatever the actual extent of the abolitionist presence in the slaveholding South, it seemed clear to South Carolinians that their commitment to control of the Negro was again being tested, this time by open violence. Their reply was a predictable popular revulsion, coupled with an unprecedented mass vigilance movement aimed at utterly destroying these serpents and their poison of disaffection.[13]

[12] *Courier,* November 14, 1859, quoting the Columbia *Guardian; ibid.,* November 15, 1859, quoting the Savannah *Republican; ibid.,* December 2, 1859, quoting the Montgomery *Mail; ibid.,* November 21, 1859, quoting the Chattanooga *Advertiser.*

[13] *Courier,* October 25, 1859. See also the Spartanburg *Spartan,* November 10, 1859, quoting the (Georgetown) *Pee Dee Times.* The average size of farms in South Carolina was the largest in the nation, and the isolation of

Such occasions had been marked in the past by the eruption of organized vigilance activity. In 1835 planter Robert Gage, maddened by the rhetoric of the abolitionists, swore that the only way slavery could be made secure was "to have meetings to form committees of vigilance in every quarter—to visit with the strong arm of the law & if it must be with Lynches law every man who meddles with our private relations." Fourteen years later, with the state again embroiled in protest against the North, James E. Henry, a Spartanburg farmer gave similar warning. "Incendiaries," he reported, were being arrested and examined in his upcountry village. "Examples are thought necessary," and he did not doubt that "the first clear case that arises will furnish one for summary execution." Henry was not interested in whether a suspected "incendiary" could be proved guilty legally; but he was certain of one thing—no abolitionist would leave South Carolina "without carrying with him its sovereign *marks* of displeasure." The resort to violence and intimidation by frightened men was not peculiar to the South. But there was a unique quality in the evolution of a pattern of response to assaults against slavery, a ritual understood by every South Carolinian. These men and women had never become inured to this challenge because it struck at their most "intimate relations," their deepest fears. Still, having lived with an impending crisis for two generations and more, they had evolved a traditional, structured way of dealing with the verbal, and now physical, antislavery attacks. Self-constituted vigilance committees were an accustomed agency of local race control in the antebellum South involving the great mass of the white population, not a contrivance of radical activists. Their widespread emergence across South Carolina marked the first step in this, the penultimate secession crisis.[14]

With newspapers of every political complexion calling the

families, which was a common feature of agricultural regions, was more intense. See Tommy W. Rogers, "The Great Population Exodus from South Carolina, 1850–1860," *South Carolina Historical Magazine*, LXXVIII (January 1968), 14–21.

[14] Robert Gage to James Gage, August 31, 1835, James M. Gage Papers, SHC; James E. Henry to Samuel Finley Patterson, August 8, 1849, Samuel Finley Patterson Papers, DU. John Hope Franklin examines aspects of Southern aggressiveness in *The Militant South* (Cambridge, Mass., 1956).

white population to arms, the flood tide of vigilance activity broke in the final months of 1859 and did not recede again. From town to town there were differences in the manner by which committees of safety were formed, but most were established at public meetings called by prominent men in the district. The impulse to create these extralegal groups was neither confined to those areas of traditional political radicalism and high slave density, the low country, nor to the slaveholding class. Active vigilance committees leaped to the defense of whites in every parish and district in the state.[15] Disagreement as to means would continue to divide whites, but the base line of race fear stretched unbroken across the state, embracing patrician planter and yeoman farmer in an unyielding agreement upon the necessity for the rigid control of the blacks. To be sure, South Carolina was not free of the class and sectional antagonisms that divided other regions. Polarized to some extent between parish and piedmont, such conflict between the gentry and lower classes of whites over political representation and power, and economic policy had long presented an obstacle to the achievement of complete political unity. But below these real disagreements lay the profound and inescapable fact of massive African slavery, and a dread of the potential for mutual disaster arising out of that presence. Politicians would ignore it, openly attempt to rise above it, or try to tap it for their own advantage, but in the end fear of the Negro—physical dread, and fear of the consequences of emancipation—would control the course of the state.[16]

The ways in which the vigilance committees operated often depended on their location. Rural districts already had an instrument for the regulation of Negro affairs in slaveholding commu-

[15] *Courier,* October 29, 1859, quoting the Wilmington *Journal; ibid.,* quoting the (Georgetown) *Pee Dee Times; ibid.,* November 21, 1859, quoting the Savannah *Express; ibid.,* December 30, 1859, quoting the (Pickens) *Keowee Courier;* Spartanburg *Spartan,* November 24, 1859.

[16] Census returns show a decided out migration of poorer whites in the period 1850–1860. An historian who has noted this also reports that the size of plantations was growing progressively larger in the middle and up-country districts, in an east to west pattern. These demographic and agricultural statistics suggest an increasing agreement on economic policy was in the offing, as the state became more homogeneous in economic and social structure. See Rogers, "Great Population Exodus."

nities, the patrol. Based upon compulsory membership in the state militia, the patrol was manned by units of the local militia company. These units, divided by beat, rode through the country-side, arresting and punishing slaves caught without passes, in-specting slave quarters for weapons, and barring assemblies of Negroes. Originating in provincial Carolina statutes of 1686 and 1690, which made every white man legally responsible for good order around the plantations, the patrol was the institutionaliza-tion of the white community's fear of Negro misbehavior. In quieter times implementation of patrol surveillance weakened; men became inattentive and sought paid substitutes. In periods of crisis this deterioration was reversed.[17] In the aftermath of Harpers Ferry rural vigilance committees usually moved either to ensure that the patrol laws were carried out, or to become ad-ditional patrols themselves, outside the framework of the militia. Committees of vigilantes were regarded as more flexible than pa-trols formally instituted by statute law. The traditional patrol was concerned with the subordination of Negroes. Vigilance commit-tees looked beyond this to the activities and beliefs of fellow whites. When a vigilance patrol broke up a nest of whites secretly trading with slaves in coastal Georgetown, there was some grum-bling about this use of their authority. A local editor promptly dis-missed such opposition as a "puerile and distempered sentiment which confounds a prudential and necessary vigilance with higher-law doings." The scoundrels were probably indoctrinating the Negroes with the lies of abolitionism while pocketing their illicit gains, and for the *Pee Dee Times* this was enough to justify any arbitrary action.[18]

A meeting at Gillisonville, in the heart of coastal Beaufort dis-trict was an early and typical response to the Harpers Ferry raid. On October 31 the people of the township, men and women, masters and overseers, merchants and artisans, gathered together

[17] See "An Act to reduce all Acts and Clauses of Acts, in relation to the Patrol of this State, into one Act, and to alter and amend the same," printed in *The Militia and Patrol Laws of South Carolina, December, 1841. Pub-lished by order of the General Assembly* (Columbia, 1842), pp. 39–42.
[18] *Courier*, December 23, 1859, quoting from the (Georgetown) *Pee Dee Times*.

to hear their leaders rage at the abolitionist challenge. This very community had been marked on John Brown's frightening map. In a grim chorus, five new vigilance committees were created to better enforce the patrol laws, and their ranks were quickly filled. This atmosphere of anxiety and determination was soon being recreated in virtually every community of the state. Sometimes the town council was ordered to examine or actually expel strangers whose real purpose, as the people of Sumterville said, "may be to act as spies and abolition emissaries." In smaller rural villages, like Blackville in Barnwell district, groups of men were simply named at meetings in the public square to test the "soundness" of itinerants. Occasionally a vigilance committee was created in the wake of excitement over suspected abolitionist activity. Great feeling was stirred up in Abbeville when one James Woods was arrested and jailed with his wife and child, "under positive proof of tampering with slaves." A mob sought to remove Woods from the city jail, but calmer heads prevailed and resolutions were accepted acknowledging that existing laws were adequate to handle the case; at the same time a vigilance committee was set up to deal with any future agitator who might try to disrupt the natural docility of the slaves.[19]

With both the state legislature and the national Congress in session, and the trials and executions of John Brown and his followers going on in Virginia, public sentiment in South Carolina remained disturbed. Committees of public safety continued to form throughout the state in December and into January 1860. Resolutions drawn up at a meeting on January 3, at Black Oak, St. John's Parish, Berkeley District, suggest how strong and deep ran the current of apprehension. Some of the most influential families in the state made their plantation homes in this rich district, which lay along the Cooper River north of Charleston. Noted botanist Henry William Ravenel attended the meeting and recorded the event in his journal. Ravenel observed that the state

[19] *Courier*, December 3, 1859; *ibid.*, November 3, 1859; *ibid.*, November 23, 1859, quoting the Sumter *Watchman; ibid.*, November 28, 1859, quoting the Barnwell *Sentinel; ibid.*, quoting the Columbia *Guardian; ibid.*, November 24, 1859, quoting the Orangeburg *Southron;* Edgefield *Advertiser*, December 7, 1859. No further evidence was found to indicate whether Woods was guilty or innocent, or what disposition was made of his case.

had been thrown into an uproar by Brown's insane attempt to incite insurrection among the slaves of northern Virginia. The sympathy of Northerners for Brown must be perfectly evident to all Southerners; and it seemed equally clear to Ravenel that secession was "the only means of safety to our institutions." For the present, there was "a general feeling of vigilance against all Northern men & especially itinera[n]ts. Associations have been formed for the purpose, & for cutting off as much as possible all commercial intercourse with the North."[20]

Ravenel's diary taciturnly recorded the response of his own community. The people of Black Oak had come together to counsel. They were determined to unveil Northern abolitionists disguised as ministers, teachers, and salesmen, and to thwart their attempts to plant the seeds of insubordination and rebellion among the slaves. And these conservative men insisted that insurrectionary agents were there: "We must not shrink from the imputation of being suspicious; we have been made so." Thus a vigilance committee system was established, but not without a hard look at the conspicuous pitfalls of vigilance justice. Committees of five were appointed in each beat[21] to enforce police regulations, and to draft new ones where necessary. To resist the temptations of overzealous action which inevitably arose in a nervous and angry community, the members swore to take action only as a group, and even then only under the sanction of majority voting. With this proviso each Black Oak vigilante pledged mutual financial support should legal action result from any proceeding of the association. They were unwilling to forgo the advantages such extralegal devices brought to the purging of dangerous men and ideas from their society, but they could not help worrying about social responsibility and damage suits.[22]

The normal uneasiness of slaveholding communities was turned to a higher pitch, and it did not take much to trigger assaults against suspected abolitionists anywhere. But it was in the towns

[20] Henry William Ravenel MS Journal, USC, December 31, 1859, and January 3, 1860.
[21] The beat was the geographic area for which the patrol was responsible, and early became the local governmental unit.
[22] Resolutions of the Black Oak meeting were reported in the *Mercury*, January 20, 1860; see also Isaac DuBose Porcher MS Diary, in the Stoney-Porcher Papers, SHC, January 3, 1860.

and villages that vigilance committees seemed to act most dramatically. The vigilantes of Orangeburg seized fellow Carolinians from adjoining districts, expelled visitors merely because they were strangers, and arrested unknown men for such crimes as "being in a negro house conversing with negros [sic]."[23] In Yorkville, sealed letters were purloined and opened in the frantic search for damning evidence. A friend of Senator James Hammond worriedly wrote of the fear and excitement that had convulsed nearby Savannah following a rampage by the new vigilance committee, and he cried "Where will all this end!"[24] The potential for violence implicit in the activities of these committees was well revealed in an incident which took place in Columbia. An Irish stonecutter at the new state capitol building was suddenly ordered to leave after allegedly using "seditious language" concerning slavery. Fearing for his life, the man, James Powers, left at once; but the self-constituted protectors of the city were not satisfied. Nine miles below Columbia he was seized by vigilantes, brought back to town, and put in jail. That Saturday, December 17, Powers was removed from jail (by whose authority it was unclear), marched into the city square, and before a throng of spectators, was given thirty-nine lashes by two Negro "operators," coated with tar and feathers, and shipped out of town on the evening train for Charleston. After being confined in jail there for several days, Powers was at last shipped to New York, thereby removing this alleged threat to slavery.[25] The atmosphere in the state capital had apparently not cleared after a month. Leaving his former home, one-time senator William Campbell Preston exclaimed that the town had "become distasteful to me by its being a focus of slave traders, disunionists and lynching societies which possess it entirely."[26]

[23] *Courier,* November 24, 1859; *ibid.,* December 15, 1859, quoting the Orangeburg *Southron;* Edgefield *Advertiser,* December 14, 1859.
[24] *Courier,* December 3, 1859, quoting the Yorkville *Enquirer;* W. Duncan to J. H. Hammond, December 2, 1859, James H. Hammond Papers, LC.
[25] *Courier,* December 19, 1859; New York *Herald,* January 4, 1860; James Sanders Guignard to his son James Guignard, III, December 17, 1859, in Arney R. Childs, ed., *Planters and Business Men. The Guignard Family of South Carolina, 1795–1930* (Columbia, 1957), p. 88.
[26] William Campbell Preston to Waddy Thompson, January 27, 1860, William Campbell Preston Papers, USC. See also the *Courier,* December 22, 1859, quoting the Marion *Star; Mercury,* December 7, 1859.

– 3 –

In Charleston itself, the movement to form a vigilance committee precipitated a debate over necessity and technique that dramatized the dilemma of freedom of thought and speech in the slave states. For a time the very leader of South Carolina disunionists, Robert Barnwell Rhett, found himself in opposition to the establishment of these vigilance societies, and even after he reluctantly reversed his stand, Rhett remained a spokesman of caution. Nevertheless, with committees being formed throughout the state in the closing days of November, Charleston, for almost two centuries the focal point of Carolina leadership, would not remain silent.

On November 23, in an editorial entitled "Measures of Securing Southern Safety," Rhett discussed the renewed debate over two of the allegedly gravest threats to that security, illicit trading with slaves, and the presence within the South of disguised abolitionists. While admitting that these evils were present, Rhett was confident that existing laws could eliminate the problem of trading. As for abolitionists, Rhett eagerly politicized the issue by denying the possibility of any remedy "in the false and humiliating position in the Union as it now is." He pointed out that since Americans, North and South, lived under the same national government, free interstate travel could never be effectively controlled. But Rhett's analysis fell short. The hypertense desire for added precautions in Charleston would not be put off. An aggressive letter signed "Slaveowner" on the very same page of the *Mercury* demanded vigilance action for Charleston, and spelled out the reasons. A vigilance association could protect the security of the city by "marking" all suspicious persons "so as to make a speedy and proper disposal of them." All that was needed, he concluded, was concerted action by each and every Southern community. "Defence of home is a matter that takes precedence of every other consideration and is antecedent in men's minds to the formality and technicality of law."[27]

[27] *Mercury*, November 23, 1859. The Charleston *Mercury*, edited by Rhett's son Robert Barnwell, Jr., was for many years his organ. It is well to note that

In the days that followed, the establishment of vigilance committees in South Carolina ceased to be a sporadic local phenomenon. Coupled with other aspects of the reaction to Brown's raid, it became a politically significant movement, sparked by the assault at Harpers Ferry, generated by deep personal and community race fears, and growing rather than abating in intensity. This was the most important expression of popular feeling in the state since the secession crisis that had opened the decade. Rhett surely observed these things. As a political man anxious to avoid being left behind by a movement he had helped to create, he recognized the obvious value of tapping this powerful current for his own radical ends. Along with every white man and woman of South Carolina he fully shared a sense of the need for vigorous enforcement of the Negro laws, and he saw repeated demonstrations of the broad uses to which vigilance committees could put their authority. But as a genuine, if self-conscious, sentinel of liberty, he was also compelled to stand witness to the often arbitrary abuse of that authority.

Rhett was visibly moved by a demonstration of the dangers inherent in vigilance justice which occurred at this time. On November 22 a meeting was held near Kingstree, in Williamsburg District, to expel two Northern school teachers. As the story unraveled in lengthy, embittered letters printed in the Charleston newspapers, it not only became clear that there had been no concrete evidence to prove that these men harbored abolitionist sentiments, but also that personal and religious controversies which antedated the Harpers Ferry attack had already created antagonism in the community towards the two. The editor of the Kingstree *Star*, a principal instigator of the expulsion, admitted that nothing certain was known of their alleged hostility to slavery beyond the sole belief that they were Northerners, *"and therefore necessarily imbued with doctrines hostile to our institutions."* The progress of anxiety had come a long way in Kingstree when suspicion of Northern birth could arouse a community to expel two

---

Rhett was not alone in his concern. The Marion *Star* cautioned its readers on the need for positive proof, since a real hardship might be inflicted on a man wrongly expelled from the community. *Courier*, December 22, 1859, quoting the *Star*.

apparently inoffensive school teachers. Although violence was averted by negotiation with the employers of the two men, they were, in the end, forced to leave.[28]

Rhett was perplexed by the Kingstree incident. He observed that most of the citizens of the district were determined to drive the men out on mere suspicion, while their employers and others seemed equally determined to defend them. (Estimates of the size of the mob varied from fifteen to one hundred but it is clear that armed conflict in the community was only narrowly avoided.) "This is a sad state of things," Rhett lamented. "In our indignation at the aggression of the North we are in danger of dealing with men as if they were guilty without proof." Rhett was concerned over the way vigilance activity was dividing Southerners, draining their potential for unified action. But with events sweeping past him Rhett had to speak, and on Decmber 5 he reluctantly came out for a formal system of vigilance committees.

> The newspapers from all parts of the South bring unmistakable evidence of the excitement of the people against abolition emissaries. Persons are seized and sometimes rudely examined—sometimes to be warned off and sometimes treated with great violence. There is danger that injustice will be done to innocent individuals by the irresponsible and disorganized bodies who, by their voluntary action, are seeking to secure the safety of the people of the South. Whilst there is unquestionable cause for their proceeding, we beg leave to suggest that they had better be carried on by a regular system of organization.[29]

[28] *Courier,* November 26, 1859, quoting from the Kingstree *Star;* letter from T. B. Logan, editor of the *Star,* in the *Courier,* November 29, 1859. Also see the joint letter refuting Logan's allegations in the *Courier,* December 22, 1859 and other charges and counter-charges in the *Courier,* January 6, 1860, January 10, 1860, and January 13, 1860, quoting from the Greenville *Patriot; Mercury,* January 6, 1860, and December 5, 1859; *Spartan,* December 15, 1859. R. P. A. Hamilton, one of the ostracized teachers, was not to have peace after leaving Kingstree. He was soon hounded out of Sumter on suspicion of being an abolitionist, and was last noted on his way to the hoped-for anonymity of Charleston. Subsequent letters indicated that Hamilton was in fact the son of a Virginia minister. There is a description of the affair in Howell Meadoes Henry, *The Police Control of the Slave in South Carolina* (Emory, Va., 1914), pp. 162–64.

[29] *Mercury,* December 5, 1859.

Rhett sought a program that would not hamper the formation of vigilance committees but which might help avoid the dangers inherent in that movement. Let "Committees of Safety" made up of the elder leaders in each community be formed to examine the attitudes of all suspicious strangers, he declared; and let "Committees of Vigilance" composed of the young men be organized to capture and punish the guilty. This was Rhett's solution. He hoped that an interconnected and mutually responsible system would achieve the elusive goal of internal security, while preserving a measure of harmony and justice that no crude, improvised action against individuals could duplicate. It remained to be seen whether even South Carolina was ready for such a para-military network.

The very next morning residents of Charleston read an unsigned address published in both the *Mercury* and *Daily Courier*, asking for a public meeting to establish a vigilance association with committees in each ward. Rhett could not have congratulated himself, however, for the words of this solicitation reflected none of his caution. The sponsors of the association proposed to examine every man in the city to "learn whether he is for us or against us in the conflict now waged by the North against our property and our rights." There were men now living in the city who questioned the Cause, and this could not be allowed to continue. "The times demand that all men South should be above suspicion," they reasoned, "but above all should Charleston." One week later it was announced that a Vigilance Association had been established with branches in each ward of the city. Attesting to the character and responsibility of the leaders, Richard Yeadon, editor of the *Daily Courier*, promised that they would detect and impart "proper treatment" not alone to hidden abolitionists, but to every sympathizer as well. "Responsible citizens" were invited to communicate information through the office of the *Daily Courier*.[30]

[30] *Courier*, December 6, 1859; *ibid.*, December 13, 1859. Yeadon apparently came to regret encouraging the vigilance movement. On December 29 he published copies of the Negro laws of 1805, 1820, and an act just passed by the General Assembly, with the remark that it was important for every citizen to know what provision existed in statute law for the protection of the

Enforcement of a public orthodoxy on the peculiar institution was among the most effective instruments of race control. Founded in a fear that division and consequent weakness among whites on the slave question would invite rebellion by the blacks and aggression by abolitionists, the organized attack on free thought in the antebellum South was a lamentable product of African slavery. As in comparable systems of intellectual tyranny, the achievement of maximum effectiveness depended on the participation of a preponderant majority in the community. Each individual was made to feel, more or less keenly, a commitment to protect the system and to resist all threats to its perpetuation, whether these came from without or, more insidiously, from within. Any issue touching slavery, however lightly, aroused the fiercest suspicions. Such social pressure compelled a group in the town of Due West to terminate a subscription to the *African Repository*, the organ of the American Colonization Society. Although the object of the Society—gradual resettlement of Negroes in Liberia—seemed tame enough, the journal had excited "ignorant & unreasonable" fears in the postmaster and others in the Abbeville community. "Those opposed to it," wrote a local Society supporter, "are free to admit their ignorance of the whole matter, & yet seem to have a kind of *instinctive dread* of it, as of something *pestilential.*"[31]

The attack on dissension arose not so much from any repressed sense of guilt over the morality of slavery, as from a more realistic and tangible fear that division would inevitably lead to insur-

---

security of the state, in order to "avoid any resort to those measures of redress which override the law and lead to violence and disorder. It would seem," Yeadon significantly concluded, "that these statutes provide for all those cases which are likely to occur and if the citizens will guide themselves accordingly, our community can easily rid itself of all who would interfere with our peace and domestic tranquility." *Courier,* December 29, 1859. Yeadon had been a Unionist until the 1850's, and was to support cooperationism in 1860. He voted for secession at the last. John Calhoun Ellen, "The Public Life of Richard Yeadon," (Unpublished master's thesis, the University of South Carolina, 1953).

[31] J. S. Pressly to W. R. Hemphill, July 6, 1840, Hemphill Family Papers, DU. See also George Adams to ———, September 15, 1846, George Adams Papers, USC; and F. W. Pickens to B. F. Perry, June 27, 1857, Benjamin F. Perry Papers, Ala.Arc.

rection and emancipation. Orthodoxy was a bulwark against annihilation. This was clear to Senator Robert Woodward Barnwell. He had been called upon to rationalize a similiar witch-hunt during the secession crisis of 1851. "The South was putting its house in order not to die," Barnwell had declared, "but to live." Such statements of principle from on high were one thing, however, their application in local communities quite another. R. C. Grier, a minister in Abbeville whose devotion to slavery was justifiably impugned, suddenly found his character and personal security threatened by those who presumed to apply Barnwell's principle of self-preservation. Reverend Grier's accusers were convinced that self-preservation obliged every Southerner to declare himself on slavery. "And if any person or persons are found not prepared to act in unison with their neighbors in defending the honor, rights and *institutions* of their state to the last extremity, that District or County should be purged of such spuriousness."[32] Together with other expressions of popular anxiety, this protracted "reign of terror" was brought to a peak in the winter of 1859.[33]

Nevertheless, the spirit of self-restraint was not wholly lost. On December 9 the vigilantes of Orangeburg publicly complained of receiving anonymous letters incriminating citizens of the district as abolitionist agents or sympathizers. Even the zealous

[32] Printed in "Public Communication by [Rev.] R. C. Grier," Due West, S. C., October 1, 1850, in Southern Broadsides Collection, Duke University Library.
[33] "We are under a reign of terror," William Campbell Preston wrote his friend Waddy Thompson, "and the public mind exists in a panic." N.d. [c. 1858], William Campbell Preston Papers, USC. Francis Lieber, a renowned German-born scholar then teaching at South Carolina College was aware of the terrible strength of the public orthodoxy on slavery and secession. "A time is fast approaching here when every man, especially in my position will be stigmatized if he does not openly, positively and loudly come out for disunion—" Lieber wrote privately in 1850, "a time like the reformation when a man was called and treated as a heretic unless he loudly pronounced himself for pope and cardinals. A time may come, perhaps soon, when I may no longer feel perfectly at ease to write frankly from my heart in any letter." Lieber to "My dear Ruggles," August 23, 1850, Francis Lieber Papers, DU. For similar sentiments, see Lieber to Alexis de Tocqueville, November 7, 1844, and Mathew Williams to Lieber, February 12, 1850, Francis Lieber Papers, USC.

Orangeburg committee could see how easily the desire for personal revenge or self-interest could be gratified through unsigned accusations. Taking the hint, the Charleston Vigilance Association insisted that letters to them also be signed. But this was no real protection. Before long a jointly written declaration was on Mayor Charles Macbeth's desk, denouncing the entire process of vigilance justice as a usurpation of the law, a veritable appeal to a "higher law" of self-preservation.[34] Based on a broader sort of legalism, opposition to vigilance justice also came from members of the planter class who dreaded any popular movement that threatened good order and patrician political control. The solution in nearly every case was to assume leadership themselves; as suggested, fear of the disruption of slavery was felt at once by all classes, gentry and poor white alike, and the danger of rebellion against ingrained habits of obedience to planter leadership subsided as long as all were travelling the same road to security against the Negro. Still, deeply conservative slaveowners like David Gavin of Colleton Parish who cursed political democracy as the source of all the ills of the Republic, opposed vigilance work because it operated beyond the reassuring frontiers of statute law.[35]

Vigilance advocates were quick to counterattack and, impelled by the general sense of insecurity, were not to be denied. Letters to the citizens of Charleston signed "Some of the Safety Committee," and "One of Them" denied any desire to challenge established authority. They were all gentlemen, they said, "to the manor born;" the least of the members of the committee was a slaveowner. What better proof could there be of absolute loyalty? Throwing caution to the wind, "One of Them" warned that those who had expressed concern over the creation of a vigilance committee in Charleston had good reason to do so: they were Northern sympathizers, he charged, men with "abolitionist proclivities." The new association would work with the police and other vigilance groups, as Rhett wanted, but they would not be deterred "by nervous gentlemen or Abolition sympathizers from ferreting

[34] *Courier,* December 9, 1859, quoting the Orangeburg *Southron; ibid.,* December 14, 1859.
[35] David Gavin MS Diary, SHC, December 17, 1859.

out these friends of 'Old JOHN BROWN' and aiding to convict them."[36]

— 4 —

However furious was this mutual incrimination, chief concern still centered on the docility of the slaves. Despite John Brown's own denials, the people of South Carolina from the very first believed that his aim had been to incite a slave rebellion. The news that the slaves of Virginia had not joined him as he expected was ostensibly greeted less by thanksgiving than by a well publicized sense of satisfaction. The Richmond *Whig* now explained that Harpers Ferry was not an insurrection at all but simply a fanatical excursion by Northern abolitionists. The slaves of the South would never engage in insurrection, the Virginia paper remarked, they wanted only to live in peace; no thought of freedom stirred these naturally quiet waters. If only the abolitionists would cease their attempts to force or incite the blacks to murderous rebellion—a thought which would never occur to a slave were it not for the instigation of Northern incendiaries—Southern slaveholders, their families and neighbors would live in a state of complete security. "The Southern whites would live undisturbed, even without a firearm in their houses or a lock upon their doors." With naturally loyal slaves, and the South secure against open, armed attacks, the real danger clearly lay beyond the South in the hands of those emissaries who were trying to deceive and inflame the Negroes. Reading these sentiments in their home newspapers, South Carolinians could only breathe a hopeful amen.[37]

The aim of the vigilantes in the winter of 1859 was, as it had always been, to prevent the poison of abolition ideas from being disseminated among the blacks. Negroes were looked upon on one level as naturally obedient and faithful, though infantile, but on

[36] *Courier*, December 15, 1859.
[37] *Ibid.*, October 26, 1859, quoting the Richmond *Whig*. See also *ibid.*, December 8, 1859, Message No. 1 of Virginia governor John Wise; and David Gavin MS Diary, SHC, October 30, 1859. It was even suggested that the outcome of Brown's scheme proved that slaves would be loyal and would "sustain their young masters in the field" in the event of a Civil War. Address of A. B. Longstreet, *Courier*, December 13, 1859.

another as potentially bestial and destructive. Men who crossed the Mason and Dixon line were hated because they could communicate directly with slaves, bridging the carefully fabricated barrier of myths and intimidation which was the engine of slavery, and disturbing that latent potential for violence conceived to be smoldering in the psyche of the slave.[38]

Since the slaves reputedly were illiterate, Northern conservatives wondered why their Southern friends were so concerned that public agitation of the slavery question would influence the Negroes. James Hammond made clear in a letter written shortly after secession that there were thousands of literate slaves in the South, taught by careless whites, by free blacks, and by one another. Hammond professed to be undisturbed by such illegal practices, since the few who were able to learn were "not only the most intelligent but usually the most loyal and faithful, for for the most part [they] read only the Bible, the Catechism, and the Prayer and Hymn books." Perhaps some blacks did read the abolitionist New York *Tribune*. Hammond freely admitted that sources of information about the sectional controversy were even closer at hand than that. At least ten percent of the audience at any political rally or public discussion was made up of Negroes who heard everything. "In addition, daily at our tables and our firesides we discuss these matters with Negroes all around. We

---

[38] In rendering a sentence in the case against Francis Michel, a man convicted of aiding a slave to escape, Judge Francis Withers provided real insight into the Southern concept of this dichotomy in the nature of the slave.

"There is a peculiar duty on the part of the Government which holds slaves to protect that description of property. Slaves are capable of being seduced, swerved from their allegiance to their masters; capable of evil purposes as well as good. They are, to a certain extent, free agents. They have brains, nerves, hands, and thereby can conceive and execute a malignant purpose. When, therefore, you or any other person shall succeed in corrupting a slave, in swerving him from allegiance, what have you done but turn loose an enemy to society in its very bosom. You have prepared him for 'treason, stratagem and spoils,' have armed him as with a dagger, and placed about a master and his family an enemy capable of conceiving their destruction."

State *vs.* Francis Michel, Court of General Sessions and Common Pleas, Sentence delivered by Judge Thomas J. Withers, printed in the *Courier*, January 30, 1859.

can't help it." Still, there was no fear that the proper subordination of the blacks would be altered by their learning the Northern version of the "truth" this way. Far more disturbing was the potential of an actual abolitionist instigator, travelling through the South, spreading his evil notions of disaffection. "What we do fear," Hammond told his Northern correspondent, "is your abolition emissaries who like the Serpent in Eden, whisper *lies*. We hang all of them we can catch."[39]

The burden of public and private correspondence in the aftermath of the attack at Harpers Ferry indicates that Carolinians believed the slaves had in fact been "tampered with" in their own communities, and had grown less docile. An essential part of the public orthodoxy on the slavery question was that the attitude of the Southerner of the 1850's was not the attitude of his forebears of the early nineteenth century. Having lived through a trial of conscience, economics, and fire, the typical Southerner had abandoned his supposed earlier belief in universal liberty and equality for the safety and stability of an harmonious but rigid social order. There was a sound reason for this. As one slaveholder bluntly put it, "had Jefferson and Washington lived to the [Nat Turner] outbreak at Jeruselem in Southhampton County, it is probable they may have recanted their errors."[40] In a similar manner, a new generation of slaves had been nurtured under the auspices of this recommitment to the peculiar institution. Raised under a system of expanding plantations, where bonds were tighter, personal "liberties" curtailed, and whites themselves agreeing to proscribe dissension, Negro slaves perhaps came closest in the late antebellum period to fulfilling the idealized image of them held by whites. This "new Negro"—part wishful thinking and part wish fulfilled—was an indispensable element in the structure of race

[39] Hammond to F. A. Allen, February 2, 1861, Hammond Papers, LC. Hammond's confidence was not shared by all. During the last excited weeks before secession the up-country Spartanburg Grand Jury called for legislation to bar "all negroes, Free negroes, and Slaves from attending musters and political meetings." The legislature recognized the dangers, but suggested that existing military and civil officials already had the power to keep blacks away from such meetings. Spartanburg Grand Jury Presentments, November 1860, SCArc.

[40] Letter from "*SALEM*" in the *Mercury*, January 5, 1860.

control. The abolitionists were conceived to be willfully shaking this pillar, with no understanding of the inevitable consequences of its collapse.

Two letters written to the *Mercury* in mid-November by unnamed slaveowners give a striking picture of the state of mind at this time. The first, styling himself "Vigilance," was no longer confident that the growing Northern challenge to white mastery of the Negro could be surmounted. Many planters had laughed too quickly at the suggestion that the fidelity of the slaves could be undermined. That was quite all right so long as the Negroes remained isolated in the slave system, "but when they are constantly tampered with it is rather too flimsy a defense and one which might lead to many fatal mistakes as experience has proved." The abolitionists were entreating the slaves to cut white throats, so slaveholders must prepare for the worst. There were ways to excite even the contented Negroes to violence.

> History teaches us that the most effectual mode to rouse an ignorant people is to appeal to their superstition and to their lust. *Nat Turner* made his followers in Virginia believe that the vengeance of God was about to fall upon the white people because it had about that time rained blood and it was a powerful instrument in his hands.

"Vigilance" claimed that the slaves in his very district (Beaufort) had been corrupted by abolitionists. His own slaves were recently told by a free Negro to regard the *Aurora borealis* as a sign of war! He groaned at how easily Northerners travelled across the South; any one of these men could be abolitionists from Ohio, bearing arms for the slaves. "Vigilance" was convinced that only full-scale preparedness would save the state. Women must be taught self-defense, the militia offices filled, patrol duty performed vigorously, "but in no case to leave any family exposed without one man at home."[41]

Writing two weeks later, "A Countryman" agreed that emissaries were moving all over the state, replacing the usual affection and loyalty in the hearts of "our laborers" with hatred and rebel-

[41] *Mercury,* November 11, 1859.

41

liousness. Although he refused to believe that the result would be widespread insurrection, he admitted that this poison was having its effect. To it could be attributed the "impertinent demeanor or reluctant submission" that had shown itself in recent months among a portion of the slave population. He was confident that most of the blacks were content, but he wondered aloud whether anyone expected that there were no Negroes who would be receptive to the evil but enticing words of abolition agents. "Is their nature so other than human," he rightly asked, "as to be proof against the tempting lie and the promise, though false, of better things?" These recent developments were necessitating changes in the allegedly relaxed and patriarchal rule of slavery in South Carolina; it must become more harsh, more severe. Where there had been indulgent confidence from the master and contented loyalty from the slave, the treachery of the abolitionists was compelling the diminution of privilege and the strengthening of discipline on the one hand, to counter growing insubordination and indolence on the other.[42]

Just as they had done so often in the past, particularly in the critical years from 1822 to 1832, the whites of South Carolina were joining hands on the race question. Under the aegis of this profound and disturbing continuity, the people of the state—shaken by the assault on Virginia and concerned over the potential rebelliousness of their own slaves—were coming together to protect their vital and indispensable institution.

Complementing the efforts of vigilance committees, the initial response naturally came from the traditional line of defense, the patrol. Residents of slaveholding communities were quick to strengthen patrols. Ministers warned their flocks of suspicious behavior by the Negroes. Planters became more sensitive to the need for surveillance and were noticeably less inclined to leave the task to others. Writing to Postmaster-General Joseph Holt during the winter holiday season, Alfred Huger, venerable head of the Charleston post office, apologized for missing Holt while the latter was in the city, because with other planters he "preferred at this *particular moment* to be with the Negroes during the Holy

[42] *Ibid.*, November 22, 1859.

days when excitement was most likely to be manifested." At the same time Huger's son noted uncomfortably that the Negroes of Charleston, appearing to sense the tension in the air, "have been as though under a cloud, & less seen in the streets, in gay attire, & less merrymakings."[43]

Difficulty of detection, particularly in towns and villages, had long made arson a favorite form of retaliation by discontented Negroes. It was the rare newspaper report of fire that failed to lay the cause to "incendiarism." In addition to the usual daily alarms in Charleston, and a destructive fire in 1838, the "Queen City" of the South was intermittently stirred by rumors of arson plots.[44] In the summer of 1842 the mayor received anonymous warning of a plot to burn down the city, and such an attempt was apparently made.[45] In 1855 cases of suspected arson were so frequent that Charleston insurance companies joined with the city council to offer an award of two thousand dollars for information about the perpetrators. A modern fire alarm and police telegraph system were subsequently installed, but the danger remained ever present.[46] It was natural that anxiety over this threat worsened after the raid at Harpers Ferry, particularly in the cities and towns of the state where whites and Negroes alike were aware that a single match could create a holocaust. In fact, reports of so-called incendiary attempts appeared to increase in Charleston. Jacob Schirmer, a Charleston merchant, was moved to comment in late October that fire alarms were breaking the quiet of the fall evenings "almost nightly." Weeks later, suspicion had not vanished. From the coastal town of Beaufort a man who signed him-

---

[43] Jane Pettigrew to Charles Pettigrew, October 30, 1859, Pettigrew Family Papers, SHC; Alfred Huger to Joseph Holt, January 3, 1860, Joseph Holt Papers, LC; S. P. Huger to N. R. Middleton, January 3, 1860, Nathaniel R. Middleton Papers, SHC.

[44] See above, footnote 9.

[45] Richard M. Middleton to Nathaniel R. Middleton, August 2, 1842, Middleton Papers, SHC.

[46] "C.W.H." to Louis Manigault, September 3, 1855, Louis Manigault Papers, DU; J. N. Gamewell & Company to "The Mayor and City Council of Charleston," n.d., South Carolina County Papers, DU; A. O. Andrews to [Mayor] William Porcher Miles, n.d., Miles Papers, SHC. The crux of this sequence came in December 1861, when a huge fire storm destroyed much of the city. The cause was generally laid to pro-Union blacks in the city.

43

self "Palmetto" spoke in the *Courier* about arson there. "The threatened work of revenge has commenced and the startling cry of fire strikes alarm in our community." But the town was now alert to the emergency. "Fear blanches no cheek; *we are ready.*" The citizens of Beaufort were not alone. The events of the past weeks were to excite a debate in Charleston over the effectiveness of race controls that was not laid to rest even by secession.[47]

The *Mercury* opened one important line of discussion in its issue of November 7 by noting that the last session of the state legislature had abolished an old instrument of security, the Charleston Fire Guard. Created many decades before, the Guard was a volunteer military brigade called out to protect property and suppress possible Negro insurrection in case of a great fire. Elimination of the allegedly decrepit system a year before had attracted little notice. But in the winter of 1859 the fact was suddenly regarded in a new light. The city was startled by this news concerning the Fire Guard. Writing in the *Courier* the next day, "Citizen" defended the Guard and called on the legislature to restore it. "If the people of Harpers Ferry could have had such a system," he nervously concluded, "the ringing of the fire bell would have summoned a sufficient number of armed citizens to have at once put an end to 'Old Brown's' murderous plans."[48]

The city's newspapers were quickly filled with charges over the disbandment of the Fire Guard. Many seconded the appeal for reestablishing the organization, while a few wondered aloud why their fellow townspeople were so wrought up over their personal security, and scoffed at the defense offered by such a volunteer company. Yet there was no denying the genuineness of general concern over the action of the legislature, and under this popular pressure, Mayor Charles Macbeth was quick to act. Within a few days he arranged for the printing of an exchange of letters between his office and the commander of the local militia division, Major General John Schnierle, and at once it became clear that the original alarmed notice in the *Mercury* of the dissolution of the Fire Guard had misconstrued the action of the 1858 legisla-

[47] *Courier*, November 7, and December 14, 1859; Jacob Sass Schirmer MS Diary, SCHS, October 30, 1859.
[48] *Mercury*, November 7, 1859; *Courier*, November 8, 1859.

ture. The General Assembly had abolished the Guard, but at the same time had authorized the Mayor of Charleston to request assistance from the senior officer of the district militia to suppress insurrection or riot. Macbeth now proclaimed that because of "the frequent incendiary attempts at present," he was requesting that two or three militia companies be placed at his service in *every* fire alarm. This was preparedness with a vengeance, and a satisfied writer in the *Courier* told the people of Charleston that they had been lulled into a false sense of security by the original Fire Guard; before the 1858 reorganization it was impotent to defend the town, inadequately armed and manned. As now constituted the Guard was well armed, better trained, better led, and more easily called into service in emergencies by the Mayor. A satisfactory end to this story came in late December, when the 1859 session of the legislature, then sitting in Columbia, gave its official blessing to the reconstituted Fire Guard.[49]

− 5 −

The people of Charleston also moved to strengthen other local instruments aimed at the difficult task of controlling Negroes. The abolitionist raid in October had raised troubling questions about the soundness of controls over the masses of African slaves laboring on plantations and farms; the answer to those questions appeared to be more of the traditional regimen. Less significant, but perhaps more perplexing for contemporaries was the problem of maintaining race controls in the urban environment. This was especially so in seaport Charleston. Here was the scene of the Denmark Vesey insurrection scare in 1822, which had sparked both the enactment of a more rigorous slave code and the first in a series of Negro seaman acts designed to isolate the city's large black population from the dangerous touch of free Negro sailors. The city never again relaxed the outward forms of vigilance. It

[49] *Courier,* November 12 and 14, 1859; *Mercury,* November 11 and 14, 1859. It is interesting to note that the author of the letter in the *Mercury* for November 14 declined to go into excessive detail in public print because, he said, it was best to maintain secrecy about such affairs of internal security. See also *Courier,* December 23, 1859.

was here in 1839 that a young Episcopal minister, Rev. John Cornish, fresh from New England, first saw African slaves and was moved to wonder at the seeming paradox of quiescent Negroes living under a strict system of curfews and street patrols.[50] Ten years seemed only to have strengthened these controls when, in 1849, James Johnston Pettigrew, a future Civil War general, described the city to his family in North Carolina. Pettigrew remarked upon the unusual appearance of Charleston, especially the armed guard, the strict enforcement of Negro curfews and the patrolling of churches on Sundays.

> The watchmen here are not provided simply with alarming weapons, such as rattles, etc, but are accoutred as soldiers, with muskets, uniform and bayonet, all of which you may rightly conjecture is for the black population. . . . Such precautions are absolutely necessary in a city of which more than a majority of the population are slaves, lible [sic] in sea port town to be corrupted and tampered with [in] every possible manner.[51]

Finally, it is interesting to note that radical leader William Porcher Miles, secessionist and Congressional representative from Charleston District in 1860, made his first mark in politics when he enlarged the City Guard and inaugurated a mounted police force while mayor of Charleston, from 1856 to 1858.[52]

The Fire Guard satisfied the need for protection against massive rioting in time of fire, but it clearly was not the solution to the more subtle, mundane corrosion of race controls at work in the city. In a process made the more irreversible by its sheer lack of drama, the Negroes of Charleston, slave and free, had been steadily expanding the frontiers of freedom and privilege. In their speech and dress, in their businesses and trades, in their pursuit of literacy and education, their traveling, and their cir-

---

[50] Rev. John Hamilton Cornish MS Diary, SHC, November 1839.
[51] James Johnston Pettigrew to ———, April 16, 1849, Pettigrew Family Papers, SHC.
[52] W. P. Miles to Gov. James H. Adams, March 31, 1856, William Mc-Burney to Miles, April 29, 1858, and J. Maxwell Pringle to Miles, January 31, 1859, all in Miles Papers, SHC.

cumvention of laws against emancipation, Charleston Negroes were exerting a growing pressure upon barriers of statute and custom aimed at their perpetual subjugation. That much of this was accomplished through the connivance of a minority of whites, and the inattentive acquiescence of the majority made a return to earlier standards of behavior all the more difficult. But the essential first step of a renewed awareness of the problem was reached in large part because of the impact of John Brown's raid. The black community in the city, which had been either transparent to white eyes, or dismissed as "merry thoughtless domestics," suddenly leaped into view, and the scene was disconcerting.[53]

The indictment raised against Charleston Negroes following Harpers Ferry illustrates not only the extent of black pressure upon the Negro code, but also the broad sensitivity to racial issues on the part of the white community. Charlestonians began publicly questioning the gross violations of municipal law. How could they explain the flocks of Negro children on their way to schools with books under their arms every morning? What of the countless breaches of liquor laws, which allowed blacks to congregate in grog shops where "moral and physical instruction is dealt out in such shape as to ripen them for stratagem and strife." In this frantic analysis of race relations, Charlestonians gave evidence of the depth of postwar racial attitudes and practices. The local Grand Jury in this winter session spoke out against the practice of free Negroes and slaves being permitted to travel on public conveyances, vehicles often driven by whites. And the Grand Jury warned, "It is proper that the line of demarcation between the castes should be broad and distinct, more particularly at this time for reasons which need not be mentioned. It is full time that slaves and free persons of color should know and understand their position."[54]

As far as most slaveholders were personally concerned, the key threat was to control and supervision, but the expansion of Negro enterprise also threatened the livelihood of white laborers and

[53] S. P. Huger to N. R. Middleton, January 3, 1860, Middleton Papers, SHC.
[54] *Mercury*, October 25–27, 1859; *Courier*, November 29, 1859; Charleston Grand Jury Presentments, January 1860, SCArc.

merchants. Numerous letters published in the daily newspapers alluded to this grasp for wider opportunities by the slaves of the city. Renewed alarm was felt over the old practice of slaves becoming virtually independent workers by hiring out their own labor, "not only the equal but superior even, in some regards, to his employer, and entirely beyond control and supervision." As slaves they were keeping bank accounts, travelling north and south with impunity, and, most disconcerting of all, "entering into competition with the worthy white citizens for the best patronage of the city." What had been mere nuisances were now adjudged real dangers, and the fertile imagination of many uneasy whites knew no bounds.[55]

Suspicions over declining Negro subordination inspired some ludicrous charges. Scant days after the Virginia raid became known, a group signing themselves "Many Voters" pledged their vote in the upcoming election to the mayoral candidate who swore to enforce certain hoary statutes concerning Negro apparel, rules which had been brought to their attention by the "late outrage at Harpers Ferry."[56] Negroes free and slave in most Southern cities, especially style-conscious New Orleans and Charleston, were eager to imitate the fashions of the day. Perhaps there was more to this than just an escape from the drabness and drudgery of farm and city labor. Concerned whites looked upon it as part of the affirmation of independence that characterized black insubordination in Charleston. On weekdays King Street and the Battery were thronged with white ladies and gentlemen promenading in the bright sun. But Sunday was "negro day," and, as George Gordon, a newcomer to the beautiful city vividly wrote, "the negro wenches crowd the streets in the height of fashion.

[55] *Mercury,* October 25–27, 1859; *Courier,* November 29, 1859.
[56] *Mercury,* October 21, 1859. This letter cited the statute of 1740, which enjoined slaves against wearing clothing finer than coarse fabrics because, as the framers wrote, "many of the slaves in this Province wear clothes much above the condition of slaves, for the procuring whereof, they use sinister and evil methods." *The Public Laws of the State of South Carolina, from its first establishment as a British Province down to the Year 1790, inclusive . . . ,* edited by John Faucheraud Grimké (Philadelphia, 1790), p. 164. This issue was sarcastically dismissed by "MANY OTHER VOTERS," in the *Mercury,* October 24, 1859.

. . . The nigger bucks act just the same. All through the week they sweat and bark in the sun with a slouch hat, shirt sleeves rolled up & on Sundays they dress up in fine clothes, wear a silk hat and gloves." It was "enough to make a horse laugh!" Gordon mocked, but it is remarkable how very often "unnatural" dress by Negroes was a target of condemnation.[57]

Still the slaves were not satisfied. They wanted freedom itself, and with some success were circumventing state laws against emancipation not only in spirit but in fact. Operating through associations which functioned either in entire secrecy or through nominally social organizations, so-called "negro class societies," with the surreptitious aid of whites were actually buying fellow blacks out of bondage. Taken together with the wide range of nervous allegations levelled against free and slave Negroes, and "traitorous" whites in Charleston, slavery was being undermined in the city. Not only were instruments of race control being frustrated, but the will of whites to maintain them was being eroded as well.[58]

With evidence of recalcitrance so flagrantly manifest, solutions were eagerly sought. Readers of the *Mercury* were invited to think back over the past twenty years, to the time when the black population was purportedly more secure. What was to be done? "A Slaveowner" spoke for many when he wrote on October 25:

> We are no alarmists; neither are we *agitated or surprised* at the recent disturbances in Virginia; but we would speak the word of caution to our citizens. We would have them examine into what has been too long neglected. We would purge our community and punish its lawbreakers. Neither talents, social position or wealth should screen them from public exposure and denunciation.[59]

[57] George A. Gordon to his wife, August 12 [1857], George A. Gordon Papers, DU. It is interesting to note that this same fear that finer clothing tended to blur essential distinctions between the races was present in other slave societies. The Spanish crown adopted a code concerning proper dress for Negroes as early as 1571. See Herbert S. Klein, *Slavery in the Americas; A Comparative Study of Virginia and Cuba* (Chicago, 1967), p. 205.
[58] *Mercury*, October 26, 1859.
[59] *Ibid.*, October 25, 1859.

One response was a call for the enlargement of the police force, which "recent events" had proved inadequate "in a moment of sudden peril." But the character of the letter from "A Slaveowner" suggested the delicacy of the problem involved. More to the point was an inquiry about the defunct South Carolina Association.[60] Arising out of the Denmark Vesey insurrection plot, this voluntary organization of low country planters was formed in July 1823 to aid in the enforcement of newly strengthened slave codes. A leading newspaper of the day had defended the extralegal organization as merely the embodiment of the spirit of vigilance felt by every loyal South Carolinian. Well endowed with money and talent, the Association played an important role in ensuing years as a defender of racial orthodoxy, but fell into disuse before the end of the antebellum period. Now the white population of Charleston wanted that "wholesome vigilance" restored. The new Charleston Vigilance Association inherited the mantle laid down by the earlier South Carolina Association.[61]

This fact becomes evident upon reading the action proposed by the Charleston committee. Vigilance groups organized in the state following Harpers Ferry were chiefly concerned with the detection of Northern abolition emissaries, and Southern sympathizers. However, like its venerated predecessor, the Charleston Vigilant Association was concerned perhaps more with Negro behavior than with white. Very likely this was a function of the severe impediments posed by the urban environment to effective race control. A recent study has shown that one approach to security in the 1850's was the expulsion of male slaves into the countryside.[62] Nevertheless, the continued presence of masses of slaves and free Negroes made for apparently undiminished anxiety.

The city association of vigilance committees promised action on a variety of issues. Of the seven subjects for investigation listed

[60] *Ibid.*, October 26, 1859.
[61] Charleston *City Gazette and Commercial Daily Advertiser,* July 26–29, 1823, quoted in Susan Teague Speare, "The Law of Self-Preservation: The South Carolina Negro Seamen Acts, 1822–1856" (Unpublished master's thesis, the University of North Carolina, 1965), pp. 14–18. See also Freehling, *Prelude to Civil War,* pp. 113–16.
[62] Richard C. Wade, *Slavery in the Cities, the South, 1820–1860* (New York, 1964).

by the association, three involved persisting conditions in the Negro community, and the remainder aimed at checking that Northern intervention into the private sanctum of Southern race relations which was the paramount inspiration for most vigilance activity at this time. First, they proposed to examine the condition and certification of Negro schools run by whites. The principal worry here was probably literacy, for the next two complaints concerned the subscription of city Negroes to such newspapers as the New York *Tribune* and the *Colonization Herald,* and the unhindered circulation of such books as James Redpath's antislavery biography of John Brown. The association wanted to investigate the operation of grog shops, still exerting their evil influence despite the efforts of police. In line with the usual pattern of such proposals, the Charleston vigilantes intended to consider the presence of Northern salesmen, and, more alarmingly, to inquire "as to whether strangers ought not to be prevented from publicly expressing their peculiar opinions."

The last item on this agenda illustrates the continuing pressure for expanded liberty which obtained in the Charleston Negro community, along with the difficulty of constraining it. As was so often the case, Negroes achieved a measure of simple day-to-day freedom by withdrawing from white supervision and control. This largely explains the existence of separate Negro congregations in the city's churches. The Charleston Vigilance Association chose to intervene in this process. The association sought to investigate the propriety of buildings being occupied by as many as one or two hundred Negroes with no white supervision. Negroes (independent slaves avoiding the constant surveillance of their masters at home, and free Negroes escaping from the vigilance of legal and self-constituted authorities) were clearly seeking all-black dwellings for the personal satisfaction and greater liberty they offered. What appeared to be segregation—an expression of disgust and a technique of race control by whites—was in part the reverse. This was to a large extent a Negro-initiated, willful "segregation" aimed at thwarting the instrument of race control that had been the predominant weapon of whites since the coming of African slaves to America, namely, immediate, intimate white supervision. That this antebellum technique of the Negro community should, through the vagaries of history, be twisted to fit the new conditions of white anxiety after emancipation is one of the ironies of Southern history.[63]

—6—

Initial reaction to the attack at Harpers Ferry had been local, and largely spontaneous. Focus and direction were given to the response in December by the legislature convening in Columbia. Here, political leaders from all over South Carolina met for the first time since John Brown's raid to discuss this latest crisis. The grim atmosphere of debate was repeatedly broken by appeals for violent action. Impelled by public opinion and its own anxious perception of the dilemma, the Assembly did move against what was believed to be immediate threats to slavery in South Carolina.

Even before the legislature met on November 28, it was clear that the people of the state expected concrete action. "Our Legislature is about to assemble," a slaveowner admonished the *Mercury*. "We expect the State in its sovereign capacity to speak out in terms not to be mistaken. We look for stringent measures calculated to put down these concerted emissaries of mischief—to award them full justice—that is, a speedy trial—quick execution." Slaveholders were determined to see measures adopted to secure their property.[64] A large number of bills were proposed, remarkably similar measures offered by representatives from districts as diverse as the sea island parish of St. Helena and piedmont Greenville. Out of this broad statewide agreement came two major statutes, "An Act to regulate the granting of licenses to itinerant Salesmen and Travelling agents," and "An Act to provide for the Peace and Security of this State." As its title indicates, the former sought to restrict the free mobility of drummers, book and clothing agents, and the like. Such visitors now had to obtain a license under pain of a $2,000 fine or six months in jail. A statement of his business intentions, backed by two letters of recommendation by South Carolina citizens, together with a $3,000

[63] *Courier,* December 15, 1859.
[64] *Mercury,* November 23, 1859. See also David Gavin MS Diary, SHC, December 17, 1859.

bond were the guarantee to the state of a visiting businessman's moral conduct.[65]

The implications of the second act were far more sweeping. By its five provisions the state sought to do away with all possible contact between a slave and any source of disaffecting ideas, whether these might come from a book, pamphlet, newspaper, picture, a play, a whispered phrase, a cypher, in short, from every conceivable source. No inducement to insurrection of any sort could be produced, circulated, subscribed to, or uttered, "with evil intent," without committing a high misdemeanor, with the punishment left to the discretion of the court.[66] Just how intensely alive the people of the state were to what they chose to call the "demoralization" of the slaves may be seen in an amendment to the general tax bill, which added a levy of $100 per day on traveling circuses to the existing license fee. The heavy fine was readily agreed to when its proponent, O. E. Edwards of piedmont Spartanburg district attacked the alleged influence of these roving companies upon the slaves. No institution, no association was exempt from this sort of denunciation.[67]

The General Assembly also passed numerous effective, if less dramatic, measures for the immediate strengthening of internal security. The tone of the proceedings had been set by Governor William Gist's opening message. Gist was concerned that owners of plantations with fewer than fifteen slaves were not required to remain in residence for more than six months each year, and were not compelled to keep overseers on them the year round. "It seems to me," the Governor continued,

that as much damage might be done by leaving fifteen hands

[65] Spartanburg *Spartan,* January 19, 1860. The purpose of the statute was made clear by the requirement that any applicant for a license must swear that he "will not in any way infringe or interfere with the laws and regulations of the State, or of any municipal authority, made for the government of slaves and free persons of color."
[66] *Ibid.*
[67] *Courier,* December 21, 1859. Bills were also introduced into the General Assembly restricting Negro apparel, barring the sale of liquor by itinerant salesmen, prohibiting the delivery of mail to slaves and free Negroes, and other such acts. See the *Journal of the House of Representatives of the State of South Carolina: Being the Session of 1859* (Columbia, 1859), December 1, et passim.

without a proper supervision, as a larger number, and in the present state of affairs, exposed as we are to secret emissaries inciting our slaves to insubordination and insurrection, the law should be altered so as to compel every one that owns a farm, with any quantity of negroes, to reside thereon all the year round, or keep a white man constantly on the place.[68]

Such an act had to wait for the more urgent quest for security of the war years. But the General Assembly was moved to adopt such legislation as "An Act to punish attempts to poison," a resolution creating the Georgetown Night Police Guard, acts providing for the formation of a rifle regiment and a "proper Fire Guard" in Charleston, and a variety of adjustments in the state militia.[69]

Consciousness of the need for close supervision was naturally greater in the tidewater parishes, where the resident whites were vastly outnumbered by slaves. A debate over state support for western railroads in this session of the legislature demonstrates how this basic fact of life in South Carolina was used to advantage by special pleaders. In 1830 William Aiken, a wealthy planter and president of a new railroad and canal company, had petitioned Senator Daniel Webster for support in obtaining a land grant. Among the benefits to the government offered by Aiken was the facility of transporting troops from the more dense white population of the interior to the coast of Carolina, whether to repel "foreign invasion or domestic insurrection."[70] Aiken's fears were not idle. In 1836 numbers of volunteers from the tidewater parishes for the Seminole wars in Florida were not permitted to go because, as one frustrated volunteer put it, with the "very dense *Black* population in the low country, too many whites cannot be removed from this section of country with safety."[71]

[68] *House Journal*, pp. 12–24; *Senate Journal*, pp. 11–23.
[69] *House Journal*, December 6, 1859; *Courier*, December 23, 1859.
[70] William Aiken to Senator Daniel Webster, January 9, 1830, William Aiken Papers, USC.
[71] John Burbidge to Rosina Mix, February 23, 1836, Rosina Mix Papers, SHC. Similar sentiments were expressed by James Louis Petigru during the Mexican War in a letter to Ebenezer Pettigrew, January 8, 1846, Pettigrew Family Papers, SHC. See also James Hemphill to William Hemphill, March 17, 1836, Hemphill Family Papers, DU.

Race anxieties remained a paramount political factor a generation later. In the 1859 legislature Christopher Memminger and others used Aiken's time-honored appeal to gain low country support for the trans-Appalachian Blue Ridge Railroad. Memminger was convinced that secession, if it came, would precipitate civil war, and he was particularly concerned about the defense of the Carolina sea coast. Writing on this theme, the Columbia correspondent of the *Mercury* appealed more directly to the peculiar weakness of the tidewater parishes. The tidewater parishes favored secession, he wrote, and it was clear that as an independent nation the South would be exposed to foreign invasion. The *Mercury* reporter warned his readers that throughout the South, the coast line of South Carolina was the most likely target for such an attack because of the multitude of slaves and the paucity of the white population. It was clear to this correspondent how manifest was the need to establish a stronger link with the "great hives of the white population in Tennessee and Kentucky." The sense of security alone would be worth the cost of construction. He called upon the parishes to support this railroad if they seriously looked towards ending the Union, *"or even security in it."* The first year of Civil War would show how well Memminger and the *Mercury* had prophesied.[72]

— 7 —

South Carolinians did not live in constant and conscious dread of murder at the hands of their slaves, either before or after John Brown's fateful raid. There is no question that most Carolinians believed slavery to be a necessary *and* proper condition for the Negro. It seems equally clear that by 1859 under undisturbed circumstances most slaves were persuaded if not to accept, at least to suffer the institution in relative silence. Whites were quick to praise the loyalty of their bondsmen. When the buildings of a women's school in Edgefield were destroyed by fire, the local

[72] *Courier,* December 10, 1859; *Mercury,* December 7, 1859. The Assembly eventually approved funds for railroad construction to the northwestern town of Walhalla. *South Carolina Reports and Resolutions, 1859* (Columbia, 1859).

editor was eager to applaud the courage of the faithful slaves who labored to save the buildings. Here was proof to fling back at those Northern tormentors who claimed that Southern homes were infested by deadly enemies of the whites. "They are our friends—our sworn allies. . . . The ties that bind slave to master —mutual affection and mutual dependence—grow more perfect every year."[73] Here was the yearning to have reality conform absolutely to the idealized concept of the social relations of slavery. History could be made to lend substance to this vision, as in the fact that most slave plots had been averted by warnings from faithful slaves. Day to day evidence of these ties of mutual affection and dependence was plentiful in most districts most of the time. So true was this that some whites urged that the laws be changed to permit roving abolitionists to be convicted on Negro evidence. As the Greenville *Patriot and Mountaineer* explained, "The Negro is as equally entitled to belief as the Abolitionist, for the latter seeks to place the former on a political equality with himself. Why not, then, let a negro, a good, faithful negro, give testimony against the infamous wretch who would consign to ashes the home of his master."[74]

What then was the matter? For some there was the gnawing consciousness of the contradictions inherent in the perpetuation of African slavery in a society whose public dogma was political democracy, or at least equality.[75] But for the great majority of South Carolinians, whether they held slaves or not, this painful sense of being a party to a moral wrong was not a significant factor since the Negro, in their view, was distinctly not a civilized man, and for centuries past slavery had been assumed to be the proper status for the African.[76] A more important cause of the disturbed state of the public mind, however, was an awareness of the gap between the idealized state of slave-master relations,

[73] Edgefield *Advertiser*, January 11, 1860.
[74] *Courier*, December 2, 1859, quoting the Greenville *Patriot and Mountaineer*.
[75] Charles Grier Sellers, Jr., "The Travail of Slavery," in Sellers, ed., *The Southerner as American* (Chapel Hill, 1960), pp. 40–71.
[76] For a comprehensive examination of the origins of white attitudes towards the African and slavery, see Winthrop D. Jordan, *White Over Black: American Attitudes Toward the Negro, 1550–1812* (Chapel Hill, 1968).

where slaves lived docile and contented, and the reality which in a thousand ways bespoke danger and insecurity. In the winter of 1859 the white community was pervaded with a sense of a loss of mastery over the blacks. In part this derived from unforgotten past and present slave recalcitrance; but South Carolina had successfully handled this problem before. No, the dreadful and portentous sense of apprehension that now filled the pages of newspapers and private correspondence was produced by Carolina's belief that abolitionism was boldly thrusting itself into the slaveholding community, indeed, into the very home and family of every white man, woman and child. Such was the immediate and practical meaning of Harpers Ferry.

CHAPTER TWO

Memories and Forebodings

In formulating an elaborate defense of slavery, Southern writers had drawn from all the records of human experience. In the same manner, when these men donned the prophet's mantle and sought to envision and describe the consequences of emancipation they spoke through quasi-science and philosophy to prove their vision of apocalypse. So awful was this prophecy, so extreme the language, that a modern observer is compelled to question the depth of fear that lay beneath it. Yet there is little doubt that from the first, abolition was regarded as an unthinkable horror, attendant with boundless physical, economic, social, and political disasters. Apprehension of abolition darkly colored the attitude of South Carolinians toward northern society, and explained the frantic response of the state to the rise of the Republican party. Secession cannot be understood apart from this intense foreboding.

— 1 —

The specter of black insurrection which slept uneasily in the bosom of whites powerfully affected their vision of emancipation. Carolinians had come to believe the most immediate response by the slaves to emancipation would be a violent, murderous uprising. Among the most comprehensive defenses of slavery was William Drayton's *The South Vindicated from the Treason and Fanaticism of the Northern Abolitionists*. Although he was a Unionist who left South Carolina after the Nullification crisis, Drayton's hatred and fear of abolition made this book an enduring contribution to pro-slavery literature. Written in 1836, following two decades of intense slave unrest in his native state, Drayton's "vindication" was suffused with a dread of race war. He believed emancipation would break the essential bonds that held the Negro in check, and inject into society an irrational being filled with bitter hatred for all whites; a black insurrection would inevitably follow.[1] Still more widely read was a "Memoir on Slavery," written by state Chancellor William Harper in 1837. Elaborating on the theme of race war, Harper likened the great mass of African slaves in the South to a barbaric tribe pressing on the frontiers of a civilized nation. Whatever other functions the institution of slavery served, it was a "Great Wall" of protection for every white man, woman, and child. Emancipation would destroy this safeguard, and end the only conceivable satisfactory relationship between the two races. If broken, estrangement and hostility would instantly flare up. Having learned the dogmas of human liberty and equality, and filled with a quickened sense of economic oppression, Harper was convinced the freedmen would rise up against their former masters.[2]

The first fruits of abolition, then, according to the pro-slavery argument, would be rebellion and race war. This was not entirely a surrealistic picture, utterly divorced from reality.[3] Well before

[1] [William Drayton], *The South Vindicated from the Treason and Fanaticism of the Northern Abolitionists* (Philadelphia, 1836), pp. 151–52, 246–48.
[2] William Harper, "Memoir on Slavery," in *The Pro-Slavery Argument; as maintained by the most distinguished Writers of the Southern States, containing the several Essays on the subject, of Chancellor Harper, Governor Hammond, Dr. Simms, and Professor Dew* (Charleston, 1852), pp. 11–12, 89.
[3] The French student of American society, Alexis de Tocqueville, confessed that he did "not regard the abolition of slavery as a means of warding off the struggle of the two races in the Southern states. The Negroes may long remain slaves without complaining; but if they are once raised to the level of freemen, they will soon revolt at being deprived of almost all their civil rights; and as they cannot become the equal of the whites, they will speedily

1800, when antislavery pressure was confined to the tender appeals of the Quakers and a few enlightened statesmen, and the recognized pro-slavery argument was two-score years away, fear of the consequences of emancipation was already an integral part of white attitudes toward the Negro. In 1791 the slaves of Santo Domingo began their bloody decade-long revolution from French rule. By 1803 the Negroes had secured control of the colony and proclaimed their independence as the first black republic in the New World. This successful insurrection at once became the principal evidence for Southerners of the dangers of weakening the chains of slavery. In South Carolina the 1790's were marked by repeated rumors of slave plots linked to the French island colony, and Carolina congressional representative John Rutledge among others seized upon the West Indian experience as horrible proof of the insanity of abolition.[4] Yet even before the Santo Domingo rebellion began, Congressmen from South Carolina and Georgia were strenuously resisting any discussion of the foreign slave trade or petitions from antislavery groups and free Negroes

---

show themselves as enemies." The institution of slavery, for white Southerners, was a "question of life and death." Short of an unthinkable racial amalgamation, de Tocqueville could see no alternative to slavery but "the most horrible of civil wars, and perhaps . . . the extirpation of one or the other of the two races. Such is the view that the Americans of the South take of the question," the French social critic wrote in 1835, "and they act consistently with it. As they are determined not to mingle with the Negroes, they refuse to emancipate them." Alexis de Tocqueville, *Democracy in America*, edited by Phillips Bradley, 2 volumes (New York, 1945), I, 378–79.

[4] *Annals of Congress, 1789–1824*, 42 volumes (Washington, 1834–1856), X, 241. In 1793 the editor of the New York *Journal and Patriotic Register* learned from Charleston that the "NEGROES have become very insolent in so much that the citizens are alarmed, and the militia keep a constant guard. It is said that the St. Domingan Negroes have sown the seeds of revolt." Quoted in Mary Treudley, "The United States and Santo Domingo, 1789–1866," *Journal of Race Development*, VII (July and October 1916), 122–25. In a letter to the Governor of South Carolina, Secretary of State Thomas Jefferson spoke of a plot to incite a Negro insurrection in Charleston, and later in the decade Federalist congressman Robert Goodloe Harper warned his Carolina constituents of a French plot to invade the Southern states using black troops from Santo Domingo. *The Writings of Thomas Jefferson*, edited by Albert Ellery Bergh, 20 volumes (Washington, 1907), IX, 275; Harper's letter is in *The Papers of James A. Bayard, 1796–1815*, edited by Elizabeth Donnan, in American Historical Association, *Annual Report for the Year 1913*, 2 volumes (Washington, 1915), II, 90.

in the North because these, they said, were merely an "entering-wedge" for total emancipation. Slavery was the "palladium of the property of our country," intoned representatives from the two southernmost states, an institution that could never be removed without "tearing up by the roots [their] happiness, tranquility and prosperity." "Do these men expect a general emancipation of slaves by law" asked Carolina Federalist William Smith years before Eli Whitney's cotton gin began to reshape the Southern economy. "This would never be submitted to by the Southern States without a civil war."[5]

The burden of race fear grew heavier in the nineteenth century. As the dark years of slave unrest which preceded the Nullification crisis slipped into the past, fear of outright insurrection seemed to decline. But the minds of Carolinians were not greatly eased, for anxiety over threatened abolition clearly increased in this same period. There seemed to be no escape. Whereas in the 1820's slave insurrection was very real, at times imminent, and abolitionism remained for most a distant drum, the order in this scale appeared to change in the later antebellum years. By 1850 fear of a general abolition of slavery was the paramount racial concern of most Carolinians. And apprehension of Negro rebellion remained inextricably caught up in this fear. The white community seemed to have gained a measure of security from the internal enemy just when the external threat of political abolitionism began its climb toward apparent domination of the spirit of the Northern people. Thus the balance of anxiety was maintained.

South Carolina was trapped in this dilemma, and the furious

---

[5] *Annals of Congress,* I, 340; *ibid.,* II, 1228, 1453, 1458. South Carolina representatives greeted all discussion of slavery with unfeigned uneasiness. Smith attacked the admission of petitions from manumitted slaves, saying "These men are slaves and . . . not entitled to attention from [this] body; to encourage slaves to petition the House," Smith argued, "would spread an alarm throughout the Southern States; it would act as an 'entering-wedge' whose consequences could not be fore seen—This is a kind of property on which the House has no power to legislate." And in 1798 John Rutledge told the House that the people of the South already believed that the North was aiming at the destruction of slavery. There was no question in the minds of these Carolinians about the existence of a "South" at that early date. *Annals of Congress,* VI, 2015–2024; *ibid.,* VII, 667. See also William B. Hesseltine, "Some New Aspects of the Pro-Slavery Argument," *Journal of Negro History,* XXI (January 1936), 1–14.

hatred of her citizens toward the North was scarred with indignation. Private correspondence in the antebellum years is repeatedly marked by a dread of abolition. "It is not with us merely a question of principle," wrote Benjamin Yancey, brother of the leading Alabama radical, William Lowndes Yancey, "but of our very existence." "It is our death struggle," another Carolinian declared, "Our own dear South slumbering over, what seems to me here, a Volcanoe—ready to burst upon their heads—while they are slumbering, sleeping for want of action." Senator Robert Woodward Barnwell despaired at the lethargic response of Southern leaders to the rising antislavery movement in the North. "Our institutions are doomed," he warned his cousin Robert Barnwell Rhett in 1845, "and the Southern civilisation must go out in blood." Two years later, John C. Calhoun, expressing concern at political dissensions in Alabama, was clear in his own mind that the cause of these divisions could not lay in indifference to the future of slavery, "for there is not a man who is so stupid as not to feel that it is a question involving the fate of the South." A Greenville merchant was even more to the point when he explained the meaning of agitation over slavery to his son during the Secession crisis of 1851:

> This miserable matter in the dissolution of the Union is direful to think of[.] But these Abolition Fanaticks have set themselves never to cease until the Negroes are all free & regardless of the manner whether it is by cutting throats or any other manner never seem to enter their imagination or reflect on the consequence.[6]

— 2 —

According to defenders of the peculiar institution, abolition would also spell certain economic disaster, not only for the South,

[6] B. C. Yancey to the Chairman of the Committee on Delegates to the Nashville Convention, April 20, 1850, Benjamin Cudworth Yancey Papers, SHC; Wilmot N. DeSaussure to "Dear Sir," March 6, 1850, Wilmot N. DeSaussure Papers, USC; Louisa Cunningham to Sarah Yancey, March 22, 1851, Benjamin Cudworth Yancey Papers, SHC; R. W. Barnwell to R. B. Rhett, February 19, 1845, Robert Barnwell Rhett Papers, SHC; John C. Calhoun to Edmund S. Dargan, May 14, 1847, John Caldwell Calhoun Papers, DU; Vardry to Vardry A. McBee, November 26, 1850, Vardry McBee Papers, DU.

but for the North and the entire world as well. In all their doleful predictions, South Carolina polemicists never failed to draw a grotesque picture of total economic collapse based upon what James H. Hammond called the "inveterate sloth" of the black man. Since Negroes were believed to be naturally indolent, freedom could only destroy the personal security they enjoyed as slaves. According to the pro-slavery litany whites could never survive plantation labor under the Southern sun, and Negroes, who alone were able to endure this necessary ordeal, would refuse to work if freed. As Henry William Ravenel, the planter and amateur scientest explained, Africans constituted "a labouring population peculiarly adapted to the climate, & whose physical instincts lead them to subjection and control." By this convenient reasoning, emancipation would not only destroy the vast capital investment in bondsmen themselves; the entire property value of the region would vanish at the stroke of emancipation—crops, buildings, machinery, land, all rendered valueless by the annihilation of slave labor. But the South would not suffer alone. For defenders of the institution, the products of slave cultivation were the very bulwarks of Northern and European trade and prosperity.[7] Edward Thomas Heriot, one of the largest slaveholders in South Carolina, described this widely held notion for his Scottish cousin:

> Destroy the slave labour of the Southern & Western portions of the United States, and consequently the agricultural productions, and the civilized world would be shook to its very centre. Europe would feel it much more than we would—the manufacturing interests would be overturned, & destitution

[7] James H. Hammond, "Letters on Slavery," in *The Pro-Slavery Argument* . . . , p. 145 ff.; [Edward J. Pringle], *Slavery in the Southern States, By a South Carolinian* (Cambridge, 1852), p. 48; John Townsend, *The Doom of Slavery in the Union: Its Safety Out of It; An Address to the Edisto Island Vigilant Association, October 29th, 1860* (Charleston, 1860), p. 18; Drayton, *South Vindicated*, pp. 117–18; Harper, "Memoir," pp. 86–87; Henry William Ravenel, MS copy of an Address to the [Black Oak] Agricultural Society, n.d., Botany Department Papers, SHC. The letters by Hammond printed in *The Pro-Slavery Argument* were originally written to the English antislavery leader Thomas Clarkson. They were received enthusiastically in the South; Hammond delighted in the execration they aroused in the North. Hammond to Edmund Ruffin, August 7, 1845, Edmund Ruffin Papers, SHC.

& nakedness of the working classes would amount to famine. Think of the Cotton, Rice, Sugar . . . and other exports from the country consumed in different portions of the world, and the manufacturing of some of them giving employment to millions of people, and what if all were cut off —and recollect that free white labour could not be substituted—it is a monstrous question.[8]

Until the British ended slavery in Jamaica in 1833, the dramatic decline of commodity exports in Santo Domingo, dating from the beginning of the insurrection in 1791, served as principal evidence for these sweeping predictions.[9] The effort in Jamaica was widely regarded by both pro-slavery and antislavery forces as a thoughtful test, for owners were compensated, and the freedmen were given homes, good wages, and the protection of a powerful government. As with Haiti, however, plummeting staple crop export figures seemed again to stand as mute evidence of deteriorating plantations and broken fortunes. For low country planter William Elliott, as for thousands of other Carolina slaveholders, the experience in Jamaica proved conclusively that the "free black will not labor in the fields." According to Elliott, himself the owner of both rice and cotton plantations, "the only alternatives remaining to the planter are the employment of slave labor—or the abandonment of the country."[10] Indeed, Southerners believed that they need go no further than the free Negro in their own country to demonstrate the validity of their forebodings of economic disaster. The general low state of free blacks, North and South, was attributed in part to the psychological effects of slavery, telling the Negro over and over that he was an inferior being, incapable of competing in white society; as novelist William Gilmore Simms explained it, the very color of the Negro's skin had attained cultural and ethical significance, an association between

[8] Edward T. Heriot to ———, April 1853, Edward Thomas Heriot Papers, DU.
[9] Drayton, *South Vindicated*, pp. 265, 270–71.
[10] William Elliott to William Plumer, Jr., draft of letter, n.d. [Spring, 1847], Elliott-Gonzales Papers, SHC. In this letter to a Northern friend Elliott unconvincingly wrote, "To place the institution of slavery in the South on the true basis [,] the exigency of climate—if the white man could labor in the region of malaria the labor of slavery wd not be resorted to."

blackness and inferiority which Negroes themselves had internalized as the symbol of an ineradicable moral taint. But more than this were those "inherent" flaws of indolence, immorality and intellectual weakness, forever dragging the black man down to the basest levels of society, a burden to himself, and useless to the community.[11]

— 3 —

The full extent of the Negrophobia inherent in the vision of emancipation was clearly revealed in the prophecy of Southern political and social relations after slavery. According to proslavery theorists the Negro as a slave occupied a position in society commensurate with his moral and intellectual capacity. He could be an object of affection as a dependent being, and of lively interest as an article of property. But this fine patriarchal relationship would have to end with emancipation. For there was believed to exist in the bosom of every white person an unquenchable race prejudice, born of a "natural" loathing, magnified by the obviously degraded condition of blacks.[12] And freedom for the masses of slaves would be more than just a logical absurdity. It

[11] [William Gilmore Simms], *Slavery in America. Being a Brief Review of Miss Martineau on that Subject: By a South Carolinian* (Richmond, 1838), pp. 27–28 note, 78–79; Thomas Roderick Dew, "Review of the Debate in the Virginia Legislature, 1831–32," in *The Pro-Slavery Argument . . . ,* p. 435; Drayton, *South Vindicated,* p. 113.
[12] Dew, "Review of the Debate," pp. 436, 462; Townsend, *Doom of Slavery,* pp. 22–23; Iveson L. Brookes, *A Defence of Southern Slavery. Against the Attacks of Henry Clay and Alexander Campbell. In which much of the False Philanthropy and Mawkish Sentimentalism of the Abolitionists is met and refuted. In which it is moreover shown that the Association of the White and Black Races in the relation of Master and Slave is the Appointed Order of God, as set forth in the Bible, and constitutes the best social condition of both races, and the only true principle of Republicanism. By a Southern Clergyman* (Hamburg, S.C., 1851), pp. 43–44; James K. Paulding, *Slavery in the United States* (New York, 1836), pp. 65–66, 270–275; H. Bascom, *Methodism and Slavery: with other matters in Controversy between the North and South; being a Review of the Manifesto of the Majority, in reply to the Protest of the Minority, of the Late General Conference of the Methodist E. Church, in the Case of Bishop Andrew* (Frankfort, Ky., 1845), pp. 57–58; Edwin DeLeon, *Thirty Years of My Life on Three Continents, . . .* 2 Volumes (London, 1890), I, 89.

posed a threat to white political control which jeopardized the social guarantees of slavery: the guarantee which insured that no Negro would ever rise above any white man; the guarantee against Negro enfranchisement; the assurance, as Charleston-born publicist James D. B. DeBow phrased it, that the "little children of both races shall [never] be mixed in the classes and benches of the schoolhouse and [never] embrace each other filially in its outside sports"; that half-whispered guarantee for the Southern white woman against the ravages of the Negro; in short, the assurance that the Southland would remain a white man's country. It was feared that political rights would lead to pressure for social equality, and that, at last, would bring the ultimate sexual challenge.[13] Indeed, South Carolina leaders often chose to emphasize the necessity for uncompromising resistance to abolition by swearing that slavery in America could only be ended through the loathsome touch of amalgamation. William Elliott again spoke for most of his fellow Carolinians when he concluded that if it was the destiny of the Negro "to remain in the country with us there is nothing on which the Southern mind is more determined than this: that they shall not remain as equals."[14]

The threat of abolition also evoked more lofty and intangible fears. For some Southerners, slavery had come to have transcendent social and philosophical meaning. A letter by Senator Barnwell in 1844 to his cousin Barnwell Rhett well illustrates the special light in which slavery had come to be regarded. "I believe" Barnwell warned the Charleston radical leader, "that unless slavery is upheld as a political institution essential to the preservation of our civilisation and therefore to be maintained and defended in the same high strain as liberty itself we must become a degraded people."[15] For these men slavery had become an institution sanctioned not only by its venerable age in human history, but by the hand of God himself. Clearly a conservative force, it was slavery alone that was believed by many to have given tone and character

---

[13] James Dunwoody Brownson DeBow, *The Interest in Slavery of the Southern Non-Slaveholder* (Charleston, 1860), p. 9; Simms, *Slavery*, pp. 6, 26–27; Harper, "Memoir," pp. 90–99; Drayton, *South Vindicated*, pp. 228, 235–36.
[14] William Elliott, *The Letters of Agricola* . . . (Greenville, 1852), p. 10.
[15] R. W. Barnwell to R. B. Rhett, November 1, 1844, Rhett Papers, SHC.

to Southern civilization. The lowest element of society was *ipso facto* disfranchised, the rightful planter leadership sustained, and radicalism checked. The African had been led out of his heathen darkness into a land of religion and law; now his ceaseless labor was producing nourishment and employment for millions of industrial workers. Who could question this divine appointment? Who doubted that slavery was not merely the only imaginable relation between the races, and that it was wholly productive of good for black and white alike, but more, that it was divinely ordained, immutable and virtuous? With Henry William Ravenel, Carolina slaveholders called upon the entire South to rally in defense of this heritage "which God has most surely blessed, [and] resolve at all hazards to defend it, though the whole world should frown upon you."[16]

— 4 —

Here was the South at bay, perplexed and defiant. Black emancipation was an unthinkable horror, slavery a divine mission, inescapable but ennobling. Yet, ever since the formation of the Republic, leaders of South Carolina were aware that some day the ultimate question would be fairly drawn—Union or slavery—and while there was never any question of what the answer would be,[17] there was a clinging foreboding about the outcome. Discus-

[16] Alfred Huger to Allen Smith Izard, August 6, 1856, Alfred Huger Papers, DU; Alfred Huger to William Porcher Miles, July 23, 1858, William Porcher Miles Papers, SHC; David Gavin MS Diary, SHC, December 2, 1859; Brookes, *Defence*, p. 44; Henry William Ravenel MS copy of Address to the [Black Oak] Agricultural Society, n.d., Botany Department Papers, SHC.

[17] At that early day, and after, there were voices raised in opposition to the predominant pro-slavery sentiment. John Laurens was such a man, who drew his distaste for slavery from his father, merchant-planter-statesman Henry Laurens. The younger Laurens is best remembered for his courageous but unsuccessful effort to persuade the state Assembly to enlist and emancipate black troops during the Revolution. Despite military necessity, pledges of compensation from the Continental Congress, and the urging of Washington, Hamilton, and others, Laurens's plan was repeatedly rejected by the leaders of South Carolina. His untimely death in 1782 removed a potentially powerful opponent of the prevailing racial wisdom. See John Richard Alden, *The South in the Revolution, 1763–1789*, Volume III of

sion of slavery and Federal relations were increasingly pervaded not alone with a consciousness of impending crisis, but also with a gloomy sense of inevitable doom. The people of the state, slave-holding families and nonslaveholders alike, would not, and in every meaningful sense, could not ever consent to abolition, for the consequences of a general emancipation seemed too clear, too certain, too awful. Still the tide of abolitionism mounted in the North, and no argument, no threat seemed powerful enough to halt it. For reasons at once interior to Northern society, and integrally related to the essential meaning of the American experience, slavery in the South was attacked, and thoughtful South Carolina political leaders recognized the certainty of this attack. It was not the abolitionist crusade which produced an apprehension of insurrection, nor the grim vision of emancipation, nor even the fatalistic sense of impending national conflict which characterized the Southern defense of slavery. These all existed well before there was a powerful abolition movement in the North. But it was that movement which seemed finally and forcefully to compel every South Carolinian to choose between affection for the Union and the compulsive need for continued subjugation of the slaves. In the face of this logic, more and more of the state's citizens began, with Senator Barnwell, "to dispair [sic] of our institution and of course of the very existence of the Southern people as a civilised nation."[18]

Barnwell and his people were frustrated by their inability to make the Northern people understand that they must end their assault on an institution which seemed to have given life and a distinctive purpose to the South. Under this cloud Carolinians

Wendell Holmes Stephenson and E. Merton Coulter (eds.), A *History of the South* (Baton Rouge, 1957), 225–26; and the letter of Alexander Hamilton to John Jay, [March 14, 1779], describing Laurens and his plan, in *The Papers of Alexander Hamilton*, edited by Harold C. Syrett and Jacob E. Cooke, 15 Volumes (New York, 1961), II, 17–19.

[18] R. W. Barnwell to R. B. Rhett, November 1, 1844, Rhett Papers, SHC. At the same time Senator Barnwell emphasized the special position of South Carolina in maintaining slavery on the highest plateau. "South Carolina and her offshoots have hitherto given dignity to the position of the South. The greater part of the slaveholders in the other states are mere negro-drivers believing themselves wrong and only holding on to their negroes as something to make money out of."

rapidly progressed from confusion and dismay to hatred of the North, and on to a conviction of inevitable sectional conflict. Many were those who foresaw where the growth of Northern abolitionism would lead. One such was the Reverend Iveson Brookes. He was a Baptist minister born in North Carolina who permanently left both his state and his youthful opposition to slavery when he came to live in Hamburg, South Carolina. In February 1836 Brookes wrote to his wife about a peculiar vision he had seen.

I have been dreaming since leaving home and I suppose you will think it a plausible dream—The substance is that in some twenty or thirty years a division of the Northern & Southern States will be produced by the Abolitionists and then a war will ensue between the Yankees & slaveholders [.][19]

Brookes believed that the Yankee army would quickly be joined by the slaves "who would shew more savage cruelty than the blood thirsty Indians," and those Southerners who ultimately escaped would gladly abandon their homeland to those who were once bondsmen in it. Brookes's vision was not unique to this ardent pro-slavery minister. More and more Carolinians came to believe that the Union could not survive the abolitionist attack on slavery, and, as one of them foresaw in 1839, "Civil War must follow from which the Lord deliver us."[20] In 1859 William Henry Trescot, a planter and amateur diplomat who was to play his own special role in the coming drama, clarified the meaning of the sectional struggle for his friend William Porcher Miles. "The only question . . ." he insisted, "is can the Union and slavery exist together?" Trescot, always the patrician, doubted that they could, for he considered the institution indispensable to the preservation of the existing social order in the South. But James Hammond spoke for the whole of the state when he asked Edmund Ruffin

---

[19] Iveson L. Brookes to his wife, February 25, 1836, Iveson L. Brookes Papers, DU; see also James H. Hammond to his brother Marcellus, February 21, 1836, James H. Hammond Papers, USC.
[20] Parmenas Bird to Iveson Brookes, January 27, 1839, Brookes Papers, SHC; see also Charles Pelham to Benjamin F. Perry, n.d., Benjamin F. Perry Papers, SHC.

"How any sane man can have any hope of our saving ourselves from the fate of Jamaica but by cutting ourselves loose from the [Union] as speedily as possible." In his own writings Ruffin cited the fate of Santo Domingo.[21]

There always were South Carolinians who would have taken issue with Hammond's appraisal of what a "sane man" must perceive. Many thousands of them continued to deny the imminent and fearful quality of the Northern antislavery crusade. Some of the older and more sensitive men saw, with William Campbell Preston, how the "fanaticism of abolitionism has generated an equal fanaticism in our own section." These conservatives lamented the violent and seemingly irrational political behavior of their people, produced by "a kind of instinctive dread" of all discussion of the issue, and, as Unionist Joel R. Poinsett bitterly wrote in 1850, by the goading of her radical leaders. Insofar as men like Preston and Poinsett correctly labelled fear of abolitionism as unjustified, they performed a necessary and beneficial task. But if those fears were appropriate, if radical leaders in South Carolina were correct in identifying the antislavery cause as a genuine menace to the security of slavery, a menace which truly threatened the lives and happiness of every white Southern man, woman, and child, then these "radicals" may perhaps be lauded as real patriots by the standards of the antebellum South.[22]

– 5 –

The development of a strong abolitionist movement in the North had obvious and fearful implications. Yet there was not always the same degree of state-wide agreement on the seriousness of the threat. This was because the antislavery movement

[21] W. H. Trescot to W. P. Miles, February 8, 1859, Miles Papers, SHC; James H. Hammond to Edmund Ruffin, February 8, 1859, Ruffin Papers, SHC. See Edmund Ruffin, *The Political Economy of Slavery; or, The Institution Considered in Regard to its Influence on Public Wealth and the General Welfare* (Washington, 1853).

[22] W. C. Preston to Francis Lieber, March 6, 1859, Francis Lieber Papers, USC; Joel R. Poinsett to J. J. Albert, June 26, 1850, Joel Roberts Poinsett Papers, USC. See also J. S. Pressly to William R. Hemphill, July 6, 1840, Hemphill Family Papers, DU.

did not enjoy immediate success in the North. Support for radicalism in South Carolina rose in direct and exaggerated proportion to the apparent growth of abolitionism among the Northern people. Following a decade of slave unrest, the state was thrown into political convulsion by the events of the early 1830's. The dispersion of David Walker's *Appeal* to slave insurrection, the launching of William Lloyd Garrison's *Liberator*, the debates on emancipation in the Virginia legislature, and the open debate with the Federal Government over Nullification—all underscored by Nat Turner's horrifying rebellion—provided painful evidence of an apparently resurgent antislavery spirit in the North. Still, many leading South Carolinians could not yet see how this movement would seriously affect their secure place in the Union. In 1836, for example, William Elliott attended the 200th anniversary of his *alma mater*, Harvard, and was pleased to report the enthusiastic applause which greeted one of the poems delivered at the celebration. It was, Elliott later wrote his wife, "a hard hit at the abolitionists," and its hearty reception "satisfied me that I was right in thinking the intelligent classes in this community decided in their hostility to that fanatical sect." So long as abolitionism remained only a sect, Elliott's confidence would persist. In fact, that same year, John C. Calhoun himself remarked that recent agitation of the slavery question was a healthy thing. Calhoun believed the South was united and rendered "sounder" on the issue, and "the nature of the question is better understood both north and South than it has ever been."[23]

Calm analyses of the attitudes of Northerners persisted in South Carolina. Writing to his wife in Columbia while on a trip to Rhode Island in 1849, the Reverend Samuel T. Jones told about a good-humored argument he had with a professed abolitionist. He only mentioned this as an exceptional incident, Jones said, for he rarely heard slavery mentioned and never denounced. With insight, Jones concluded "I began to think that the subject was more agitated at home than with the Yankees." Confidence in the essential conservatism of the majority of North-

[23] William Elliott to his wife, September 1, 1836, Elliott-Gonzales Papers, SHC; John C. Calhoun to Armistead Burt, June 28, 1836, Calhoun Papers, DU.

erners remained an important fact of political life in South Carolina. Moderates were convinced that the political issues raised by the abolitionists were understood to pose a choice between union or disunion as much by most Northerners as they surely were by all Southerners. As James Simons, speaker of the state House of Representatives, explained to his son late in 1858, "the battle on that question [abolition] will be fought for us at the North— The body of the Northern people will not swallow that—& it is only necessary for them to apprehend the depth and vitality of the issue & they will put [abolitionism] down beyond a doubt." It was this same confidence, as substantiated by the pro-Southern policy of Presidents Franklin Pierce and James Buchanan, which underlay the continued strength of the National Democratic party, an attitude which led such men as Simons to write in 1858 that he "knew no distinction between a states rights Democrat and a National Democrat."[24]

Moreover, it was clear to Southerners that racism knew no sectional boundaries. South Carolina Unionists often cited this national agreement on the propriety of racism to prove the reliability of Northern support for the peculiar institution. James Simons was sure that avaricious Northerners would soon forget their romance with moralism and would clamor for a share of a reopened foreign slave trade. We would then hear no more talk of the evils of the trade, he promised his son, nor of "the question of 'niggerdom' . . . except with a [few] *Damphools* at the North, who would vote more bibles to benighted greasy Cuffy." On the very day that John Brown was captured, J. D. Allen, a state senator from Barnwell District still unaware of the attack, calmly assured a local audience that the whole sectional controversy was merely the traditional struggle of the sections to control the central government. Abolitionism, he predicted, would be destroyed by national unity on the underlying race question. Everywhere Allen saw signs of the progressive revelation of racism. The Dred Scott decision assured that no Negro would ever be a citizen, "Hayti and St. Domingo are daily announcing verdicts in

24 Samuel T. Jones to his wife, September 1, 1836, Samuel T. Jones Papers, DU; James Simons to James Simons, Jr., November 11, and September 2, 1858, James Simons Papers, SHC.

favor of slavery," while free Negroes in America were languishing and the experiment in Liberia was collapsing into barbarism. According to Allen, these happy signs pointed to an imminent recognition by the entire nation of the necessity for slavery. With the South united and in control of the Federal Government, with the North divided by the pangs of rampant capitalism, and with the entire country moving towards an open avowal of the need for Negro subjugation, the future for slavery in the Union legitimately seemed secure.[25]

Unfortunately for the future of the American Union, this confidence was shared by fewer and fewer South Carolinians and even less by their leaders as the antebellum period wore on. To be sure, the perception by Carolinians of the strength and intentions of abolitionism, and ultimately of the Northern people, was grossly distorted and exaggerated. The disrupting Nullification crisis, as a recent historian has shown, was in large measure a feverish search for constitutional safeguards for slavery, which arose out of an overreaction to real slave unrest and generally illusory abolitionist activity.[26] As late as 1844 the active adherents of political abolitionism numbered only in the tens of thousands, and few were those who would have supported the kind of violent destruction of slavery feared most by the people of South Carolina. Still, by the time of the war with Mexico, it was clear that the antislavery crusade was growing in support, and that it was compelling an alteration in the political complexion of the nation.

The anxiety and dismay generated in the state by these developments can be glimpsed in the words of Isaac E. Holmes, congressman from the Charleston District in the 1840's. In a long and thoughtful letter written in 1848 Holmes reflected on the enormous impact which the antislavery appeal had already made upon national politics. The Southern people had been watching

[25] James Simons to James Simons, Jr., August 19, 1858, Simons Papers, SHC; letter of J. D. Allen, October 18, 1859, in the Charleston *Daily Courier*, October 27, 1859. See also Francis W. Pickens to B. F. Perry, June 27, 1857, Perry Papers, Ala.Arc.
[26] William W. Freehling, *Prelude to Civil War. The Nullification Controversy in South Carolina, 1816–1836* (New York, 1966).

the progress of the abolitionist cause for over twenty years, Holmes's letter began, yet none anticipated the dramatic advances which now loomed before the South. Holmes remembered the condition of things in the 1820's. He was labeled an "alarmist" then by friends who dismissed the Northern abolitionists as a scattering of factious spirits, fanatics who were contemptuously ignored in their own communities. "I *then* replied," Holmes dramatically recalled, " 'They may be so *now*—but they must increase because they base their action upon an abstract proposition yielded up by the larger portion of the world & promulged in the declaration of Independence—' " Holmes thus identified that quality of the abolitionist argument that defenders of slavery could never understand, and which perhaps appealed most to Northern supporters of the movement. The "self-evident truth" of the sin of slavery intuited by abolitionists made argument by Southerners futile. So much of the fuming rage generated in the sectional controversy derived from this simple and apparently irreconcilable disagreement. Instead of admitting to the practice of inequality throughout the nation, more and more Northerners came to regard slavery as an immoral denial of an abstract natural right of equality. For Southerners, the "fact" of the natural inferiority of Negroes was demonstrated by history and the plain evidence of their own eyes. They never could comprehend how and why the sensible folk of the North were led to believe the arrant and foul nonsense of abolitionists.[27]

It also took time for South Carolinians to realize just how dynamic was the abolitionist dogma. Small as the movement was in 1836, Calhoun was careful to caution his lieutenants against relaxing their vigil against the "numerous, zealous & active" abolitionists. Within two years, John P. Richardson, member of a leading Sumter family, nurtured a still more lurid perception of the danger. "The wealth—the talents—the enterprise—and religion of the whole North," he warned fellow planter Richard Singleton, "are concentrating to effect the subversion of our Domestic Institutions. It has never entered our imagination to conceive the zeal and earnestness with which a very large proportion of the

[27] Isaac Holmes to Mitchell King, July 13, 1848, Mitchell King Papers, SHC.

intelligence of the North is devoted to this object." Richardson was convinced that so powerful an excitement could not pass without producing a disruptive political reaction. "You may rest assured," he advised Singleton, "that we are not to be allowed to enjoy our property in peace and quietude."[28]

It seems clear in hindsight that such wholesale condemnation of the Northern people was unjustified. Nevertheless, by the 1850's it appeared that most South Carolinians had come to regard Northerners with an uncritical gaze of hostility and suspicion. In a letter that perfectly described an underlying assumption of Southern Unionists, a constituent of Carolina congressman Lawrence M. Keitt attacked political conservatism. "It is sometimes said even by Southern politicians that the large mass at the North are all right, that they are indifferent [,] believing there is no danger, that whenever they perceive a difficulty they will rise in the majesty of their strength and casting aside subordinate issues will rally to the support of the Constitution and Laws." Yet even as he wrote these words in 1855 he knew that "Those who entertain these sentiments are not wise."[29]

Sympathetic Northerners often tried to gloss over or dismiss the critical nature of the sectional conflict. The results were frequently a hardening of attitudes on both sides. An interesting exchange took place in 1847 between Carolina planter William Elliott and William Plumer, son of the New Hampshire Federalist Senator. Plumer was eager to explain away the growing animosity of his native section toward slaveholders. There were fanatics on both sides, Plumer truly observed, but their language distorted the "true state of feeling in the mass of the people here," and even more the sentiments of the intelligent classes. Yet the more Plumer wrote, the wider the gap stretched between himself and his erstwhile Southern friend. Indeed, Plumer admitted, we do believe slavery to be a moral evil, but we recognize your predicament; if we had grown up in the South we would surely

[28] John C. Calhoun to Armistead Burt, June 28, 1836, Calhoun Papers, DU; John P. Richardson to Richard Singleton, February 23, 1838, Singleton Family Papers, SHC.
[29] Joseph Tenhet to Lawrence Keitt, October 18, 1855, Lawrence M. Keitt Papers, DU. See also David Gavin MS Diary, SHC, August 8, 1857.

accept slavery, just as you would challenge it if you were a Northerner. Elliott had charged that the entire movement which now threatened to destroy the Union had been created by artful politicians. But Plumer gave away the game when he defended the virtue of the antislavery movement from such charges. "Opposition to slavery did not begin with the politicians here. It is a moral feeling which has been growing stronger & stronger for many years," and which, Plumer fondly hoped, would eventually work its way through the entire Union. Elliott could take but cold comfort from this promise.[30]

Carolinians naturally found the excoriation of slavery by Northerners immensely distasteful. Still, in the end, abolitionism had to be perceived as a practical political threat before it would provide the full measure of anxiety for slaveholders. And however uncertain abolitionist leaders really were about the best way to achieve their ends,[31] most South Carolina observers never doubted that the attack on slavery would come through the Federal Government. As noted earlier, representatives from the state to the very first sessions of Congress reacted with unnecessary public alarm to the mere idea of the Congress receiving Quaker petitions on slavery; such alarms did not exaggerate sentiment at home, for most citizens felt the same trepidation at any hint of Federal interference with the institution. Slavery, noted the eminent Charles Cotesworth Pinckney in 1790, "is altogether a matter of domestic regulation."[32] With the perspective of half a century, such politicians as Hammond, Calhoun, and Holmes could see just how clear a threat the national government posed to slavery.

By 1845 Hammond had lost patience for Southerners who could still say, Let the Northern politicians touch slavery and we shall fight. "Let them *touch* it," Hammond barked. "Has it not been a question of the utmost political moment for 10 years discussed

[30] William Plumer, Jr., to William Elliott, April 15, 1847, Elliott-Gonzales Papers, SHC.
[31] The abolitionists's search for means to implement their moral indignation is succinctly discussed by Norman A. Graebner, "The Politicians and Slavery," in Norman A. Graebner, ed., *Politics and the Crisis of 1860* (Urbana, 1961).
[32] Charles Cotesworth Pinckney to "My Dear General," March 31, 1790, Charles Cotesworth Pinckney Papers, USC.

from Canada to Mexico?" Contemptuously he asked when "our 'Chivalry'" would decide to resist. Two years later Calhoun had become convinced that all further discussion of the issue by Congress must cease. "It is high time we should know where we are to stand in the Union, if we are to continue in it." Watching the acrid clouds stirred up by the Mexican War and the Wilmot Proviso billow on the political horizon, Congressman Holmes agreed with Calhoun. Slavery—secure for so long—was now imperiled by the great sectional party Holmes now clearly saw emerging in the North. Abolitionism, which he regarded at once as a "religious conviction" and a moralistic cloak for political and economic ambition, seemed to be moving rapidly toward that long-feared elevation to Federal power.[33] This ultimate apprehension—with all the grieving, the fatalism, and the inescapable implications formed by two generations of South Carolinians—was movingly expressed by William Campbell Preston in 1857.

At the foundation . . . is the deep conviction which we all participate in that the General Government controled [sic] by a northern sentiment has a fatal tendency to Abolition and that thus our property and everything we hold dear in society is subjected to the mad caprice of a blind & reckless fanaticism. This I confess is my own opinion and altho I think the Institution of slavery is a most unfortunate one, yet no foreign panacea can be permitted to meddle with it. Blood and burning and unuterrable [sic] calamity would be the inevitable consequence. . . . We are a magazine round which crackers are exploding.[34]

— 6 —

The perception by most South Carolinians of the strength and character of forces threatening to destroy slavery was always imperfect; they never failed to exaggerate the unity and purpose

[33] James H. Hammond to Armistead Burt, February 11, 1845, Armistead Burt Papers, DU; John C. Calhoun to Armistead Burt, September 21, 1847, Calhoun Papers, DU; Isaac Holmes to Mitchell King, July 13, 1848, King Papers, SHC. See also Louisa Cunningham to Sarah Yancey March 8, 1850, and *id.* to Benjamin C. Yancey, March 27, 1850, Yancey Papers, SHC.
[34] W. C. Preston to David Campbell, August 22, 1857, David Campbell Papers, DU.

of the Northern people in this regard. Yet their fear was not a paranoid vision of the outside world, completely dissociated from reality. Apprehension of a loss of control over the slave masses, and of ultimate emancipation was intimately related to the intrinsic instability of slavery and the presence of an expanding, strident, and even violent abolitionist spirit in the Northern states. The image of the attitudes of Northerners which gained increasing acceptance in the state, particularly after the abortive secession attempt at the beginning of the 1850's, was formed in a highly charged climate. The normal uneasiness of slaveholding communities was heightened by the apparent presence of abolitionist instigators; the wearying grind of ceaseless agitation and ridicule rubbed away at the sensitivities of self-respecting men and women; and withal, a frustrating inability to establish genuine communication with the North on the fundamental race question. Considering this hypertension, the excessive picture of Northern unity and fanaticism which had taken hold in Carolina can only be judged a tragedy. Like the act of secession which was its consequence, this impression of unrelieved external hostility was the product of logical reasoning within a framework of irrational perception.

Nowhere was this aberrant perception more apparent, and nowhere were the consequences more fatal than in the way South Carolinians viewed the rise of the Republican party. Whatever the true nature of Republican policy, the party was from its inception regarded as the coalescence of decades-old antislavery and free soil factions. That great Northern abolitionist party which had been apprehended for so many years had emerged at last. South Carolina leaders could see that the Northern wings of the Whig and American parties had dissolved in the potent reagent of abolitionism. Until the fall of 1859 and the calamitous events which followed, no two occurrences appeared to have a greater effect in reinforcing this notion than the Presidential election of 1856, and the enunciation of the doctrine of an "irrepressible conflict" by William Henry Seward, in his famous speech at Rochester, New York, in 1858.

Never did the dread prospect of the fulfillment of abolitionist ambitions seem so close as when John C. Frémont garnered almost half the votes of the Northern states in the election of 1856. Frémont was a perfect representative of the youthful aggressiveness and hostile intentions of the new party. South Carolinians looked their long awaited adversary in the face with a sense of anxiety and excitement. "The great issue is now joined between the defenders of Equal rights in reference to slavery on the one side," intoned Abbeville legislator Samuel McGowan, "and the abolition Black Republicans on the other." McGowan, a supporter of the National Democratic party, was confident that every Southern vote would go for Buchanan, leader of the party of state rights and the Virginia and Kentucky resolutions. For McGowan there was no choice. What man of the South would support a party that intended to repeal the fugitive slave act, bar slavery from the territories, and, inevitably, "accomplish in some way or affair the abolition of slavery." McGowan wrote these words in June 1856, but by October the outcome of the election seemed less certain. Alfred Huger, speculating on the possible consequences of a Republican victory, foresaw almost certain sectional war. The deeply conservative Charlestonian hoped that the South would pause and await the overt enactment of the antislavery plot. But, Huger lamented, if Frémont were elected and he did not "play traitor to his friends," if, in short, the "Black" Republicans did "half that they threaten, we shall be in a state of Revolution."[35]

As with the general perception of a totally "abolitionized" North, there were considerable numbers of South Carolinians who denied that the new sectional party solely represented political antislavery sentiment, or that Frémont's election would necessitate a bloody conflict. A "Friend of the Union," writing to Presbyterian minister and fellow Unionist William R. Hemphill, professed to see no significant difference between the Presidential candidates. Even Frémont said that "slavery where it exists in the States *must not be interfered with*," Hemphill's correspondent affirmed, and Buchanan and Fillmore had made similar pledges. Like most, this "Friend of the Union" was not pre-

---

[35] Samuel McGowan to James Johnston Pettigrew, June 23, 1856, Pettigrew Family Papers, NCArc; Alfred Huger to James J. McCarter, October 4, 1856, Alfred Huger Papers, DU.

pared to believe this promise, nor to battle for Constitution and Union, out of any doubts about the soundness of the Southern position. As "Friend" concluded, what could "Frémont or any other man elected president not proslavery . . . do to injure Southern interests while we have a democratic senate and House of Representatives?" Still, there were some who were not equivocal in condemning all "little minded disunionists," and asserting that the state would be willing to " 'Try Frémont a while.' "[36]

All the same, there is no question that the overwhelming number of the people of South Carolina, up country and low, looked upon the new Republican party as the political representation of the abolitionist impulse which had been growing in the North for over a generation. In one sense they were justified in doing so. Although vital economic aspirations and fears were involved in the sudden success of the party, it seems clear that it was above all the heir of moral and idealistic forces generated by the anti-slavery crusade. "Only the steady growth of a Northern concensus on the moral unacceptibility of slavery," writes one recent student, "explains . . . the rise of Republicanism or its brilliant success in contrast with the disintegration of Whiggery, the failure of Know-Nothingism, and the disruption of the Democracy."[37]

[36] "Friend of the Union' to William R. Hemphill, October 29, 1856, and S. Conley to *id.,* November 3, 1856, Hemphill Family Papers, DU. The sentiments expressed by "Friend" exemplify the rationale of many Unionists. A letter written by Francis W. Pickens to Benjamin F. Perry in the summer of 1857 states this well. "We have the Executive with us," Pickens declared, "and the Senate & in all probability the H.R. too. Besides we have repealed the Missouri line & the Supreme Court in a decision of great power, has declared it, & all kindred measures on the part of the Federal Govt. unconstitutional null & void. So, that before our enemies can reach us, they must first break down the Supreme court—change the Senate & seize the Executive & by an open appeal to Revolution, restore the Missouri line, repeal the Fugitive slave law & change in fact the whole governt. *As long as the Govt. is on our side I am for sustaining it, & using its power for our benefit,* & placing the screws upon the throats of our opponents." (Italics added.) Pickens to Perry, June 27, 1857, Perry Papers, Ala.Arc.
[37] Don E. Fehrenbacher, "The Republican Decision at Chicago," in Graebner, *Crisis of 1860,* p. 36. See also Avery O. Craven, *Civil War in the Making, 1815–1860* (Baton Rouge, 1959), pp. 30–32; and Glyndon G. Van Deusen, "Why the Republican Party Came to Power," in George Harmon Knoles, ed., *The Crisis of the Union, 1860–1861* (Baton Rouge, 1965), pp. 19–20.

South Carolina secessionists were convinced that the last vestige of false conservatism fell away on October 25, 1858, when William Seward mounted the platform at a political rally to announce the approach of an inevitable war between free and slave labor. The New York senator had long been looked upon as a leading exponent of abolitionist doctrine, and by 1858 he was regarded as his party's first figure, and certain to be its standard bearer in 1860.[38] His speech asserted Republican hostility to slaveholders so blatantly that Senator Hammond, who fancied himself an instigator of Seward's address, expressed the vain hope that the immature party organization of the Republicans would disintegrate at once.[39] Writing in a more deliberate mood to his friend William Porcher Miles, Hammond sketched the full shape of the coming secession crisis, standing forth, stark and implacable. Seward, "the leader of the Abolition Political Party with every appearance of full consideration," had finally decided to make the "great final issue." Here for Hammond, Miles, and all of South Carolina, was the ultimatum of the Republican party:

> The South is to be Africanized [Hammond wrote,] & the elections of 1860 are to decide the question. In other words it is emancipation or disunion after 1860, unless Seward is repudiated. If he is there is an end to political abolition. If he is not we shall make jelly of him & his party in 1860, if we

[38] "Seward's 'irrepressible conflict' speech of 1858 was, in the judgment of the extremists, no less than an official declaration of the Republican party, and they tried to persuade South Carolina and the South that it exposed the end sought by 'Black Republicanism.'" Harold S. Schultz, *Nationalism and Sectionalism in South Carolina, 1852–1860; A Study of the Movement for Southern Independence* (Durham, 1950), p. 186. Seward's speech was so judged by far more than just "extremists," and little persuasion was needed to convince most South Carolinians that the end of Republicanism was abolition and consequent race war. See the letter of "Vigilance" in the Charleston *Mercury*, November 11, 1859; and the speech in the Senate by James Chesnut, Senator from South Carolina, in December 1859, wherein Chesnut called Seward's promise that the fields of South Carolina and Louisiana would soon be tilled by free labor a "declaration of war." *The Congressional Globe: Containing the Debates and Proceedings of the First Session of the Thirty-Sixth Congress* (Washington, 1860), p. 37.

[39] "Seward's speech is great for us. I fear that they will repudiate him. If they do he can break up the Black Republican Party." Hammond to G. W. J. DeRenne, November 20, 1858, George Wymberley Jones De-Renne Papers, DU.

promptly accept & fight the battle right through on the issue tendered, or failing in that we are consolidated organized & trained for a So. Republic.[40]

The long night of waiting, filled with confused jousting over tangential issues was drawing to an end.

— 7 —

The approach of winter in 1859 saw Carolina still distracted and divided. Never had the elusive goal of Southern unity seemed so remote. The bitter factional discord created in the state by the abortive secession attempt at the beginning of the decade had not entirely passed away. Despite widespread agreement on the reality of the threat to slavery there was still considerable disagreement on the best means to secure the peculiar institution from attack. Secessionists continued their search for a mechanism to gain their violent end, while more moderate leaders doggedly hoped for the reprieve of Democratic victory in upcoming Northern state and national elections. In fact, by this time the future of politics in the state seemed to lie in the hands of the Northern people, for conservatism in South Carolina only made sense so long as there could be a realistic belief in the fundamental moderation of the North.[41]

The confused despair felt by many was well expressed by David Flavel Jamison. Jamison was a respected planter and a long-time secessionist who in little more than a year's time would be elected president of the state's Secession Convention. In a letter written in September 1859 Jamison condemned the distracted counsels and public apathy which were crippling the ability of the state to meet the inescapable threat to, as he phrased it, "our very political and social existence." Instead of

[40] Hammond, who had been looking towards 1864 as the year of decision, was moved by Seward's address to "set my sights at '60 for a final adjustment." He was no longer the fire-eater, however. Seward's "transcendant folly" had given the country two years to openly discuss this ultimate question, and Hammond never lost confidence that the Republicans would be repudiated at the polls. At the same time, he did not doubt that the sectional controversy would end either in "disunion or the end of abolition." Hammond to Miles, November 5, 1858, Miles Papers, SHC.
[41] Laura A. White, *Robert Barnwell Rhett: Father of Secession* (New York, 1931), pp. 152–56.

acting boldly, he remarked with unconscious irony, "we are looking to some sudden turn of fortune we know not what to rescue
us from the doom we have not the courage to avert." He refused
to prophesy as to what shape this coming thrust of Northern
hostility would take. But one thing was clear: the time for polemical debates on the Constitution or the equal rights of the sections
was passed. The issue between the North and the South had been
"narrowed down to the safety of our institutions and the preservation of our existence as a nation." Only one month later "the next
storm of Northern hatred and fanaticism" foreseen by Jamison
"burst upon the South."[42]

The news from Harpers Ferry appeared to have a mixed effect
on sentiment in the state. Radicals and so-called cooperationists
(those who opposed the separate secession of the state but who
would support the secession of a united South, presumably as a
last resort), greeted news of the senseless attack less with surprise
and fear, than with a knowing, embittered flush of anger; for
these secessionists John Brown was merely an expected actor in a
long-fated drama. The raid had a more significant impact upon
the apolitical masses of the state, as well as upon her pale
Unionists. The effect of the attack, and the dramatic illustration
it seemed to afford of Northern opinion was to seal that fateful
connection between the concepts of Insurrection, Abolition, and
the Republican party in the minds of even the most insensitive
observer. The ranks of thoughtful Unionists were depleted as
fewer and fewer Carolinians could honestly feel confidence in the
firmness and integrity of Northern moderation.[43]

Aside from the practical response which has been discussed,
the three months following the news from Harpers Ferry saw the
state convulsed by a prolonged debate over the central question
of Northern conservatism. There never was much doubt that the
attack was at least condoned by Republican leaders as a natural
expression of the "irrepressible conflict" doctrine. Still, perplexing
problems remained about the general sentiment of the Northern

[42] Letter of September 23, 1859, published in the *Courier*, November 3,
1859.
[43] White, *Rhett*, pp. 157–58; Schultz, *Nationalism and Sectionalism*, pp.
189–91. For a summary of Northern newspaper opinion, see Lawrence T.
Lowrey, "Northern Opinion of Approaching Secession, October 1859–November 1860," *Smith College Studies in History*, III (July 1918), 191–203.

people. Did they realize in their hearts and minds the profound implications of a war for abolition? Did they admire or repudiate John Brown? Would the mass of them support or acquiesce in the rise of a political party pledged to unremitting sectional conflict aimed at a general emancipation? And were they aware of the inevitable consequences of such a catastrophe? Finally, by supporting a party supposedly created for and committed to achieving the total and immediate abolition of Negro slavery in the South, did the people of the North genuinely understand that this could compel the destruction of the Union? These were fundamental questions, and John Brown's raid opened the last stage of the catechism.

The argument for the defense began at once. Newspapers associated with the Democratic party, as well as other conservative papers in the North, quickly put forth a steady stream of words ranging from attacks upon Brown and the Republican party which allegedly spawned the raid, to gentle reminders of the essential conservatism of the North. The commercial Charleston *Daily Courier* for October 24 printed a large selection of such editorials for the benefit of its readers. Here those frightened Charlestonians who sought soothing reassurance for continued confidence in Northern sentiment found what they were seeking. The Hartford *Times*, Boston *Courier*, and New York *Herald* confirmed that the recent attempt to incite insurrection should indeed be charged to the teachings of Seward, Sumner, and their ilk, while the New Haven *Morning Times* hoped that abolitionists would learn the futility of disturbing the harmonious social relations of slavery. The most significant editorial opinion of the lot came from Henry J. Raymond's Republican New York *Times*. To the probable joy of South Carolina Unionists, Raymond asserted that "the great mass of the people North," whatever their party affiliation, "regard every such attempt to emancipate Southern slaves as that which has just been crushed in Virginia with horror and execration." The business community of New York City with its close commercial ties to the South, as well as similar groups all across the nation, suddenly came forward publicly to preach the same doctrine. With the New York *Herald* in the lead, spokesmen for the city's businessmen condemned the fanatical attack, loudly proclaimed their dependence upon Southern markets, and declared their ardent support for the South and slavery.[44]

Less obviously self-interested assurances of the peaceful sentiment of Northerners soon reached South Carolina. Over the years, the gentry had established warm personal connections with wealthy friends in the North, notably through travels to such popular summer resorts as Newport and Saratoga Springs.[45] Recognizing perhaps more than most the dreadful meaning of the Harpers Ferry excitement, many of these Northerners moved promptly to testify to the essential conservatism of their section. Francis W. Pickens, then serving as ambassador to Russia, learned of Brown's attack in letters written early in November by Elias Burrows, a Northern friend. Burrows tried to comfort Pickens by stressing the political value of the raid. The sectional controversy had only been a war of words until this attack, Burrows wrote, but now all the world could see the truth of Southern allegations —that Northern interference with slavery would lead to bloodshed. And Burrows was optimistic about the outcome. By demonstrating the fatal consequence of supporting the Republican party, the assault on Harpers Ferry would help "avert the wicked war made at the North on the rights & lives of our Southern brethren." The antislavery movement, and the imminence of disunion would be stopped at the North.[46]

[44] *Courier*, October 24, 1859; *ibid.*, November 1, 1859, quoting the New York *Herald*. During the winter Southern newspapers contained innumerable letters and editorials calling for measures to secure economic self-sufficiency, such as direct trade with Europe, home manufacture, and commercial nonintercourse with the North. There was even a list circulated indicating the alleged political affiliations of leading New York mercantile houses. The list was noticed by those merchants and many were quick to deny the accusation of harboring abolitionist tendencies. One of them, J. L. Seixas & Brothers, was defended by Richard Yeadon, editor of the Charleston *Daily Courier*, who affirmed that "this house is true on the Southern question." *Courier*, January 28, 1860. See Philip S. Foner, *Business and Slavery. The New York Merchants and the Irrepressible Conflict* (Chapel Hill, 1941).

[45] Thomas H. O'Connor provides a good picture of the warm relationships established at such places between Southern planters and New England conservative businessmen, in *Lords of the Loom; The Cotton Whigs and the Coming of the Civil War* (New York, 1968), pp. 47–50.

[46] Elias Burrows to F. W. Pickens, November 5, and November 12, 1859, Francis W. Pickens Papers, DU. Burrows closed his letter of November 12 with the hope that the abolitionists had learned from the Harpers Ferry fiasco "that the servants of the South are not retained by their Masters by

Similar letters penned by Northern conservatives streamed Southward, all of them strenuously protesting that the Harpers Ferry incident signified nothing about the preponderant sentiment of the Northern people. William Porcher Miles was assured by New York business leader Charles Augustus Davis that the long-awaited conservative reaction had already set in. Davis reported that Brown's foray, "this comparatively trifling and insane affair, has already worked *wonderful results,*" by arousing the latent but allegedly predominant conservatism of the Northern people. He urged upon Miles and his radical cohorts a policy of silence and forbearance; indiscriminate denunciation and premature action would only worsen the existing severe sectional strains. Davis was confident that this program would destroy both the Republican party and abolitionism itself, because the Northern people would certainly *"smash down"* any element hostile to the Constitution *"as it is* & with all its *compromises* and *guarantees."* To a doubting Miles, Davis swore that this was the true state of opinion at the North.[47]

Although these assurances had no visible effect on Miles, they held the only real hope for more moderately inclined Carolinians. From the remoteness of St. Petersburg, Francis Pickens expressed his feelings to that staunchest of South Carolina Unionists, Ben Perry. The news from Harpers Ferry, and its still more dreadful implications had frightened Pickens. Yet a month after the event he was prepared to hope that it had set the stage for a genuine test of Northern intentions. Should the people of the North fail to rebuke the demagogues who fostered such schemes, Pickens warned Perry that the cause of political moderation in the South

fear and trembling, but as Gov Wise said 'by a Patriarchal tenure.' But the South have now a right to demand of the North some pledge of security that their emmissaries [*sic*] will not arrouse [*sic*] them—inhabitants of Slaveholding States—from their sleep by the shrieks of families or the burning of their dwellings."

[47] C. A. Davis to W. P. Miles, December 8, 1859, Miles Papers, SHC. Miles received many such reassuring letters from Northern conservatives. For example, from Boston he heard from one Ives G. Bates that "even among many Republicans that he knows of there is the strong feeling for the Union, and the desire to grant to the South the Constitutional protection they want." Ives G. Bates to W. P. Miles, January 28, 1860, Miles Papers, SHC. See also John Wool to Miles, February 11, 1860, and (from England) W. H. Gregory to Miles, February 17, 1860, Miles Papers, SHC; and F. J. Kron to J. H. Hammond, April 2, 1860, Hammond Papers, USC.

would be crippled. If, instead, the "Conservative men of the North do their duty promptly, it may be the means of confirming the confidence of the South in their integrity & ability." With other South Carolina Unionists, Pickens placed safety from insurrection and abolition far above love for the Union. He called for a constitutional convention to permanently guarantee that Northern border states would not again be used as "nurseries" for abolitionist plots. However much Pickens wanted to believe that both the Union and the peace of the South could be preserved, in his own mind it remained "for the North to act now & to do their part."[48]

It is apparent that a preponderant number of South Carolinians rejected even this hope. By its principles and leaders the Republican party was condemned as the implacable enemy of the South. More important, confidence in the disinterested fairness of the mass of Northerners—so critical to the vitality of a truly national Democratic party and to the ultimate security of slavery —was dealt a body blow from which it never recovered.

Republicans were quick to deny culpability in the raid, and more, to spurn the label of abolitionists. On the floor of the House and Senate Thaddeus Stevens and Lyman Trumbull and others took issue with these charges. Stevens dismissed them as scare tactics aimed at furthering the election hopes of Northern Democrats. (Indeed, it did seem that too many Democrats, insufficiently aware of the deep fears they were toying with, were quite willing to advance their own electoral chances by frightening their constituents with allegations of Republican complicity in Brown's raid.)[49] Trumbull declared that he had no idea why some Southern leaders were threatening secession if a Republican were elected in 1860. His was not an abolitionist party, he asserted, "We have no intention of interfering with your domestic institu-

[48] F. W. Pickens to B. F. Perry, November 21, 1859, Perry Papers, Ala.Arc. See also Nathaniel R. Middleton to his wife, November 28, 1859, Nathaniel R. Middleton Papers, SHC; letter of an anonymous Charlestonian to the Boston *Courier,* in the *Courier,* December 6, 1859, quoting the New York *Herald;* James J. McCarter to W. P. Miles, January 15, 1860, Miles Papers, SHC.

[49] On the Senate floor the leading Northern Democrat, Stephen Douglas, had no hesitation in saying that Harpers Ferry was the "natural, logical, inevitable result of the doctrines and teachings of the Republican party." *Congressional Globe,* 36 Cong., 1 Sess., p. 553.

tions."[50] Such disclaimers only angered South Carolinians. Fired by John Brown's raid, Barnwell Rhett denounced the antislavery sentiment that had grown among Northerners over the past quarter century. Abolitionists had split the national churches, stolen slaves, barred the Southern people from the common western territories, and incited black insurrections. Now, Rhett continued accusingly, they had organized a political party to capture control of the Federal Government in order to complete "their purposes of emancipation." Still they denied and denied again that this was their purpose; but their stated moral and constitutional principles betrayed those denials. The Charleston leader was confident that John Brown had now shown all Southerners what awaited them should the Union come under the control of the Republican party. For Rhett the attack at Harpers Ferry was simply "fact coming to the aid of logic."[51]

This essential link between Republicanism and abolitionism was made still clearer in a vigorous speech delivered in the state legislature by William D. Simpson of Laurens. Simpson, like most of the radical leaders in South Carolina, dismissed the surface implications of Brown's attack. It would be forgotten in a minute, he said, except that everyone knew that the entire affair had been incited by the "Black" Republicans, if not directly by their teachings, then at least as the logical fruit of them. And what were the inescapable conclusions forced upon the people of South Carolina?

> The first is—that we of the South in possession of the institution of African slavery, yet by no agency of her [sic] own—but an institution that is so interwoven with every element of Southern society that we never can surrender it, either peaceably or forceably—are living under the same government with a people whose settled and deliberate judgment is that the interests of the white race demand the utter extermination of this institution of ours—peaceably if we can be persuaded to submit to it—but if not then it must be hurried on by violence and by blood. Yea, by a servile war with all its untold horrors.[52]

[50] *Ibid.*, pp. 23–24, 36–39.
[51] *Mercury*, October 31, 1859.
[52] Simpson's speech is in the *Mercury*, January 14, 1860. See also the

The second fact that the state must face, Simpson concluded, was that there was now in power at the North a political party which represented the abolitionist spirit, and which was but one step away from taking control of the national government.

— 8 —

John Brown had made that last step appear irreversible not alone by demonstrating the "true" nature of the Republican party, but by forcing upon the whole Northern people a test of their innermost convictions. And to the eyes of most South Carolinians they failed this test. In December Northern conservatives made a spectacular effort to alleviate sectional strains. In a series of Union meetings, they sought to demonstrate that the mass of Northerners continued the studied indifference to slavery which had become so essential to the preservation of the Union. The most notable Union meetings were held in Boston, Philadelphia, and New York, where statesmen and community leaders gathered to chorus their love of country, and their disgust at such excesses as those of John Brown and his abolitionist supporters. Several speakers took such advanced ground in defense of slavery as an immutable, beneficent institution, that the meetings may have discredited the cause of moderation for some Northerners.[53]

Some South Carolina conservatives were openly pleased with these Unionist effusions,[54] but for the most part the leaders of the state indignantly spurned the "Humbug Union Meetings." They

---

Mercury, November 22, 1859; Edgefield *Advertiser,* November 30, 1859, quoting the Columbia *Daily South Carolinian.*

[53] News of these meetings was very widely reported. See the *Courier,* December 6 and 10, 1859, regarding the Philadelphia meeting; *ibid.,* December 12, quoting the Philadelphia *Press* and New York *Herald,* regarding the Boston meeting; and the *Courier,* December 23, quoting the New York *Herald,* reporting the affair in New York City. Official summaries of the meetings were also published. See *Great Union Meeting, Philadelphia. December 7, 1859* (Philadelphia, 1859); and *Official Report of the Great Union Meeting held at the Academy of Music in the City of New York, December 19, 1859 . . .* (New York, 1859). There is an excellent description of this phenomenon in Allan Nevins, *The Emergence of Lincoln,* 2 volumes (New York, 1950), II, 105–107.

[54] For example, see Alfred Huger to W. P. Miles, December 12, 1859, Miles Papers, SHC; *Courier,* December 16, 1859, quoting the Greenville *Patriot and Mountaineer;* letter signed "A." in the *Courier,* January 18, 1860.

were, according to Rhett, part of a well-oiled propaganda machine, designed to appease and confuse opinion in the South. The outrage in Virginia was so blatant, and the response of the Southern states so decided, "that a pause for a time has become necessary in the Northern 'progress of civilisation.' " So-called conservatives were "the very rear-guard of *Abolitionism*," he continued. At every crisis they rose up to hold demonstrations and mouth tranquilizing slogans. They were indeed appalled at Brown's invasion, Rhett mocked. They eschewed violence; they merely wanted to bleed the wealth of the Southern people, and inexorably force slavery down into the Gulf states, to be wiped out at their pleasure. More ominous than Rhett's condemnation, however, were the remarks of Unionists such as Congressman John Ashmore, who disparaged the meetings because they were attended only by Democrats and old line Whigs, and ignored by representatives of the majority Republican party.[55]

Moderate Northerners eager to dispel what they regarded as unrealistic notions of the strength of antislavery feeling, urged their friends South to ignore the "ravings of a few fanatics like Gerrit Smith" (as Senator Hammond's friend William Hodges described him), and to look instead to the upcoming Northern state elections as a sounder measuring rod. Hammond received two such letters written on November 15, one from Hodges quoting election statistics to adduce the real weakness of the Republican party, and another from a committee sponsoring a Union meeting in New York City, warmly assuring him that "the People, North, are sound upon the great subject which agitates this Country at the time and would so express their opinions through the Ballotbox." In South Carolina itself one of the most vocal Unionists, Arthur Simkins, editor of the Edgefield *Advertiser*, voiced similar confidence that the Harpers Ferry uprising would help return control of New York and other Northern states to Democratic hands.[56] Clearly, there were thousands of men in the

[55] *Mercury*, December 9, 1859; John Ashmore to B. F. Perry, January 14, 1860, Perry Papers, Ala.Arc. See also the letter from "Some of the Safety Committee," in the *Courier*, December 15, 1859; and *ibid.*, December 24, 1859, quoting the Sumter *Watchman*.

[56] William L. Hodges to James H. Hammond, November 15, 1859, Hammond Papers, USC; G. Hunt to Hammond, November 15, 1859, Hammond

North who were not even aware that the principles they believed in, and the policies they supported, as innocent as they may have seemed at home, made them the desperate enemies of South Carolina.[57]

In the case of the Northern state elections in the winter of 1859, it appears that Democrats were not merely imprudent but misguided in attempting to picture these elections as public tests of Northern indifference to the slavery question. Their groundless optimism only dramatized the helpless condition of conservatives North and South. State elections were frequently used as measuring rods. In a *Mercury* editorial Rhett recalled that after Seward had delivered his Rochester speech in 1858, many who still fondly believed that abolitionism had not taken hold of the Northern people, had looked to the ensuing New York State elections for proof of the expected repudiation of Seward; they were surprised instead to see the Republicans gain a sweeping victory. In the same manner, Rhett went on, the attack at Harpers Ferry was followed by legislative elections, including a contest for Seward's own seat. Again, Rhett noted, there were those who called on the South to observe these elections as true tests of Northern conservatism. But how had these important elections gone? The "Black" Republicans increased their strength in the state legisla-

---

Papers, LC; Edgefield *Advertiser,* October 26, 1859. Former President Franklin Pierce understood the limitations of the Union meetings, and wrote his brother in December that the Southern people were sure to look closely at Northern state elections as the true guide to public sentiment. Pierce to H. D. Pierce, December 21, 1859, in "Some Papers of Franklin Pierce, 1852–1862," *American Historical Review,* X (January 1905), 362–63.

[57] *Mercury,* December 17, 1859. Many Northerners were well aware of the growing hostility for the South above the Mason and Dixon line. They, too, could see the interracial masses held for John Brown, and could read the broadsides from out of the New England hills deifying Brown. See "PINK," the New York correspondent of the *Courier,* December 5, 1859; "Treason!" a broadside dated November 4, 1859, in the Stephen A. Douglas Papers, UChic; William Plumer, Jr., to William Elliott, December 8, 1859, Elliott-Gonzales Papers, SHC; Lewis Cass to F. W. Pickens, December 12, 1859, Pickens Papers, DU; James Morrow to Christopher Memminger, January 24, 1860, Christopher G. Memminger Papers, SHC. These letters despaired of an end to the sectional controversy short of civil war, and suggested that Northern conservatives were all but reconciled to a secession of the Southern states. Here were the "signals" reaching the eyes and ears of intelligent South Carolinians during the winter of 1859.

tures, and Seward was resoundingly returned to office. What was the lesson to be learned, according to the *Mercury?* That there *were* conservatives at the North, but that they constituted a distinct minority. They were men who were "powerless to arrest the growing fanaticism and aggressive predominance of the North"; men, Rhett acidly concluded, who were "worth nothing without power."[58]

— 9 —

What was the outcome of the attack at Harpers Ferry and the critical debate over Northern intransigence which followed? It is clear what the raid did *not* do. By February 1 the immediate chain of events set in motion in October had ended. The movement for a Southern convention was dead.[59] On the level of practical politics the hysterical fears and the frenzied debate which swept across the nation that bleak winter seem to collapse onto the pile of sectional abuses and excitements that had been building for over a generation. The real importance of Harpers Ferry lay in its profound impact upon the entire range of political sentiment in South Carolina. Although secessionists greeted the news from Virginia and the Northern reaction to it with grim understanding, they were nonetheless aroused by the possibility that their dream was to be fulfilled. Radicals were emboldened, the most violent of them calling for immediate secession, or an open attack at the seat of government to precipitate a wholesale disruption of the Union. They believed that the final stage of the "irrepressible conflict" had begun. The evidence was unmistakably clear to James H. Taylor and his fellow radicals:

> that the doctrines which have been taught in the pulpit, from the rostrum, in sabbath schools and by the fireside that slavery is a sin which should be removed from our land at

[58] *Mercury*, November 24, 1859; *ibid.*, December 15, 1859. Despite the apparent evidence presented by the 1858 election results indicating that the North was not basically "conservative," some Carolinians were not dissuaded from their confidence in Northern moderation. In a letter of November 11, 1858, written to his son James, Jr., House Speaker James Simons denied that the late elections proved that the slavery issue had come to control Northern politics. Simons Papers, SHC.
[59] See Chapter III.

every hazard are now producing their bitter fruit in lawless aggression, violence and death. *This state of things cannot endure.* Will the conservative sentiment in the free States be able to roll back the tide of wild fanaticism which finds its *root in the conscience of a people?* Never. For the conservatism itself is rotten in the core. Not one perhaps of all those men who would thus sweep back the ocean of abolitionism with a broom, but are conscientiously convinced that slavery in principle is wrong and that the institution is evil.[60]

Lifelong Unionists in the state were thrown into despair, and men dedicated to forbearance searched frantically for those all-important signs of real conservatism in the Northern states. To the eyes of most Carolinians the entire North did seem maddened with that strange hatred described by James Taylor. With state and church joined in such a moral crusade, how could men reason together? For perplexed and well-meaning (and equally dogmatic) South Carolinians, there simply was "too much of a religious element in the schemes of the Black Republicans."[61] Augustus Baldwin Longstreet, then President of South Carolina College, warned the graduating class in December 1859 that they were about to enter a world already embroiled in revolution, "a Revolution from which there was no escape." A generation before, John Brown's raid would surely have brought forth a burst of denunciation from the North. Longstreet now looked in vain for that reaction.[62] For the moment many thousands of conservative Carolinians abandoned the hope of preserving their secure world in a Union which brought only tumult and grief. Harpers Ferry did not utterly destroy the confidence that slavery could still be safe in the Union. The saving grace of political apathy, and the more potent fear of secession prevailed. But thanks to John Brown, who could doubt what the Republican party symbolized? Look to Santo Domingo.

[60] Ironically, Taylor's remarks were made in a speech to the Charleston New England Society on December 22, printed in the *Mercury*, December 23, 1859.
[61] Letter from "A Son of the South," in the *Courier*, November 16, 1859; letter from "Our Offspring," in *ibid.*, December 14, 1859; W. Duncan to James Hammond, December 2, 1859, Hammond Papers, LC.
[62] Address of A. B. Longstreet, *Courier*, December 13, 1859.

CHAPTER THREE

Cooperationism
Is Laid to Rest

It was an anxious group of legislators who came together in Columbia in late November 1859 to sit in the General Assembly. The hysterical reaction to the attack at Harpers Ferry was only then reaching its peak. Nervous murmurings drifted through the chambers of the old capitol building, forming a muted echo to the angry chorus of vigilance committees rising across the state. Conservatives in the legislature grumbled over this latest assault by the North but were yet indisposed to second the aggressive action coveted by their radical colleagues. There was a wide gradation of sentiment in the South Carolina Assembly, from the secessionism of Edward Rhett to the unflinching Unionism of Benjamin F. Perry. But, in the three weeks of the short session, these men, despite their differences, were able to agree on practical legislation to provide better security against Negro insubordination. Still, more than this was needed. Nearly every legislator seemed to feel that a public stand had to be made on the aggravated condition of the sectional controversy. It soon became evident that most of the state's representatives were prepared to go beyond a mere declaration to substantive action.

— 1 —

The tone of the proceedings was set in the opening message of Governor William Gist. The Governor had made his position clear months before in a public letter which called for the immediate secession of South Carolina should a Republican president be elected "on the Seward Platform." Gist coolly looked upon secession as a measure calculated to secure permanent concessions to the South, or failing in this, as the first step towards a Southern Confederacy. Now with the opening of the General Assembly the people of his state were looking to the legislature for leadership, and the Governor's message was awaited with a measure of interest "almost amounting to anxiety."[1] Gist offered no clear solutions. The North had finally gone beyond mere slave stealing and economic exploitation, he cried, they had "crossed the Rubicon" by openly trying to incite slave insurrection. The evidence of Northern hostility was too blatant for the South again to be seduced by the hypnotic appeal of the National Democratic party. "Can we still hug the delusive phantom to our breasts that all is well," he asked, "and that the Democratic Party . . . will work out our salvation by platforms and resolutions?" Yet the alternative proposed by Gist was not persuasive. He merely issued a lame call for Southern unity. Together with most radicals, the Governor had learned well the lesson of the abortive 1851 secession attempt, in which the state had advanced to the brink of disunion, only to withdraw when it became clear that no other state would follow. Disunionists were certain that the mass of Carolinians would support their cause when the final issue was made. But moderates were equally certain that the separate action of the state would be rejected so long as any alternative to secession existed. The result was frustration and stalemate.[2]

Although the Governor's message represented the epitome of futile rage, there were many in the Assembly who were more confident that definite action could be taken to unite the Southern

[1] Charleston *Daily Courier*, October 6, 1859; *ibid.*, November 26, 1859.
[2] Governor's Message No. 1 (November 29, 1859), *Journal of the House of Representatives of South Carolina: Being the Session of 1859* (Columbia, 1859), pp. 12–24.

states. The problem was what sort of steps leading to what result? From the opening rap of the gavel, resolutions poured onto the dockets of the House and Senate calling for everything from vague and truculent proclamations to pledges of arms and men for Virginia, and even demands for immediate secession. The crisis atmosphere in which the Assembly worked is suggested by the essential agreement of resolutions submitted by James Hammond's son Edward, and by Benjamin F. Perry, a man who in ordinary circumstances would have been found on the opposite end of the political spectrum. Hammond, a representative from Barnwell District, condemned John Brown's raid as an expression of unmitigated hostility by the Republican party, and proof of "the apparent state of public sentiment in the so-called Free States." The South must anticipate renewed attacks upon slavery, he insisted, and he called on the House officially to declare to the world that the American Union "would be scarcely an atom in the scale against the perpetual maintenance of our system of African slave labor."[3]

The similarity of Perry's resolution offered persuasive evidence of the fundamental agreement of South Carolina whites on the race question, whatever their position on disunion. Since the 1820's Perry had remained the most outspoken opponent of disunionism in the state; this was a role in which he took clear satisfaction, and one which he played with stoic determination. Nevertheless, he was plainly shaken by Harpers Ferry. "*Resolved,*" Perry's declaration of conscience began,

That the people of South Carolina feel no apprehension as to the permanent existence, safety and security of their domestic institution of African slavery, founded, as it is, in the best interests and happiness of the white and black races, and which they are prepared to protect and defend at any and every sacrifice of their political relations with the Federal Government and the Northern States, should it be invaded or assailed in any manner or form whatever.

The Greenville lawyer testified to the disdain felt by Carolinians for the hypocritical expressions of sympathy from the North for

[3] *House Journal,* pp. 56–57.

John Brown, and the unbelievable deification of a man he considered to be a murderer. Perry would come to regret the vehemence of his words, but in December 1859 he spoke for the whole state when he demanded an end to such outrageous attacks upon the essential institution of slavery, even to threatening secession itself.[4] All over the state Unionists like Perry were seriously questioning their hope that the peace and safety of the South could remain secure in the Union.[5] But what could be more dramatic, or more welcome to radicals than an avowal of despair by this particular man. The editor of the *Mercury* could hardly suppress his delight. "We frankly acknowledge that Mr. Perry's resolution has given us more gratification than any other offered in the legislature, not so much on account of its substance, as of the man who offered it."[6]

Despite this real agreement on the fundamental issue, the subsequent rejection of Rhett's own proposals by the legislature indicated that there was still a disinclination to have the state take the lead in any radical action. The essence of Rhett's program at this time was to prevent the state's participation in the upcoming National Democratic Convention. He and his followers were counselling the state to remain aloof from the contaminating association of convention with the Northern Democracy. South Carolina politicians were already looking toward the presidential nominating convention, and adherents of the *Mercury* program believed that only a simon-pure Southern convention could present a sound platform and candidate. Resolutions declaring this to be state policy were presented in the Senate by Rhett's brother, Edmund. Yet even in the more radical Senate[7] the painful isola-

---

[4] *Ibid.*, pp. 72–73.
[5] For example, see Daniel H. Hamilton, Federal Marshal in Charleston, to William Porcher Miles, December 9, 1859, William Porcher Miles Papers, SHC. Hamilton referred to the conversion of "a rank disunionist F. I. Moses," a state senator from Sumter. Moses, chairman of the Committee on Federal Relations, was now ready to endorse secession. "I had not believed that I would see the day when I would ask to be delivered from this Union," Moses declared, "but it has come." *Courier*, December 10, 1859.
[6] Charleston *Mercury*, December 5, 1859.
[7] The Senate was traditionally more disposed to support radical proposals than the House, for it was based upon the direct representation of districts and the numerous low country parishes, rather than population.

tion of South Carolina in the secession effort of seven years before had taught a memorable lesson. Secessionists were defeated then because of the obvious unwillingness of other states to join South Carolina in the fearful plunge. Since that time the hallmark of national politics had been the determination to cooperate with the rest of the Southern states. Senator B. H. Wilson, a low country moderate, well expressed this determination not to be stampeded into separate secession by "self-appointed leaders." Attacking Rhett's resolutions, Wilson caustically reminded the Senate that the other slaveholding states were just as aware of present dangers as was South Carolina; any effective action had to come through a united South. "I am a secessionist," Wilson concluded with peculiar logic, "but I am a law-abiding man." In the end, despite an unremitting barrage of criticism by the *Mercury* for inaction on the "greater issues" of the national party platform and the Presidential nomination, the Senate was persuaded to agree with Wilson. South Carolina would participate in the Democratic convention to assure the nomination of another conservative president. What other security was there in the Union?[8]

— 2 —

For the present there was general agreement on certain lines of action. For one, there was statewide acceptance of the need for better military preparedness. The first reports of John Brown's seizure of the armory at Harpers Ferry had elicited expressions of fear over the inadequacies of the state's military posture.[9] A month after the attack, Governor Henry A. Wise of Virginia, fearing threats by Northern abolitionists to recover Brown and his cohorts, advised Governor Gist to arm South Carolina.[10]

---

[8] Edmund Rhett's resolutions are in the *Courier*, December 5, 1859. The debate which it sparked was reviewed in *ibid.*, December 10 and 17, 1859. On opposition to the state's participation in the convention, see Rhett's editorials in the *Mercury* for December 5, 6, and 7, 1859. Commenting on the confusion of sentiment in the legislature, the Columbia correspondent for the *Mercury* warned that the present opportunity for action might be "frittered away upon immaterial and insignificant measures leaving to the Nationals [Democrats] and politicians of the South every opportunity for patching up hollow truces." *Mercury*, December 7, 1859.
[9] *Courier*, October 25, 1859.
[10] Beaufort Taylor Watts to James H. Hammond, November 27, 1859, James H. Hammond Papers, LC.

Within the state there was a quickened sense of the military weakness of the South, and of the danger of reliance upon Northern gunpowder and arms. In the same spirit, the palpable inefficiency of the militia system came under review at a time when new companies were rapidly being formed.[11] The result was an immediate demand by the House for a full report on the military stores and general defensive condition of the state's arsenals, along with resolutions seeking an increase in the military contingency fund. Members of the legislature also seemed united on the desirability of extending moral, or even material aid to Virginia, and to the other border states.[12]

But the issue that evoked the most resolutions and the angriest debate was the question of achieving Southern unity, with the shadow of secession behind it. The first resolution introduced in the lower chamber proclaimed the readiness of the state to form a Southern confederacy. During the following week numerous resolutions were submitted to the General Assembly expressing the desire of the people of South Carolina for cooperative action against the North. Some of these resolutions would have authorized the Governor, or a state-wide "Committee of Safety," to convene the legislature when the time came for disunion; others were certain that time had arrived, and would have invited Virginia to lead off on the path of secession. One of the few resolutions on this issue of Southern cooperation and disunion which came to a vote in the House was perhaps the most advanced. William Whaley of Charleston proposed that the state appropriate $100,000 to the military fund, since "fraternal relations" between the sections had already ceased, and a formal dissolution of the Federal ties was all that remained to be done. The

---

[11] *Courier*, December 7, 1859, quoting the [Pickens] *Keowee Courier;* letter of Lewis Hatch to William Porcher Miles, December 6, 1859, Miles Papers, SHC; "Resolutions of the Students of South Carolina College," in *Courier*, December 7, 1859. These aggressive resolutions which accompanied the formation of a militia company among the students explained that every man was obliged to be a "citizen soldier" in these days when "our most cherished institution of African slavery" was under attack. See also the article by James Johnston Pettigrew calling for militia reform in this hour of crisis. [James Johnston Pettigrew], "The Militia System of South Carolina," *Russell's Magazine*, VI (March 1860), 529–40.

[12] *House Journal*, pp. 43, 52–53, 56–57, 70, 90–91; *Senate Journal*, p. 43; *Courier*, December 5, 1859.

86270

House voted to table this presumptuous suggestion by a vote of sixty to forty-four. In the upper chamber parish senator Alexander Mazyck laid down the basis for debate in resolutions which described slavery as immutable and perpetual, lamented that the Federal Government was about to fall into the control of a popular majority hostile to the institution, and deduced secession from the syllogism as "essential to the very existence of the Southern states as civilized communities."[13]

The voting on various resolutions indicated that the House was by no means ready to rush the state out onto another precarious limb to be peremptorily cut down by the tenacious conservatism of the Southern people.[14] However much their confidence in Northern moderation had been shaken by recent events, the majority of the leaders of the state sitting in Columbia had not abandoned a reasonable belief that the South was still politically strong in the Union, and that Southern unity must precede any irrevocable disunion move. While the vocal fraction of outright secessionists fumed at lost opportunities, it was apparent that most South Carolinians still agreed with this analysis. Accordingly, the numerous resolutions looking hopefully toward some sort of concert of action by the Southern states, with an undefined hint of "security" promised thereby, were received gratefully by the House. Nevertheless, for two more weeks the legislature was the scene of often bitter wrangling over the proper course to take.[15] It was not until Christopher Memminger accepted the necessity for positive action that the state of South Carolina committed itself to the next step towards secession.

The impact of Harpers Ferry upon political sentiment in the state was made clear when Memminger rose on December 3 to question the need for the flood of resolutions being proposed.

[13] *House Journal*, pp. 42–43, 53, 58, 85, 91–92, 174–75; *Senate Journal*, pp. 36–65. Senator Mazyck's opening resolution described slavery as "essential to the maintenance of order and industry" in the South. See the *Courier*, December 5, 1859, and the *Mercury*, December 28, 1859.

[14] There is an analysis of the voting on a number of these resolutions in Harold S. Schultz, *Nationalism and Sectionalism in South Carolina, 1852–1860; A Study of the Movement for Southern Independence* (Durham, 1950), pp. 193–99.

[15] *House Journal*, pp. 70–71, 83, 99; *Senate Journal*, p. 36; Daniel H. Hamilton to W. P. Miles, December 9, 1859, Miles Papers, SHC.

Memminger clearly dominated the lower chamber by the force of his integrity and experience; his leadership was acceptable to a House divided by state sectionalism, economic interests, and conflicting attitudes about federal relations.[16] Still, more than a few members must have sat up sharply in their seats to see this lifelong moderate arguing with Benjamin F. Perry about the desirability of taking a public stand on the present emergency. In contrast to the Greenville Unionist, Memminger at this time believed only in silent preparedness. Memminger, who had helped defeat disunionists seven years before, now pledged to vote for any amount of money sufficient to put the state in readiness for a call to secession; but he was convinced that the call had to come from outside the state.

For the next two weeks Memminger observed the rising debate among his colleagues. The unity of South Carolina was imperative, but there was no unity. This was a controversy arising not from any disagreement on the fundamental problem of security for slavery, nor from any serious flare-up in the traditional schism between up country and low. Rather, this was a division springing out of the deep and justifiable reluctance of most to have South Carolina take the lead in a "resistance" movement. J. D. Pope, chairman of the House Committee on Federal Relations, for example, defended "masterly inactivity" as the very policy of Calhoun. He admitted that "the great freesoil, abolition party of the North has made all of us disunionists, not by choice, but by compulsion." But the St. Helena legislator cautioned that "Revolutions are not planned," and try as they did, radicals were unable to convince a majority in the Assembly that the people of the South recognized the extent of the present crisis, or that separate state action at this time would be anything but insanity.[17]

With the legislature entering its final week, the House still found itself locked in debate. At last Memminger asked for the floor. As reporters noted, the Assembly always listened silently

[16] Memminger was chairman of the Committee on Ways and Means, and the Committee of the Whole. See the *Mercury*, December 15, 1859.
[17] *Courier*, December 5, 1859; *ibid.*, December 7, 1859; *ibid.*, December 22, 1859, quoting the Columbia *Daily South Carolinian; Courier*, December 16, 1859; Mary Doline O'Connor, *The Life and Letters of M[ichael] P. O'Connor* (New York, 1893), pp. 18–19.

and intently to every speaker; surely this was so when the familiar Charlestonian rose. "We are all agreed that in this Union there is no safety for South Carolina," he began calmly. Noting that at Union meetings in the North even former Presidents had queued up to condemn the expansion of slavery, and to degrade the South, Memminger now called for new terms to restore Southern security in the Union. But it was not for Carolina to take the lead. Virginia was attacked, he exclaimed, she must be encouraged to give direction. Memminger was alive to the principles that divided his state, and he attempted to shape his analysis so as to mollify conservatives and attract disunionists. Secession *per se* would mean cutting South Carolina off from her only allies in the world, he cautioned. And, he demanded of his more aggressive colleagues, who could hope that the secession of South Carolina at this moment would arouse the South to join the movement?

Having thus disposed of potential opposition, Memminger motioned to the Clerk to read a set of proposed resolutions. There was little in them that was original. He had simply absorbed the mass of propositions, the bold and the timid, and established a common ground on which all the people of the state could stand. In essence, Memminger would: have the state call for a Southern convention "to concert measures for united action"; carry special words of sympathy and inducement to Virginia through a high commissioner; invigorate the military condition of the state by an appropriation of $100,000, and appoint an executive officer to oversee military preparedness. So perfectly had Memminger judged the temper of the House that by late that same afternoon, December 16, the House accepted his resolutions unanimously. The Senate at first balked at the program, preferring its own vague and impractical declaration of the "need" for secession. As the official day of adjournment drew near each chamber still refused to accept the resolutions of the other. It was Memminger again who proposed and participated in a House-Senate Committee of Free Conference which convened on the last working day of the session. Late that night, December 21, the Committee agreed to issue the Senate's preamble and the Memminger resolutions together as a single proclamation. With their leaders joining hands in a satisfying display of unanimity, the people of South Carolina looked towards the new year with hope and fear.[18]

— 3 —

The secession of South Carolina was eventually effected as the separate act of the state. Accordingly, the attention of this study is focused for the most part on what was done and said by Carolinians, and how events beyond their borders were perceived and interpreted. Indeed, much of the rhetoric of state leaders betrayed a desire to turn away from outside affairs, even to isolate the state from them. Nonetheless, isolation was impossible. Most of the representatives in Columbia were aware of this, for they haggled over their own resolutions under the shadow of a controversy at the seat of the national government, a controversy that threatened to bring the Republic crashing down about them. The conflict over the election of the Speaker in the House of Representatives—a debate which lasted from early December to the first of February, 1860—was a more than incidental background to Memminger's mission to Virginia.[19]

The approaching session of Congress had been awaited with anxiety. Charlestonians read such resolutions as those passed by the Tennessee state legislature condemning Seward as the moral instigator of John Brown's attack, and enjoining the state's congressional representatives against any affiliation with "Black" Republicans. The 36th Congress, coming as it did in the midst of continuing excitement over the Harpers Ferry affair (and intensified jostling for position in the approaching party conventions), took on added importance in the minds of all observers. Senator James H. Hammond was persuaded to postpone plans

[18] *House Journal*, pp. 197–204; *Senate Journal*, p. 168; *Courier*, December 19, 1859; *ibid.*, December 23, 1859; *ibid.*, December 24, 1859. The initial roll calls on Memminger's resolutions were overwhelmingly in favor, and the first four were adopted unanimously shortly thereafter. The fifth, concerning a director of military defenses, was withdrawn after consultation.

[19] Accounts of both incidents may be consulted in Ollinger Crenshaw, "The Speakership Contest of 1859–1860. John Sherman's Election a Cause of Disruption," *Mississippi Valley Historical Review*, XXIX (December 1942), 323–38; and the same author's, "C. G. Memminger's Mission to Virginia in 1860," *Journal of Southern History*, VIII (August 1942), 334–50.

for retirement because of John Brown's raid. His constituents were certain that the slavery issue would be raised in greater fury than ever before. And, as William Henry Trescot predicted to Hammond, the crucial events of the upcoming session would compel a "development of opinion especially Southern opinion as will allow one to make some calculation for the future."[20]

Trescot's high estimate of the importance of this session was suddenly underscored by a vitriolic national controversy over Hinton Rowan Helper's antislavery book, *The Impending Crisis of the South: How to Meet It*. Helper was a North Carolina non-slaveholder whose violent Negrophobia may have exceeded the feelings of most Southern defenders of the institution. His book, made more impressive by an extensive use of census statistics, was particularly frightening to Southern slaveholders because it attacked slavery not on moral grounds but as an aristocratic institution which destroyed the economic and social opportunities of the mass of white yeoman farmers. Such a matter-of-fact antislavery appeal by a native of the region was appalling, and Helper was roundly denounced as a traitor to his section. Helper's critique struck defenders of slavery in a sensitive point—the persistent fear that the Southern non-slaveholder would not support the institution to the death. John Durat Ashmore, congressional representative from Pendleton, a piedmont district containing relatively few slaves, was especially alert to this threat. Ashmore took the floor of Congress to denounce the misrepresentations of *The Impending Crisis;* but in a private letter to his brother he worried over the "evil effect" the book might have on his own constituents.[21]

---

[20] *Mercury*, November 5, 1859; William Henry Trescot to James H. Hammond, October 31, 1859, George P. Elliott to Hammond, November 5, 1859, and Hammond to William Gilmore Simms, December 19, 1859, Hammond Papers, LC.

[21] *Courier*, December 1, 1859; John D. Ashmore to his brother, January 12, 1860, in Rosser Howard Taylor, ed., "Letters Dealing with the Secession Movement in South Carolina," *Furman University Faculty Studies Bulletin*, XVI (1934), 3–12. Ashmore's fears seemed to be substantiated by the arrest during the previous month of a Greenville farmer named Harold Willis. A. B. Crook, president of the local vigilance committee investigated rumors that Willis had been circulating copies of the *Impending Crisis* in Greenville. Two copies of the book were found in his home, and two more were

When the book was first published two years earlier, it had attracted little notice. But in the winter of 1859 it quickly became common knowledge that sixty-eight Republicans, many of them leading congressmen, had endorsed the book, and that a condensed "Compendium" had been prepared and distributed by the tens of thousands as a Republican party tract. Helper's name was soon on everyone's lips.[22] The full measure of the crisis was reached when it was realized that John Sherman—now the Republican candidate for the Speaker's chair—had endorsed the book. After his endorsement was seized upon as the basis for uncompromising opposition to his election, Sherman claimed that he had signed his name to the book without knowing its contents. But the damage was done. Even before news of the unfortunate connection between Helper's *Impending Crisis* and John Sherman became well known, Democrats assembling in Washington had been apprehensive about Republican control of the House. As a leading political historian of this period has noted, the House Speaker was of greater importance in those years, for he controlled committee appointments. With the Presidential election approaching, Republicans were planning a vigorous search for fraud in the Buchanan Administration, as well as a concerted effort to obtain tariff revision; and all sides were aware of the real possibility that multiple candidates in the Presidential election might throw the decision into the House of Representatives

---

known to have been sent to friends of Willis "by a reading negro preacher." Under the authority of the vigilance committee Willis had been jailed, and was awaiting trial. In a letter to Ben Perry, Crook made the mood of the district clear. "We shall resist his *being* bailed. I think when you have examined the book you will agree with me that no man who will give aid to its circulation should be permitted to go at large in our community, but that he should be kept in a safe place until he can be tried and hung. . . . I do not believe that his presence, at large, will be tolerated by our people. Willis' safety personally, and his security for a fair trial depends in my estimation on his remaining in jaol until next court." Willis was eventually sentenced to a year's imprisonment. A. B. Crook to B. F. Perry, December 4, 1859, Benjamin F. Perry Papers, Ala.Arc. See also James Wylie Gettys, "Mobilization for Secession in Greenville District," (Unpublished master's thesis, the University of South Carolina, 1967), pp. 22–51.

[22] In the previously cited letter to Perry, for example, Crook condemned the Republican party's endorsement and circulation of *The Impending Crisis*, which he had learned of through the New York *Herald*.

next winter. For all of these reasons Democrats were convinced that Republican control of the House would not be a mere party shift, but an event somehow fraught with danger to the very life of the Republic; many Northern Democrats had come to believe their own rash charges about the nature of their opposition.[23]

Now the news of Sherman's incautious endorsement steeled the will of Democrats North and South against any break in their ranks. Through the long emotion-filled weeks of midwinter Sherman's denials of foreknowledge of the contents of Helper's book, or support for abolition in the states became almost ritualistic. Nevertheless, his apparent approval of a book that was generally misinterpreted to be a typical moralistic antislavery tract lent added confirmation to the abolitionist image of all Republicans. "The whole work," intoned the *Mercury*, "proves beyond a doubt that this party has for its distinct object and end the emancipation of the slaves of the South." Thus the election of John Sherman as Speaker would raise the antislavery party to the next high plateau of power, and bring the inevitable success of abolitionism nearer. "The election of Sherman," wrote the Washington correspondent of the *Mercury*, "will be regarded as the triumph of Seward and the *avant courier* of the success of Seward in 1860." And, he pointedly asked, "Is the South ready to allow the power of the Government to be wielded for her subjugation and to promote a war of races? Is she ready to subject herself to this sign of abolitionism?"[24]

The emotional meaning of the election to South Carolinians was dramatized by the frenzy of steps taken to meet it. Most important, Sherman's candidacy was adamantly, and in the end, successfully resisted. As one political savant noted at the outset, the Southern contingent was "resolved to draw a broad and impassable line between themselves and the Republicans and any chance of their voting with them is nil." During the next two months

[23] Roy Franklin Nichols, *The Disruption of American Democracy* (New York, 1962), p. 271. Also see the *Courier*, December 1, 1859; *ibid.*, December 5, 1859.
[24] *Mercury*, December 6, 1859; See also the speech of Lawrence M. Keitt, December 8, 1859, *The Congressional Globe: Containing the Debates and Proceedings of the First Session of the Thirty-Sixth Congress* (Washington, 1860), pp. 23–24.

over forty ballots were held, with Sherman often only a tantalizing three or four votes short of victory. Despite the fact that opposition to the Republicans came from a potpourri of sections and parties, the line held; Sherman's managers were unable to find the necessary votes among their disparate opposition. But fusion of pro-Administration and pro-Douglas Democrats, Whigs, and members of the American (Know-Nothing) party behind one candidate to oppose Sherman was even more unlikely,[25] and at last an exhausted House chose a weak and colorless Whig convert to Republicanism, William Pennington of New Jersey, to break the logjam. "Nine radical Southerners"—most of them South Carolinians—"had preferred destroying their party's chance of victory to voting for a Douglas man. The spirit foreshadowed the fate of the Charleston convention."[26]

[25] The strained effort to unite these parties and factions upon a mutually acceptable man is described by two South Carolina participants, the radical Lawrence Keitt, and the Unionist John Ashmore. See the letters of Ashmore to Ben Perry, December 25, 1859, and January 14, 1860, Perry Papers, Ala. Arc; and Keitt to O. M. Dantzler, January 18, 1860, O. M. Dantzler Papers, Calhoun County Historical Commission.

[26] Nichols, *Disruption*, p. 276. Northern Democrats never appreciated the intense fear among their Southern party colleagues. Whether Administration or Douglas supporters they were ready to do business in the traditional manner to advance their special interests. In December and January cabinet members received covert offers to "make a few votes" for one or another Democratic candidate. (See, for example, the letter of John F. Cowan to Jeremiah S. Black, December 24, 1859, Jeremiah S. Black Papers, LC.) Better evidence of this fatal incapacity to appreciate the uncompromising attitude of Southern radicals may be found in the Miles Papers, SHC. George Nicholas Sanders, then Navy Agent in New York City and a would-be president maker for Stephen A. Douglas since 1851, attempted to bribe William Porcher Miles with money and the offer of the very Speakership at issue, in exchange for his support for Douglas. Sanders assured Miles and his colleague, Lawrence Keitt, that the controversy in Washington was causing a conservative reaction at the North. "Dont organise" he telegraphed the two Carolinians on December 16, "earnest revolution going on all over the North adjourn Congress until after holidays & all come here." There is no evidence to indicate that Douglas was even aware of, much less behind, this plot. Sanders had a penchant for this skulduggery; at various times he assured the Vice-Presidential nomination to both William Lowndes Yancey and South Carolina politician Francis W. Pickens with the same motive. Nevertheless, as late as December 24 the intrepid Sanders appeared to be hopeful, as exhibited by this fascinating and purposely obscure letter to Miles:

"The unique enclosure will satisfy you that you exhibited profound

— 4 —

A more ominous spirit, which looked toward secession itself, was evinced by attitudes on the home front. With the exception of conservatives who were eager for compromise, and some extremists who hoped for Sherman's success as a way to arouse the South, the unyielding line taken by the state's representatives appears to have been strongly supported at home.[27] E. W. Marshall, for example, a Charleston merchant, whose past politics had been marked by moderation, cheered on his friend and congressman, Miles. While on a trip to New York City, Marshall gleefully noted signs of financial unrest related to the inability of Congress to pass appropriation bills. *"We have them,"* Marshall exulted, "don't yield unless a man can be elected who is acceptable to the South—*We of the South can stand it*—The North can-

---

sagacity in the selection of your Ambassador Extraordinary—return the billet doux by first mail allowing Mrs. K. and the 'Immortal' [Keitt] a glance only. You must not allow such vulgar considerations as the want of a Sergant [sic] at arms to delay you a moment in coming here, as you now sight on me, limit $1,500,000 [sic?].

Your expenses will necessarily be large as you are expected, yes required to have in your suite Madames Douglas & Keitt. Write on the receipt of this & give me a detailed account how you intend to move & telegraph when you start. The excitement must be kept up at all hazzards, studiously avoiding the slow corduroy ways that beset B[uchanan?] on every turn in his expectations—'Steam & Lightning' is our motto.

Adjourn Congress until after the holiday & haste here to perfect my negotiations, and I'll return with you in one week & elect you Speaker Sure.

[P.S.] No allusion to the enclosed—your answer must be a show document to Bank on—and on no consideration must it be deemed possible that the little note could get out of my possession."

[27] Letters to Porcher Miles from W. Alston Pringle, December 22, 1859, Isaac W. Hayne, January 5, 1860, Edward Bell, January 6, 1860, William Russell, January 10, 1860, E. W. Marshall, January 13, 1860, and Robert F. W. Allston, February 13, 1860, Miles Papers, SHC. The letters from Russell and Bell are typical of the "signals" from the North reaching South Carolina leaders. Russell labeled Sherman a "Dam'd Black Republican Abolitionist & Endorser of the infamous Helper," while Bell assured Miles, "were I a Southerner I should be ultra rabid just now—for I think the aggressions are unjustifiable." See also William Henry Trescot to James Hammond, December 30, 1859, Hammond Papers, LC.

not." A week later, after reading a fire-eating speech by Miles, the Charleston businessman assured his representative "Your constituents will sustain you *to a man.*" Money was growing tighter, people were becoming more and more uneasy, and Marshall was confident that the "Helper party" would give way.

> Better the wheels of government should stop; the country go through a crisis similar to 1837 & 1857 than our principles, our honor be infringed upon—we have right, justice & the 'King of Kings' on our side.[28]

But for a group of Southern extremists in the House mere obstructionism was not enough. These men had been repeatedly stung by the criticism that they gave inadequate leadership to an eager constituency. Because of feelings of frustration, as well as an exaggerated sense of the precarious state of Southern security, a number of schemes began to emerge aimed at gaining some permanent value from the excitements of the current imbroglio. Despite the scarcity of surviving materials, at least two closely related revolutionary plans were promulgated by South Carolina secessionists in Congress, both schemes contingent on Sherman's election. Fortunately, the Republican shift from Sherman to Pennington forestalled the possible implementation of either measure.[29]

The more restrained, though constitutionally unprecedented, plan would have brought about a national referendum on the ultimate question of security for slavery in the Union. William Porcher Miles, who was evidently the sole instigator behind this idea, was certain that most Southerners had not yet despaired of the Union and slavery. They continued to hope that the mass of Northerners would oppose any direct move against slavery in the states; this conviction was always one of the fundamental

---

[28] E. W. Marshall to Miles, January 13 and 20, 1860, Miles Papers, SHC.

[29] For example, see the letter of Miles to Christopher Memminger, February 3, 1860, Christopher G. Memminger Papers, SHC. For Miles—one of the leading extremists—there was the added impetus of rising disaffection at home with his performance as congressman, by one side for his apparent inaction, and by the other for excessive radicalism. See letters to Miles from James Johnston Pettigrew, February 4, 1860, and William Gilmore Simms, February 5, 1860, Miles Papers, SHC.

sources of opposition to the revolution of secession. Miles wanted to use the present crisis to test this confidence and reveal its falseness by compelling every congressman, through legislation, to resign his seat upon the election of Sherman to the Speakership. The Charleston legislator demonstrated his leanings toward English political forms in this unlikely suggestion, for what he proposed, as he himself explained to Memminger, was nothing less than a "general election." Parliament, that is, Congress, would be forced out onto the country, and "if in the present excited condition of the mind of the whole Country the North sent back to Congress an increased number of [Republican] votes we would have my conviction verified and the final Q.E.D. would unite the South."[30]

Other congressional radicals were pressing for a less delicate resolution of the sectional furor. This more violent scheme involved the engineering of an open physical conflict, perhaps even in the halls of Congress itself, to greet the election of Sherman. Years of bitter debate in Congress and the state legislatures, in churches, schools, and homes had created a smoldering sense of frustrated anger North and South. In South Carolina radicals chafed at the restraints of protocol. "Are there any who look upon the present as a real practical crisis in the History of the South," asked Miles's friend Isaac Hayne, or would the immense excitement merely produce another party compromise? Daniel Hamilton, United States Marshal for Charleston, assured Miles that the people of their state were prepared for "anything," and would welcome "any measures which the Southern members may adopt to bring this contest into some positive form of action—we are tired of guarding against secret attacks." All this while moderates like John Ashmore decried the "deep, concentrated hatred" which suffused Congress. The members were arming themselves mentally and physically, preparing for what could be the long

---

[30] Miles to Memminger, January 20, 1860, Memminger Papers, SHC. The considerable surviving correspondence of South Carolina radicals names no other conspirators. The 36th Congress had its share of fire-eaters who may have been implicated. Edmund Ruffin records a conversation with members of the South Carolina, Alabama and Mississippi delegations, all of whom, he overstated, were "ready for secession." Edmund Ruffin MS Diary, December 8, 1859, LC.

awaited outburst of open conflict. In this atmosphere Southern extremists, furious at the continued disunity of their section, now seemed ready to instigate actual violence at the seat of government to precipitate secession.[31]

Details of the projected attack are contained in a letter of December 20 from Governor William Gist to Miles. The radical congressman had asked Gist whether the South Carolina legislature would support any plan being secretly deliberated in Washington. Gist replied that whatever was done by the state delegation would be backed wholeheartedly by the entire state, so long as it was done in unison with all of the other Southern states, or any large portion of them. Because of the deep significance of Sherman's endorsement of the Helper book, Gist went on to assure Miles that the legislature would even sustain a solitary withdrawal of the state's representatives from Congress if Sherman were elected Speaker.[32]

> The members of the Congress are mistaken in supposing that they ought not to move but wait for home action. I know that any thing coming from our members would almost controll the action of the state & the argument here is, that our members on the spot & at the scene of action, as sentinels should counsel us & sound the alarm.

However, Gist anticipated the course of events by cautioning Miles that the state might very well resist any such withdrawal if another Republican, one who had not signed the *Impending Crisis* endorsement, were substituted as their nominee.

He then broached the matter of the most violent plan contemplated by the extremist clique in Washington. Withdrawal,

[31] Letters to William Porcher Miles from Daniel H. Hamilton, December 9, 1859, William Elliott, December 16, 1859, Isaac W. Hayne, January 5, 1860, A. F. Warley, January 19, 1860, and Alfred Huger, January 20, 1860, Miles Papers, SHC; John D. Ashmore to his brother, January 12, 1860, in R. H. Taylor, ed., "Letters dealing with the Secession Movement."

[32] Indeed, as Gist wrote these lines in Columbia, John Harrell, a representative from Horry District was presenting a resolution to the General Assembly calling for the withdrawal of South Carolina's delegation to Congress should any Republican be elected Speaker. The day before he had submitted a petition from sundry citizens of his district calling for this withdrawal. *House Journal*, p. 227; *Courier*, December 21 and 22, 1859.

the Governor wrote, was "preferable to ejecting the speaker elect by force." That plan might precipitate a terrible confrontation, and Gist calmly explained that while he was ready to resist the abolitionists with force, "yet if a bloodless revolution can be effected, of course it would be preferable." Still, Gist wanted to be sure that Miles understood him:

> When I advise against the ejection of Sherman if elected I do not wish to be understood as not desiring the war to begin at Washington; but as I would prefer it should begin in sudden heat & with good provocation rather than a deliberate determination to perform an act of violence which might prejudice us in the eyes of the world.

Radical extremists were deliberately scheming to destroy Congress as the prelude to the unification of the slave states and the creation of an independent Southern confederacy. Here was spirit portentous enough to bring down the Republic. The withdrawal of Sherman's name prevented a test of these apocalyptic plans.[33]

— 5 —

Despite these ominous events in Washington, legislators in Columbia looked forward to the launching of their own effort to obtain Southern unity in a more traditional manner. Not every segment of the population fully accepted Memminger's compromise resolutions passed on December 22. As noted, Rhett had hoped that the state would be sufficiently aroused to hold back from the Democratic convention; this program was never seriously considered. However, Rhett was not so inflexible as to spurn the potentialities of a convention of the Southern states. As private correspondence soon made clear, it was by no means obvious to all that this was, as one historian has written, "cooperationism of the most innocuous kind."[34] Rumors that Governor Gist was planning to name Memminger to the role of Com-

[33] William Gist to William Porcher Miles, December 20, 1859, Miles Papers. Gist was willing to support any action. "If however, you upon consideration decide to make the issue of fire in Washington, write or telegraph me, & I will have a Regiment in or near Washington in the shortest possible time."
[34] Laura A. White, *Robert Barnwell Rhett: Father of Secession* (New York, 1931), p. 160.

missioner to Virginia were soon proved correct. While Rhett was disappointed to see his state running off again in vain pursuit of Southern unity, he was perhaps not dissembling when he called on the leaders of his section to participate and contribute ideas calculated to bring security.

> There nowhere exists any wish to retire from the Union [declared the *Mercury*] if the people of the Southern States can obtain equality, security and peace. If any statesman of Virginia can point out a mode of obtaining such a future, let him do it. None will object or blind their eyes to the prospect. . . . To maintain the civilization and freedom of the Southern States—not the preservation of the Union is the question of the day for us.[35]

Memminger's selection was the perfect capstone to the facade of unity drawn across the state by the legislature. While some men wondered why any action was needed, and questioned the wisdom of appearing to put South Carolina back into the lead,[36] it was clear that most moderates were deeply satisfied to see personal rancor set aside by the Memminger program, even for the moment. Past bitterness, added to traditional pressure against political dissension, had created a passion for unanimity in the state. Speaker James Simons, who was himself a National Democrat, adverted to this theme in his closing address to the House by counselling his colleagues to promote "union of sentiment" when they returned home. "Question no man's patriotism because he differs from you," he wrote, urging them to use the resulting consensus as a device to "train the public will" to respond as one man in a moment of crisis. It is more likely that he hoped these words of conciliation would help protect South Carolina mod-

[35] *Courier,* December 23, 1859; *Mercury,* December 29, 1859; *ibid.,* January 5, 1860.
[36] Piedmont congressman John Ashmore expressed dismay when he first learned of the Memminger mission. He had "begged Gist to prevent if possible any resolutions beyond the announcement that we would stand by Va. This it seems is not enough & we must again assume the attitude of pushing the state forward." Yet after three weeks of fruitless debate in Congress Ashmore was persuaded that the mission to Virginia could be the basis of a permanent adjustment of the slavery question in the Union. Ashmore to B. F. Perry, December 25, 1859, and January 14, 1860, Perry Papers, Ala. Arc.

erates who were already moving to have the state "properly" represented at the Democratic convention in April. Fellow moderate Richard Yeadon, editor of the Charleston *Daily Courier*, eagerly applauded Gist's selection of Memminger in the interest of unity. Not to be outdone, the *Mercury* bowed to the prevailing climate of opinion by also approving the nomination. The man and the occasion seemed to have properly conjoined to permit a sober statement of the "*Carolina view* of this subject" to all the people of the South.[37]

Still, there was the practical problem of what to do with this opportunity. In the general mood of relief over the fact that the state had not cut itself off from the rest of the South, there was simply a vague desire to set forth the sentiment of the state, and consult about future policy.[38] From the first, however, there was an implicit radicalism in the whole adventure. Even before Memminger's proposals had been accepted, the conditional nature of Carolina moderation was evident. Charleston planter William Elliott demonstrated this in a letter to William Porcher Miles. The legislature was quiet, he wrote on December 16, "no fire eating resolutions, etc." Elliott thought this "calm[,] dignified & firm" approach best, but without the slightest sense of contradiction he concluded the letter by asking Miles what he thought of the "probability very soon within a year of a Disolution & So Confederacy–." With this same ambiguity, the proposed convention of the Southern states was repeatedly described as a real chance to make slavery safe in the Union, or failing in that, to open the door to secession. The Memminger program spelled conditional peace.[39]

[37] *House Journal*, pp. 267–68; *Courier*, December 29, 1859; *Mercury*, December 29, 1859; Isaac W. Hayne to William Porcher Miles, January 5, 1860, Miles Papers, SHC. As Rhett and Hayne noted, Memminger's appointment as commissioner was wise for a number of reasons. He had been a lifelong opponent of secession, he was still identified with the moderate party of the state, he had never held national office, and it was he who had drawn up the resolutions.

[38] As Yeadon opaquely phrased it, the state would extend her "respectful invitation to a solemn and deliberate consultation as to the practical resources of a common defence." *Courier*, December 29, 1859.

[39] Elliott to Miles, December 16, 1859, Miles Papers, SHC; *Courier*, December 29, 1859, quoting the Cheraw *Gazette*. In February Charleston repre-

Memminger believed this, and so apparently did most aware Carolinians. The abundance of surviving letters from those troubled days provides a full picture of the mission to Virginia, and it is clear that there was considerable hope in South Carolina that a convention would assemble, and that out of it would come a statement of final terms, guarantees for the security of slavery which the free states could accept or reject under threat of a disruption of the Union.[40] Memminger assured Miles that, above all, the legislators of the state sought to advance the cause of Southern unity, believing that the safety of slavery in or out of the Union depended on that unity.[41] Followers of Rhett were correct in labeling the Memminger program as cooperationism, for as Memminger admitted, the "only positive act" authorized by his resolutions was the call for a convention. Still, he denied allegations which began to emerge that the whole scheme was a subterfuge for perpetuating the present Union. "My opinion," he wrote, "and I think the opinion of our state is that the Union cannot be preserved; and that a sectional Government such as we now have is not worthy of preservation. New terms, fresh constitutional guarantees might make another Union desirable.

---

sentative Thomas Y. Simons well recalled the prevailing attitude in the legislature toward the Memminger resolutions, as he had chaired the House committee which initially considered them. "They offered a golden opportunity to the country. If embraced and carried out in good faith, they would have resulted either in developing the conservative element of the North, through the ballot box . . . or in the formation of a Southern Confederacy, under a system of regulated liberty, where our institutions would be at peace." *Speech in Favor of South Carolina being Represented in the Democratic Convention, delivered at a Meeting of the Citizens of Charleston, held in Hibernian Hall, February 26, 1860* (Charleston, 1860).

[40] Gist sent a copy of the state's resolutions to Virginia governor John Letcher with the assurance that "The people of South Carolina look with deep interest upon his mission, and confidently expect important results to grow out of it." January 11, 1860, Executive Papers, Virginia State Library.

[41] Memminger to Miles, December 27, 1859, Miles Papers, SHC. Memminger also asked for an estimate of political sentiment in Virginia, and for advice on who to confer with when he arrived. The South Carolina delegation did meet with their counterparts from Virginia in Congress. "The meeting lasted well into the night [of December 30] and was a free and serious exchange of views, although no public agreements were reached." *Mercury,* January 4, 1860. See also John Ashmore to B. F. Perry, January 14, 1860, Perry Papers, Ala.Arc.

But in this we shall soon be deprived of every defence against the Northern section."[42]

Even Miles, violent radical though he was, harbored some expectations of beneficial results from Memminger's trip. By urging upon the people of Virginia the necessity of adopting vigorous measures of self-protection, and by proving the inevitability of secession "unless every demand of the South were satisfied and some absolute security given for the future—" Miles hoped that the cardinal principle of the preservation of slavery would be advanced. Unfortunately, the prospects for such consummation were gloomy. Miles described his own long agonizing over the question of secession. He had opposed separate state secession in 1851, but since that time he had "seen all classes and conditions of men at the North—had carefully sounded the views and sentiments of Northern members of Congress," and now felt compelled to believe that the present Union was doomed. Defeat of the Republicans in the coming election would only postpone the issue. "How can we expect," Miles asked, "that a majority bitterly hostile to slavery in its every aspect—moral, political and social— will prove willing to protect a *minority* who are struggling on the one issue of its perpetuity and extension?" He ruefully concluded that the people of the South could never "know peace and security again in this Confederacy."[43]

— 6 —

At the advice of the congressional delegation, Memminger waited in Charleston for over a week before departing for Richmond. He left with his daughter on Wednesday, January 11, and reached the Virginia capital the following evening. He had written to Governor John Letcher a few days earlier advising the new governor of his travel plans, and he was greeted at Union station by a special committee of the Virginia Assembly; the South

[42] Memminger to Miles, January 2, 18[60], Miles Papers, SHC; Richmond *Enquirer*, January 2, 1860. For Henry William Ravenel the alternative was clear. "Should the North fail to give some substantial guarantees of security for Southern institutions and constitutional rights a revolution is inevitable." H. W. Ravenel MS Journal, USC, December 31, 1859.
[43] Miles to Memminger, January 10 and 15, 1860, Memminger Papers, SHC.

Carolina commissioner was escorted by them with appropriate fanfare to stately Ballard House. Memminger was no stranger to Richmond. Only three months before he had attended the annual convention of the Episcopal Church in the city, and he was now generally praised by Old Dominion newspapers as an intelligent, calm, and conservative man. Everyone recognized the unique meaning Memminger's presence gave to this mission, for it was no secret that he had been a formidable figure among South Carolina's opponents of secession in the past. On January 14 Memminger sent Governor Letcher a copy of his resolutions, and requested an invitation to address the Virginia Assembly. The people of South Carolina regarded John Brown's raid "as a blow equally at herself," Memminger declared, and they sought to join Virginia "in measures of common defence."[44]

It was a divided Assembly that received this offer. Virginia had shared with South Carolina the pattern of reaction to the abolitionist attack at Harpers Ferry, from local vigilance committees to violent declamation by then Governor Henry A. Wise. The exploitation of the raid by Wise, together with the apparent response of the North, threw all sectors of the state into distraction. Hatred and distrust of the North became so rampant in November and December that disunionism was seriously considered for a time by conservatives and radicals alike. Although many Virginians hailed the expression of sympathy coming from Union meetings in Philadelphia and elsewhere, the old confidence in Northern feelings had clearly been undermined. In accepting a "patriotic flag" from the Unionists of Philadelphia, for example, the Virginia Assembly responded with faint praise. The legislature thanked "that heroic band of Northern conservatives who have so long maintained an unequal conflict with the assailants of our rights, and the enemies of our peace." There was, more-

[44] John Ashmore to B. F. Perry, January 14, 1860, B. F. Perry Papers, Ala. Arc; Memminger to Miles, January 9, 1860, Miles Papers, SHC; *Courier*, January 16, 1860, quoting the Richmond *Dispatch*, and the Petersburg *Express;* Memminger to Letcher, January 14, 1860, Memminger Papers, SHC; Henry D. Capers, *The Life and Times of C. G. Memminger* (Richmond, 1893), pp. 243–45, 278–79. Letcher wrote to Miles to express warm compliments for Memminger, and to say that the Assembly would hear him the following Thursday, January 19. Letcher to Miles, January 15, 1860, Miles Papers, SHC.

over, a durable core of radical sentiment in Virginia well represented by such men as agriculturist Edmund Ruffin and United States Senator James Murray Mason. South Carolinians were also glad to receive private words of encouragement from friends in that state, as well as news of substantial military appropriations and support for commercial non-intercourse by the legislature.[45] The new governor, John Letcher, well typified the mood of his state. Letcher, who was to oppose secession after Lincoln's election, was dismayed by John Brown's raid and the reaction to it in the North. "The days of the Republic were numbered," he wrote despairingly to Senator Robert M. T. Hunter early in December. "All indications seem to me to point to a dissolution of the Union and that at an early day." His only hope was for a radical change in Northern sentiment, and his annual message, delivered just as Memminger set out for Richmond, called not for a Southern conference, but for a convention of all the states, a constitutional convention for the final arbitration of the sectional controversy. If the Northern states spurned this test of their conservatism, or failed to agree to satisfactory new terms for the protection of slavery, the moderate Letcher warned that Virginia would be compelled to consider a peaceful separation from the Union.[46]

The people of South Carolina were in no mood for any such

[45] Resolutions of the Virginia Legislature, December 24, 1859, in the *Courier*, December 26, 1859; J. N. Chambliss, Jr., to Robert F. W. Allston, January 6, 1860, R. F. W. Allston Papers, SCHS; D. H. London to Memminger, January 16, 1860, Memminger Papers, SHC; John Ashmore to B. F. Perry, December 15, 1859, Perry Papers, Ala.Arc.; Henry T. Shanks, *The Secession Movement in Virginia, 1847–1861* (Richmond, 1934), pp. 85–97.
[46] John Letcher to Robert M. T. Hunter, December 9, 1859, in *The Correspondence of R. M. T. Hunter, 1826–1876*, edited by Charles Henry Ambler, in American Historical Association, *Annual Report for the Year 1916*, 2 volumes (Washington, 1918), II, 274–75. See also Edmund Ruffin MS Diary, LC, December 17, 1859; *Courier*, January 11, 1860; and F. N. Boney, *John Letcher of Virginia; The Story of Virginia's Civil War Governor* (University, Ala., 1966), pp. 92–93. In his message Letcher concluded that the election of a Republican president would be final proof of the desire of the Northern people to destroy slavery; when that election result did come to pass, he resisted his own logic. For the reaction of other Virginians, see M. R. H. Garnett to Samuel Downing, January 14, 1860, Samuel Downing Papers, LC: and William Old, Jr., to Robert M. T. Hunter, January 1, 1860, in *Hunter Correspondence*, pp. 285–86.

national confrontation. It could only lead to more demands for Southern rights and meaningless, narcotic proclamations by the free states. In fact, Memminger's mission itself was generally looked upon by Carolinians as a test. For cooperationists—who in the end would decide the course of the state—the profound appeal of Calhoun's vision of a united South was far from dead. The assault by John Brown had sparked a general outcry among all Southerners from Maryland to Texas, and thereby seemed to provide a basis for common and immediate action by a solid South. Calhoun was the ultimate cooperationist, and the impulse behind Memminger's journey to Richmond lay in Calhoun's persuasive and everlasting confidence that a truly united South could calmly and successfully proclaim the terms on which the Union could be maintained. With the self-serving political value of abolitionism destroyed by such a settlement, the antislavery movement itself would vanish like a nightmare. (Of course, if these terms were rejected the Southern states would have no honorable alternative but to secede.) While Unionists and extreme secessionists in a sense agreed that "Revolutions are not planned," most South Carolina politicos continued to believe that the deliberate unification of Southern sentiment and leadership was essential as the precursor to the achievement of permanent safeguards for slavery in or out of the Union. And the mission to Virginia was widely regarded as the inauguration of this project, or at least a conclusive testing of it.

The bankruptcy of cooperationist policy was evident from the start. Virginia had so often demonstrated her antipathy to activism that Carolina Unionists had come to look confidently to the cool temper of that state as a bulwark against secession.[47] Although Miles cherished the notion that the people of Virginia would prove to be radical, it soon became obvious to Memminger that any hope for active leadership by the state was stillborn. Realistic Virginia secessionists recognized this fact even as they encouraged South Carolina. For example, D. H. London, a fiery Virginian, offered his support to Carolina even if his own state proved "too craven-hearted to vindicate her own honour."

[47] William Campbell Preston to Francis Lieber, March 6, 1859, Francis Lieber Papers, USC.

Friends of Memminger, among them South Carolina congressman William W. Boyce, were justified in fearing that the Old Dominion was not yet prepared to look secession in the face. Within that state there was plainly a different scale of values attached to measures of resistance. Even such a strong defender of Southern rights as Congressman M. R. H. Garnett, a man who welcomed the warm and united feeling created in his state by the attack at Harpers Ferry, was unable to look beyond arming Virginia and instituting commercial non-intercourse with the North. As might be expected, Garnett's unflagging hope lay in devices to bring "our Northern brethren . . . to their senses." The violent language of Governor Wise in October and November, threatening retribution against the North, was generally distrusted by the South Carolinians and Virginians, who thought them motivated by a desire for self-aggrandizement. And politicians like James A. Seddon predicted that "in any real shock of sections, any practical disunion . . . Governor Wise will be among the first to recoil and betray."[48]

Wise's sudden reversal of position on the value of the Union soon revealed the accuracy of this prediction. In speeches delivered in late December and early January the former governor called on the South to fight in the Union to preserve the Constitution against the Republicans—to resist by force any attempt to drive the Southern states out of the Union. These speeches were received in South Carolina with scorn and derision. Charleston biologist John Bachman, prompted by Wise's declarations, wrote to his friend Edmund Ruffin to bemoan the "frenzy & madness" which seemed to rule the political stage, exemplified by Wise with his strange battle-cry. Bachman warned Ruffin that all would be lost if the South were compelled to war with the abolitionists in the Union; such a battle had been raging for decades, and the abolitionists would shortly have "their feet upon our necks and

[48] Letters to Memminger from Miles, January 10, D. H. London, January 16, and William Boyce, January 4, 1860, Memminger Papers, SHC; M. R. H. Garnett to Samuel Downing, January 11, 1860, Downing Papers, LC; James Seddon to R. M. T. Hunter, December 26, 1859, in *Hunter Correspondence*, p. 282. In his letter of January 10 Miles had specifically urged Memminger to direct Virginia away from any "practical and topical treatment" like non-intercourse.

their daggers in our throats." The Carolina scientist confessed that he had long opposed disunion. "I had long hoped against hope" he moaned, but now was forced to believe that no remedy was left but secession.

> We are all united here—there is now but one voice in So Carolina—we look with longing & hopeful eyes to our sister Virginia . . . . you have had a fair specimen of Northern sentiments in the tender mercies of old Brown. Are you waiting for something more of the same sort? You will have it before long. The endorsers of Helpers Book are too cowardly, but they will send substitutes—if they triumph they will hail them as Washingtons—if they are hung they will canonize them as martyrs.[49]

— 7 —

The date for Memminger's address had been set for January 19, and during the days immediately preceding he continued to agonize over what ground to take. William Boyce and Miles favored an aggressive appeal for substantial action, the first advising Memminger to picture the Harpers Ferry attack as the culmination of a generation of antislavery agitation, yet "only a foretaste of what is ahead of us"; and the second suggesting support for Governor Letcher's national convention, if that were all Virginia would go for. Miles looked upon the convention as a potential forum to deliberate *"new and sufficient guarantees for the future,"* but when the time arrived for the address, Memminger had come to recognize just how futile any proposal would be. Since his arrival in Richmond he had been sounding out Virginia politicians, and was disappointed to learn how far their sentiments were from what he had hoped. "Some are ready for anything," he wrote Miles, but even supposed radicals hung back from the issue of a Southern conference out of a "very great apprehension about inaugurating any thing that looks to Dis-

---

[49] *Mercury,* March 6, 1860; John Bachman to Edmund Ruffin, January 18, 1860, Edmund Ruffin Papers, SHC.

union." He had tried to link it to Letcher's proposed national convention, to no avail. Like Southerners everywhere, the leaders of Virginia were deeply divided by fear of secession, a division which was worsened here by partisan opposition from the vocal Whig party. And the Democratic party itself was split by intense factionalism stemming from the competition of ex-Governor Wise and Senator R. M. T. Hunter for the party's endorsement as favorite-son candidate in the race for the Presidential nomination. While Miles wrung his hands over the impenetrable (and, to a South Carolina radical, inexplicable) resistance of the Southern states to unification, Memminger prepared to make a vigorous statement of the nature of the present crisis.[50]

Emotionally the three and a half hour speech was an anticlimax. As Miles had earlier perceived, "Virginia [was] rapidly cooling down," and for this reason Memminger's address was not calculated to warm the failing spirit of radicalism in the Old Dominion, despite the enthusiasm of the galleries, crowded with ardent Richmond ladies. He began by reviewing earlier "friendly" communications between the two states in 1883 and 1851 as the justification for his present mission. (Actually, both of these interventions by Virginia were aimed at halting radical moves by South Carolina.) Harpers Ferry was, according to Memminger, a handy rule to measure the depth of sectional ill-feeling. And the waters ran deep. Over the past eighty years the North had mushroomed in economic and political power, and the antislavery crusade had grown with that power, drawing strength from it. Now all the constitutional safeguards for slavery were gone. There was no "more perfect Union," there was no protection for Southern life and property, and he reminded his listeners that when they sought to try John Brown and his fellow assassins they were compelled to proceed as if it were a military trial, with armed guards protecting the prison, courtroom, and scaffold from threatened attack. The death sentence was carried out to strident cries of "Martyr!" from the free states, while local elections in the

[50] Letters to Memminger from Boyce, January 4, and Miles, January 15 and 18, 1860, Memminger Papers, SHC; Memminger to Miles, January 16, 1860, Miles Papers, SHC; Edmund Ruffin MS Diary, LC, January 7, 1860; Memminger to Robert Barnwell Rhett, January 28, 1860, Memminger Papers, LC.

North went against peaceable Democrats. Memminger dramatically noted that even as he spoke over one hundred men in Congress still refused to abandon a candidate for Speaker who had, he said, endorsed anarchy and servile war. The current was running against the South and would not stop of itself.

> The South stands in the Union without any protection from the Constitution, subject to the government of a sectional party who regard our institutions as sinful and whose leaders already declare that the destruction of these institutions is only a question of time.

Memminger concluded his dismal analysis by appealing to sectional unity as the most potent resource of the South. A united South could retaliate within the Union. A conference could bring the best minds of the section together to fashion terms and devices for securing safety under the present government, even though, as he frankly admitted, South Carolinians had little confidence left that slavery could be secure in the Union. Yet they were ready to act in unison with Virginia, whatever action she adopted. "If our pace be too fast for some, we are content to walk slower; our earnest wish is that all may keep together." Memminger stood ready to endorse Governor Letcher's national convention, he was ready to back a southwide scheme of commercial non-intercourse, but however Virginia chose to act, he warned the Assembly, "We cannot consent to stand still."[51]

Memminger had been escorted to the state capital for his speech by two companies of militia, with flags flying along a route lined with enthusiastic Richmond citizens, but little fanfare greeted his return to Ballard House. A time for painful decision had come. Memminger was no longer the wizened, conservative Charlestonian; he was now a South Carolinian calling for action against the North, and, as Memminger had feared, Virginia was simply not prepared to act. The key Richmond *Enquirer* supported the convention idea only if its agenda were limited to

[51] Christopher Gustavus Memminger, *Address of the Hon. C. G. Memminger, Special Commissioner from the State of South Carolina before the Assembled Authorities of the State of Virginia, January 19, 1860* (Richmond, [1860]); Edmund Ruffin MS Diary, LC, January 19, 1860.

strengthening slavery within the Union.[52] Memminger continued to hold court in his hotel, receiving Virginians eager to express their disunionism. But few were willing to support a conference now which might save the nation the "need" to secede should a Republican be elected President in the fall. And Memminger was too realistic not to recognize that he saw only the most radical men in his suite. He was repeatedly told that the people were ahead of their political representatives. That, he ruefully noted, "is not likely to continue."

In part it was factionalism within the Democratic party over the Presidential nomination which divided the counsels of the state. But Memminger properly laid the real cause of Virginia's reluctance to join South Carolina to the "apprehension of Disunion [which] will cause the Legislature to decline our conference." In his frenetic quest for popular support, Governor Wise sounded the fatal bell. Wise came out for the conference as a way to save the Union. As Memminger described Wise's speech to Miles, the Virginian had warned that if the border states failed to lend their conservative voices to this movement, "South Carolina despairing of their assistance and disgusted with their inconstancy would go on, act alone and drag them along whether they would or no." This, Memminger sadly concluded, was very probably an accurate prediction. "It seems to me that we shall finally be brought to the point of making the issue alone and taking our chance for the other States to join us, whenever a Black Republican has the rule over us."[53]

Taking a moment from the furious squabbling in Congress, Miles applauded Memminger's address as a step toward concentrating Southern attention on the reality of the present crisis; but he had to admit that the prospect for any state acting on South Carolina's resolutions appeared dim. At home, Governor Gist lambasted the "timidity" of Virginians, and their absorption in the Presidential election. In a letter to Memminger he justly declared

---

[52] *Courier*, January 21, 1860, quoting the Richmond *Enquirer*. Privately, William Old, Jr., editor of the *Enquirer*, favored a strong stand by the state, partly to assist the presidential candidacy of Senator Hunter against ex-Governor Wise. See Old to Hunter, January 1, 1860, in *Hunter Correspondence*, pp. 285–86.

[53] Memminger to Miles, January 24, and 30, 1860, Miles Papers, SHC.

that the Old Dominion held a special place in the American Republic, and in the hearts of South Carolinians. If she would only take the lead in resistance to this "warfare on our institutions" the divided South would come together in a moment and follow her. "A united South can dictate the terms of our continuance in the union" Gist wanly asserted, "and the North will yield." Even Gist, with all of his violent oratory, had not given up the hope that a peaceful settlement was possible. (When the Governor of Maryland rejected the request for a conference on the grounds that it was a disunionist plot, Gist heatedly denied the allegation.) "If I am mistaken in this," the Governor wrote concerning his hopes for a peaceful solution, Virginia could still unite the South and lead the way towards a glorious, powerful Southern confederacy, one that could "defy a world in arms." But Virginia declined this dubious honor.[54]

After delivering his message, Memminger stayed on in Richmond for three weeks, awaiting a decision by the legislature. Committees were appointed in both houses of the Assembly to consider the proposals of Governor Letcher and of South Carolina; the divisions and apprehensions in the state were reflected in the fact that for two weeks the Senate could not even agree to convene. By February 6 Memminger's patience was exhausted. Even if a conference were dragged together, he explained to Miles, there was little hope that it could accomplish anything, "For they fear the conference so much, what chance is there of any strong measure . . . being adopted by them." Although he professed confidence that his mission was repaid by the revitalization of the "*Resistance* party in Virginia," the major objective

[54] Miles to Memminger, January 23, 1860, and Gist to Memminger, January 30, 1860, Memminger Papers, SHC; Dwight Lowell Dumond, *The Secession Movement, 1860–1861* (New York, 1931), pp. 31–32; a copy of Gist's letter to Maryland governor Hicks is in the *Mercury,* February 7, 1860. Not everyone had praise for Memminger. In a letter to Miles, Daniel Hamilton expressed doubt that the mission could accomplish anything. Memminger had merely told the people of Virginia what they already knew: that a violent abolition party in the North sought to destroy slavery and Southern civilization. "He had better told [them] that they were surrounded with those incendiary elements which if they does [*sic*] not control, will be used as the means of lighting her funeral pile. . . . The South is almost entirely hemmed in," Hamilton gasped, "and nothing is left to us but desperate fighting." Hamilton to Miles, January 23, 1860, Miles Papers, SHC.

seemed lost. With a gesture of gratitude to Letcher, Memminger and his daughter departed for Charleston and home.

There he penned a disconsolate review of his trip for Governor Gist. The conference seemed doomed out of fear of disunion, he wrote, yet that fear was unjustified. Memminger believed that only when the North overtly denied a constitutional right to the South and stripped her of some essential element of security would the fear of secession be justified. Since Virginians believed that fraternal feelings adequate to resist such an assault still existed in the North, Memminger hoped that Virginia would eventually agree to a peaceful conference.[55]

By the time he returned to South Carolina, the urgent hopes of late December had largely vanished. The reaction of Maryland typified a prevailing belief that the proposed convention looked towards the initiation of disunion. In fact, any plan coming from South Carolina was instantly tainted by its origin. But some states received the proposal more warmly. The legislatures of Florida and Alabama adopted resolutions indicating support should a convention be formally organized.[56] Most heartening of all, the Mississippi legislature completely accepted the proposal.[57] As early as December 5, the tone of Governor John Pettus's inaugural address, and the evidence of sentiment in the state, prompted a leading Mississippi newspaper to express the hope that the cotton states "will hold themselves in readiness to meet Mississippi in convention for mutual conference and joint action."[58] Reflecting

[55] Shanks, *Secession Movement in Virginia,* p. 99; Memminger to Miles, February 4, 6, and 9, 1860, Miles Papers, SHC; Memminger to Letcher, February 7, and to Governor Gist, February 13, 1860, in Capers, *Memminger,* pp. 279–81. As an example of the denial of a constitutional right, Memminger told Gist, "if a sectional party take possession of the Government."

[56] Because of the opposition of Governor Sam Houston, the radical Texas Assembly did not act on the bid. Crenshaw, "Memminger's Mission to Virginia," p. 344.

[57] Robert W. Dubay, "Mississippi and the Proposed Atlanta Convention of 1860," *Southern Quarterly,* V (April 1967), 347–62; Denman, *Secession Movement in Alabama,* p. 79. Alabama declined to nominate delegates to any convention at that time.

[58] *Semi-Weekly Mississippian* (n.d.), quoted in Dubay, "Proposed Atlanta Convention," 347–48; the resolutions of the Florida Assembly are in the *Courier,* December 26, 1859.

a similar spirit of concern and the desire for unity, state Senator Peter B. Starke, a Mississippi delta Whig, offered resolutions on January 20 calling for commissioners to join Memminger in Virginia, and despite the indifferent reception already accorded the South Carolina representative, the Mississippi State Assembly resolved on the tenth of February to send an agent to Richmond. The Assembly also suggested June 1 in Atlanta as a possible time and place for the proposed conference, and the next day Governor Pettus paralleled the action of Carolina by naming the moderate Starke as the commissioner. Thus the cooperationist attempt to establish permanent security for slavery in the Union had a second launching in 1860.[59]

These hopes, however, withered in Virginia's chilling atmosphere of Unionism and fear of secession. Although Starke was a recognized moderate who pitched his appeal to the conditional Unionism of Memminger's address, the resolutions finally adopted by the Virginia General Assembly on March 10 declared that no apparent value could come from such a convention "which can exercise no legitimate power except to debate and advise."[60] In March, congressmen from South Carolina, Alabama, and Mississippi met in a vain effort to revive the conference movement. As late as March 29, Gist was writing to the governors of Mississippi and Alabama, trying to encourage their support for a conference, even among the cotton states of the lower South. All to no avail. The movement was dead.[61]

— 8 —

The failure of this cooperationist movement was significant for the course of South Carolina to secession. In the winter and spring

[59] Dubay, "Proposed Atlanta Convention," 354–56; Percy Lee Rainwater, *Mississippi, Storm Center of Secession, 1856–1861* (Baton Rouge, 1938), pp. 105–106. The determination of the state was also indicated by the appointment of seven delegates to the proposed Atlanta convention.
[60] Shanks, *Secession Movement in Virginia,* p. 100; Dumond, *Secession Movement,* pp. 28–32.
[61] *Advertiser,* March 21, 1860; Denman, *Secession Movement in Alabama,* p. 80. In his reply to Gist's letter Alabama governor Albert B. Moore indicated that only if the platform and candidate selected at Charleston were unsatisfactory should such a meeting be held. Gist to Moore, March 29, 1860, Moore to Gist, April 2, 1860, Executive Papers, Ala.Arc.

of 1860 alternatives were collapsing in the faces of moderates all across the South. For outright secessionists the failure of the mission provided vivid proof of the folly of gaining security in the Union through Southern unity. As a spokesman for radical sentiment, the *Mercury* had long opposed dependence on Virginia or any border state for leadership. Even before Memminger abandoned his stand in Richmond, Rhett dismissed the whole scheme as proof of Virginia's incapacity for leadership, and insisted that any action must come from "one or a few cotton States."[62] By March the *Mercury* was energetically portraying the political implications of the abortive mission. It had exposed the delusion that the border states could be trusted to direct the Southern cause. "They may live and thrive without slavery," Rhett explained, but "to us the institution is indispensable." Rhett saw even more bitter consequences of the mission. The "Black" Republicans were induced to believe that all Southerners were "submissionists," and that there was no unity of purpose in the South. Now more than ever South Carolina secessionists were convinced that only secret, violent, and single state action could tear the Union apart.[63]

For Unionists in South Carolina, particularly among supporters of the Democratic party, the collapse of Memminger's cooperationist venture sharpened their awareness of the critical state of affairs and the peculiar position of their own state. Benjamin F. Perry had voted in December for the idea of a conference of the Southern states, but opposed the mission to Virginia. Perry's lifetime of opposition to radicalism enabled him to recognize, perhaps better than most, the hopelessness of putting Carolina into the lead in any resistance effort.[64] The lessons demonstrated to supporters of the National Democracy by the quixotic winter campaign were well expressed by Arthur Simkins, editor of the Edgefield *Advertiser*. Simkins had sympathized with the decision of the legislature in December, for the whole nation had been aflame

---

[62] *Mercury*, February 7, 1860; Schultz, *Nationalism and Sectionalism*, p. 203.
[63] *Mercury*, March 10 and 13, 1860; Dumond, ed., *Secession Movement*, p. 32.
[64] *House Journal*, pp. 197–204. See also Lillian Adele Kibler, *Benjamin F. Perry, South Carolina Unionist* (Durham, 1946), p. 297.

over Harpers Ferry, the Helper book, and the deadlock in Congress. Yet all those things had resolved themselves, at least to Simkins's satisfaction. The moral drawn by the Edgefield editor was simple: any move that seemed to put South Carolina into the lead was imprudent, and all such decisions ought first to be referred to a popular referendum. The people of the South were surfeited with pointless resolutions and conventions which, like the futile Memminger journey, only confirmed the fatal misconception in the North that "we are divided on the vital question." For the moderate Simkins the conclusion was obvious. The Democratic party must be supported as the last instrument capable of preserving Southern rights in the Union.[65]

In retrospect, it seems clear that a convention of the Southern states could not have agreed on acceptable terms to guarantee perpetually the security of slavery in the Union. No such terms could be formulated. But a frank conference by men of the intelligence and civility of Memminger and Starke, meeting before the National Democratic Convention in Charleston, could have provided a forum for genuine compromise and discussion; it might have produced a reasonable platform and possibly (though not likely) agreed upon a candidate to oppose Stephen A. Douglas at the convention. As William Gilmore Simms wrote months later, when secession was virtually accomplished, the treatment of Memminger's proposal by Virginia "was sufficiently cavalier, if not contemptuous, to justify Black Republicanism in the conviction that the game was its own, and that it had only to prepare itself for an easy victory—nay, for the most slavish submission!" If the Old Dominion had responded to the call from South Carolina and Mississippi, Simms reasoned, the momentum of the Republican party would have been at least temporarily suspended and the evils of the present day averted.

> Every thinking man in South Carolina discovered, as the result of the failure of that mission to Virginia, that there was but one process of safety left; that co-operation . . . was not to be expected . . . and that *secession* was the only means

[65] Edgefield *Advertiser*, February 22, March 7 and 21, 1860.

left for safety, and this involved *the appeal from the politicians to the people.*[66]

Historical "ifs" abound in the story of the coming of the Civil War. But it is possible that a calm and energetic conference in the spring of 1860 could have brought a more moderate and united South to Charleston, and helped avert the disruption of the Democratic party. That would have been a temporary and expedient resolution, and the peace which might have followed would only have postponed the inevitable confrontation over slavery. The hysteria mounting in the South, however, would not permit even such a postponement. In the wake of Memminger's failure, state leaders withdrew into the deceptive comfort of separate action, or blindly ignored the dangers of continued trust in the Democracy and Northern conservatism. In South Carolina, Calhoun's vision of security through Southern cooperation was utterly destroyed. Cooperationists and Unionists were forcibly thrown together onto the last remaining chance to avoid the cataclysm—the success of the National Democratic party. Simms overstated the decisive character of radical politics following the mission to Virginia, but radicals did begin to seek one another out more seriously in an attempt to coordinate measures for disunion.

[66] *The Letters of William Gilmore Simms,* edited by Mary C. Simms Oliphant, Alfred Taylor Odell, and T. C. Duncan Eaves, 5 volumes (Columbia, 1955), IV, 297–306. See also Francis W. Pickens to Robert M. T. Hunter, December 10, 1860, in *Hunter Correspondence,* pp. 275–77; and Arthur P. Hayne to James H. Hammond, April 12, 1860, Hammond Papers, LC.

William Porcher Miles—The most uncompromising secessionist of the state's Congressmen in 1860. He served in the Confederate legislature during the war.

SOUTH CAROLINIANA LIBRARY

Benjamin F. Perry—For thirty years the most outspoken upcountry defender of Unionism and political moderation. By December 1860, Perry stood almost alone in public opposition to secession.

Opposite top: Christopher G. Memminger—A leader in the South Carolina Assembly, and Commissioner on the ill-fated mission to Virginia in 1860. He became Confederate Secretary of the Treasury in the cabinet of Jefferson Davis.

Opposite bottom: William Henry Gist—Governor of South Carolina, 1858–1860. He played an important role in bringing on the secession crisis in the fall of 1860. The bust pictured here stands in the South Caroliniana Library, University of South Carolina.

Robert Barnwell Rhett—A life-long extremist in defense of slavery and state sovereignty. His radical counsels in the pages of his newspaper, the Charleston *Mercury*, earned him the enmity of Unionists everywhere.

Robert Barnwell Rhett, Jr.— Editor of the Charleston *Mercury*. He was an articulate spokesman in his father's campaign for Southern nationalism.

James L. Orr—South Carolina's pre-eminent Unionist, head of the state Democratic party in the 1850's and during the state and national party conventions in the spring of 1860. He came to advocate secession and served as a Senator in the Confederacy.

Francis W. Pickens—A moderate Unionist—by South Carolina standards—for much of his political life, he was ironically elected Governor on the eve of secession.

Isaac W. Hayne—Not as well known as other members of his influential family, he was one of the most powerful men in Charleston politics and a key figure in the secession movement. Officially he served as State Attorney General.

William Gilmore Simms—South Carolina's popular author of romantic poetry, novels and histories. He also wrote passionate defenses of slavery and Southern nationalist propaganda.

William Lowndes Yancey—An Alabama political leader, one of many Southern radicals born and raised in South Carolina. His main influence in 1860 was felt at the breakup of the Democratic party in Charleston.

James Louis Petigru—A familiar and much admired Charleston lawyer who represented, however silently, the persistent strain of Unionism.

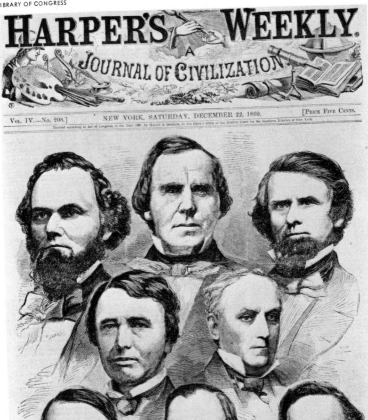

HARPER'S WEEKLY.

JOURNAL OF CIVILIZATION.

Vol. IV.—No. 208.]   NEW YORK, SATURDAY, DECEMBER 22, 1860.   [Price Five Cents.

Entered according to Act of Congress, in the Year 1860, by Harper & Brothers, in the Clerk's Office of the District Court for the Southern District of New York.

THE SECEDING SOUTH CAROLINA DELEGATION.—[Photographed by Brady.]

Only two days after the secession of South Carolina, *Harper's Weekly* magazine pictured the members of the state's Congressional delegation who had earlier withdrawn from their seats at Washington. Shown are: (top row, l. to r.) Representatives Lawrence M. Keitt, John McQueen, and Milledge L. Bonham; (middle row) Senators James Chesnut and James H. Hammond; and (bottom row, l. to r.) Representatives William W. Boyce, John D. Ashmore, and William Porcher Miles.

PART TWO

CHAPTER FOUR

The Radical Mind on the Eve of the Conventions

Little more than three months had passed since the fire bells of Harpers Ferry sounded the arrival of John Brown. At home these months were marked by hysteria, repression, and bombastic disunionist oratory. Only the potent fear of isolation prevented a more sensational display of anxiety. Since the time slavery became peculiar to the South, wise and gloomy statesmen had foreseen an impending national crisis over the perpetuation of slavery in America. Antebellum defenders of the institution were claiming that agitation of the question had burned away any lingering moral uneasiness. Yet they were aware that this same sectional agitation had educated the present generation of Northerners into a hostility which, for some, had become a burning religious conviction. The disturbing support for Frémont in 1856, and the growing strength of the Republican party in state elections since that time left little doubt that for South Carolina the election of 1860 would constitute a special test of the future of the Union. Alfred P. Aldrich, a state legislator from Barnwell, precisely described the state of politics on the eve of the conventions, as seen through the eyes of a secessionist.

If this Republican party with its platform of principles, the main feature of which is the abolition of slavery and, therefore, the destruction of the South, carries the country at the next Presidential election, shall we remain in the Union, or form a separate Confederacy? This is the great, grave issue. It is not who shall be President, it is not which party shall rule—it is a question of political and social existence.[1]

1

South Carolina radicals welcomed this challenge. The fact was that men such as Rhett, Miles, Gist, and countless others wanted nothing less than secession, and their hopes and schemes in this election year turned entirely upon ways to achieve this long-sought goal.

Secession had long seemed to offer the only guarantee of security for the kind of Southern civilization they idealized. As a separate nation, the South could perfect the suppression of incendiary ideas. It was expected that a Northern "republic" would be less disposed to meddle in the affairs of an independent South. Rhett and Hammond often depicted the essence of the entire sectional controversy as a product of the Northerner's sense of complicity in the supposed moral evil of slavery. By dissolving the national tie which was the source of that feeling of complicity in sin the New England mind would be at peace, and slavery secure. Disunionists observed that American abolitionists had no apparent interest in attacking the institution where it existed elsewhere in the hemisphere, in Brazil, or Cuba. A treaty between the two new North American nations would be more powerful than any constitutional amendment, and protective laws could be better enforced. "If we had a government of our own," Rhett dreamed, "the post office, all the avenues of intercourse, the police and the military of the country would be under our exclusive control."[2]

Secession offered more than an effective instrument to subjugate Negroes. No subject so inspired the lyrical imagination of South Carolina writers as did the vision of a Southern nation.

[1] Charleston *Daily Courier*, November 3 and 16, 1859.
[2] James Hammond to Edmund Ruffin, February 8, 1850, Edmund Ruffin Papers, SHC; Hammond to F. A. Allen, February 2, 1861, James Henry Hammond Papers, LC; Charleston *Mercury*, November 1, 1859.

Supported by the relentless logic of their new sociology, defenders of the South proclaimed that they had solved the greatest problem of the modern age—the relationship between capital and labor. With all social classes at peace under the protective arch of slavery, and with the South in command of the essential agricultural productions of the world, the future was filled with promise. Charles Pelham, a Columbia cooperationist, described his vision to Benjamin F. Perry.

> The South united in amity of feeling, and interdependence of interests, protected internally by Slavery, and externally by her noble staple productions. . . . She might practically exhibit as a nation, and so commend to the attention of the world the advantages and blessings which belong to her civilisation, and which now characterize her communities separately. . . . In nearly all—perhaps all the Southern States, society is as secure, morals as high, manners as refined & unselfish, want as little known, and the laborers as well cared for & as happy as in any portion of the globe.[3]

Clearly, the mystique of Southern nationality was not wholly produced by the post-bellum generation, which wistfully gazed back across the wreckage and revolution of Civil War. The rising anticipation of a halcyon age before the War was an integral part of the irrational but comprehensible impulse toward secession in the South.

— 2 —

This new world, however, would not come by itself. Action was needed to bring it to fulfillment. For a generation extremists in South Carolina had been lashing themselves, their colleagues, and the Southern people for their reluctance to dissolve the Union. Because 1860 was a Presidential election year of unique importance, the necessity and opportunity of choosing an effective course of action became urgent. But what action? Events since Harpers Ferry had seemed to demonstrate that a deliberate, united withdrawal of the slave states upon a platform embodying

[3] Charles Pelham to B. F. Perry, n.d. [c. 1850], Benjamin F. Perry Papers, SHC.

the central issue was impossible. The political disunity of the South following John Brown's attack, and the response to Memminger's proposals appeared to prove that. Nor did it seem possible to inaugurate an effective revolutionary movement through Congress. Miles was perturbed by the criticism of fellow radicals directed against Southern representatives after the speakership controversy. But Memminger agreed with his friend that a minority could do little to disrupt a legislative body. "A majority in either house could by leaving their seats break up the Government," Memminger wrote following the election of Pennington, "but a minority is powerless saving upon opinion; and that opinion must result in action at home. I know of no remedy but secession, and that of course must be at home."[4]

Yet the radical party in South Carolina had already tasted defeat at the hands of the people "at home." Secessionists had confidently but futilely awaited the seconding voice of the people in 1851.[5] Who could now be certain which way the people would go? For decades past the political correspondence of the leaders of South Carolina had been filled with endless speculation about the radicalism of the mass of citizens. Were they fore or aft of the state's radical politicians in devotion to Southern rights? Were they ready for revolution or would they endlessly hold back, waiting for a cooperative secession by the entire South which would never come? Writing to James Hammond after the disheartening Northern state elections in 1858, Miles had despondently divided all Southerners into two groups: absolute Unionists and secessionists *per se.* Hammond wisely retorted that this formula ignored "999 in every 1000 of the voters & 49 in 50 of the substantial & influential men of the South." It is this vast political center which controlled any momentous decision, he explained, this was where the power lay. "This immense body goes for the Union until it pinches them & then for dissolving it." And, the Senator noted "with Cotton at 10¢ & negroes at $1000 the South will know no pinch."[6]

Even the impact of events since that time had not convinced

[4] Memminger to Miles, February 6, 1860, William Porcher Miles Papers, SHC.
[5] Benjamin F. Perry, *Reminiscences of Public Men* (Philadelphia, 1883), pp. 160–62.
[6] Hammond to Miles, November 23, 1858, Miles Papers, SHC.

all disunionists that the South was ready for revolution. Writing at the end of 1859, from the isolation of his plantation on Barnwell Island, William Henry Trescot mirrored Hammond's pessimism. Trescot despaired of the idea of a united South, and scorned "the great body of the South who are even now too busy in buying negroes, clearing land and making cotton to attend to politics."[7] This generalized disdain glossed over the more sharply focused contempt felt by radicals for their Unionist opponents. But the more realistic leaders of the secession group were certainly aware that resistance to what was genuine revolution had deeper roots than mere personality or party loyalty.

For South Carolina, by the 1850's, the paramount obstacle to secession was the conviction that no other Southern state would go with her. Most Carolinians were convinced that separate secession would end in humiliating isolation for the state. In the crisis of 1851, Joel R. Poinsett and other Unionists and cooperationists were confident that no other slave state would follow South Carolina over the brink, and they depended upon this outside moderation as the surest way to allay the popular desire for secession at home.[8] Aside from waning love of the old Federal Union, there was a variety of basic attitudes which worked against the secessionist impulse.

Perhaps the most important of these was a subtle but persuasive fear of disturbing the social order. As James Hammond noted in his diary, a rage for order was an inescapable feature of Southern society.

Order is a prime necessity in every community, especially an Agricultural one & most especially a slave-holding one. To the great body of the Southern People, the Union is the only tangible & appreciable representative of Order, & it is solely on this account that they love & sustain it. Its oppressions must be grievously *felt* before they will violate Order to resist them.[9]

[7] Trescot to Hammond, December 30, 1859, Hammond Papers, LC.
[8] Joel R. Poinsett to J. J. Albert, June 26, 1850, Joel R. Poinsett Papers, USC. See also E. M. Seabrook to James Johnston Pettigrew, May 8, 1852, Pettigrew Family Papers, SHC; Waddy Thompson to James L. Orr, July 29, [1851], Orr-Patterson Papers, SHC.
[9] James H. Hammond MS Diary, USC, December 6, 1851.

Rhett and others looked eagerly to the opportunities offered by an independent confederacy for tightening the bonds of race control. But for many Southerners the temporary social disorder which might accompany a transfer of sovereignty only evoked the frightening vision of rebellious slaves. To Unionists of the Perry stripe, whose devotion to slavery was never in question, the arms and laws of the national government offered a sanctuary for the peculiar institution in a hostile world. "A most fatal blow was struck at slavery when we dissolved this Union!" Perry cried out in 1863. "We should have cherished this Union as the bulwark of slavery abroad & at home!" And, of course, it was universally understood that the very "basis of Southern Society," as a York District Grand Jury explained, was "the negro population," and its subjugation.[10]

Indeed, the ripples of potential social disorder spread beyond racial security to threaten the unique character of government and society. The sons of South Carolina families who moved west had played their part in recreating and perpetuating the attitudes that prevailed in Southern "society" on the Atlantic coast. Perhaps the culture of the Gulf states captured more the tone than the substance of the tidewater civilization they aped. But for mythmakers, conscious and unconscious, the entire South was wishfully perceived as an ideal, harmonious social system. Thus, when such conservative spokesmen as Presbyterian minister James Henley Thornwell looked across the expanse of the slaveholding South, the idea of disunion struck them with horror. Not only did secession have the potential to spark a terrible civil war, but it would surely release disrupting social and political forces. "The attempt in the present age," Thornwell wrote in 1850, "when all the elements of disorder, socialism, communism, rabid democracy and open atheism are busily at work, . . . to organize new governments and to frame new constitutions, will be perilous in the extreme."[11] No state had been so successful in the battle

---

[10] Benjamin F. Perry MS Diary, SHC, June 3, 1863; York District Grand Jury Presentments, Spring Term, 1859, SCArc.
[11] J. H. Thornwell to John B. Adger, March 8, 1850, in John B. Adger, *My Life and Times, 1810–1899* (Richmond, 1899), p. 202. See also Mathew Williams to Francis Lieber, February 12, 1850, Francis Lieber Papers, USC. The antagonism between social classes among whites in the Old South is

against democracy as was South Carolina. The special fears of "demagogic tactics," of the "undirected" political participation of the masses, and of the demands of the piedmont which beset the low country were intensified for some by the unknowable social consequences of secession.

Here then were the perplexing sources for the picture of the world held by most South Carolinians. Fear of a loss of control over the slave masses argued for secession, and yet that same fear was evoked by the turmoil which might accompany disunion. The anticipated triumph of a party supposedly devoted to immediate abolition was certainly the most pressing inducement to secession; still, the Union offered boundless sources of economic and military protection for slavery in a hostile world community. An independent confederacy seemed to offer the opportunity to perfect a durable and socially harmonious slave state; but the unnerving challenge of fabricating a new government threatened to shatter the habits, customs, and laws which had kept political power in the hands of established and known leaders. Secessionists envisioned unparalleled economic progress and prosperity, and they cursed the apparent colonial status of the South in the Union; yet these same radicals angrily criticized the busy industry of Southern planters who were enjoying prosperity in 1860. With cooperationism lying dead in Richmond and Washington, the mood of the South Carolina citizenry in the spring of 1860 was one of tense anticipation, an uneasy balance between a strong desire for full and deliberate action, and an awareness of the apparent futility of action. But frustration itself is a seedbed for revolution.

— 3 —

Disunionists had long recognized the need to find a *"practical issue"* which would compel secession. There had never been a lack of political controversies in South Carolina which justified—

discussed by Wilbur J. Cash, *The Mind of the South* (New York, 1941); and by Joseph L. Brent, III, "The Ante-Bellum Origins of Southern Totalitarianism." Paper presented at a session of the Southern Historical Association, Atlanta, Georgia, November 10, 1967.

to a growing segment of her people—the ultimate solution. The Nullification crisis of nearly thirty years before had demonstrated the special capacity of extremists to win support for an advanced and potentially revolutionary stance by the state. In the Bluffton movement of 1844 the isolation of Carolina in the Nullification controversy worked against the efforts of Rhett and Hammond, who sought a special state convention to protest the tariff and Northern opposition to Texas annexation. But the tumultuous emotional impact of the Mexican War, the clash over the Wilmot Proviso, and a threatened loss of equality in the Senate again provided the popular basis for a full-blown secession attempt in 1851; this time no one could deny that the effort would have succeeded had there been any confidence that other states would follow. The forces which operated in South Carolina to produce a high level of race fear and class anxiety, coupled with a sociopolitical elite peculiarly fitted to confuse the will of the state with its own, produced a readiness for secession unparalleled in the South.

As a result, Carolina radicals never ceased to rail at the "supineness" of their fellow Southerners. A way had to be found, as Hammond had written, to make the oppressions of the Union "grievously felt."[12] The sense of frustration was intensified after the 1851 secession debacle, when the Presidency passed into the hands of the sympathetic Democrats Franklin Pierce and James Buchanan. Their conciliatory policies seemed to cut the ground from under the arguments of Southern extremists, and the ranks of disunionists were thrown into disarray. "Some of our leading men think too much of conservatism," the brother of Congressman Milledge Bonham glowered. "They fear being thought fanatical[.] And some men of great wealth I apprehend fear something else[,] that in any change there might be danger to their possessions." Increasingly, the letters of South Carolina radicals reflected the notion that some strong antidote was needed to counteract the "torpidity" of the Southern spirit in the later 1850's.[13]

[12] James H. Hammond MS Diary, USC, December 6, 1851.
[13] M. M. Bonham to Milledge L. Bonham, August 14, 1858, Milledge L. Bonham Papers, USC.

In a vain attempt to manufacture an issue to intensify sectional feeling during the Buchanan doldrums, a number of Southern extremists began agitating for reopening the foreign slave trade. Many radicals were eager to debate the issue on its own "merits." Some based their argument on the need for slavery expansion, citing the vast western territories waiting for the beneficial hand of the Negro slave; others did not hesitate to defend reopening the trade because it purportedly would bring more benighted Africans into a land of Christian civilization (if slavery were a positive good, a ban on carrying additional Africans to America was evil and unnatural); still others drew dire pictures of the "depopulation, impoverishment, and even destruction" which seemed to await South Carolina unless ample numbers of cheap slaves were imported. Slave trade advocates did not see any "natural limit" to the utility of slavery; they sought expanded numbers of less expensive slaves not merely for planting cotton and rice, but for constructing railroads, digging mines, "even to manufacturing the coarser fabrics of cotton and wool." Concern was expressed by established planters and non-slaveholders alike that many Southerners were being denied the alleged blessings of slave ownership because of rising prices. "Under the present circumstances," wrote planter Williams Middleton, "the possession of negros [sic] in our country is becoming fast a mere aristocratic privilege."[14]

Despite these "idealistic" appeals, it is clear that most of the instigators of the hue and cry over the slave trade had a more immediate object: to destroy the Union. Charleston's Leonidas Spratt, himself a non-slaveholder who was among the leading slave trade propagandists admitted in a letter to Miles that actually reopening the trade was not desirable. "Our only object is to render the South *Sui juris* upon the subject of domestic slavery." A congressional act of 1820 had established an agreement with the British navy to eliminate continuing violations of the laws against the trade, and had condemned those violations

[14] *Courier,* November 9 and 11, 1859. One opponent of reopening the trade ridiculed such "zeal in the cause of ameliorating the condition of the 'nigger'," by equating its enthusiasm with "the progressive philanthropy of the yankee abolitionists." Samuel Leardt to James J. Pettigrew, December 4, 1857, Pettigrew Family Papers, NCArc.

as piracy. The point of debating the issue, according to Spratt, was not "whether we shall nullify an act of Congress but whether we shall let individuals be punished for an act which we cannot condemn without concurring in the censure upon our institution." Defenders of slavery, such as Daniel Hamilton, considered the act of 1820 "a heavy blow and stigma . . . designed for the Institution of Slavery," which branded the South "as the abode of 'scoundrels, Pirates, and whores.'" Spratt, Miles, and others of their radical ilk hoped that pressing the question would demonstrate "the fact that the Union is inconsistent with our objects." If the government persisted in enforcing the laws against the trade, Spratt grandiloquently ended his letter to Miles, it "will run the gauntlet of another Lexin[g]ton."[15]

The potential of the slave trade issue for causing such trouble was dramatized by the case of the "Wanderer," a slave ship which landed on the coast of Georgia in 1858 and promptly dispersed its illicit cargo into Carolina and the Gulf states.[16] One of the outstanding spokesmen for reopening the trade was James H. Adams, governor of South Carolina from 1856 to 1858. As he explained the implications of the "Wanderer" case in a revealing letter to Senator James Chesnut, it was clear that "many of the first men and families in our own State and men of equal standing in Geo., Ala. and Miss." had promoted the illegal entry. Adams believed the most urgent question was not the constitutionality of the 1820 Slave Trade Piracy Act, but the possibility that the Federal Government would attempt to recover the distributed Africans. The Buchanan Administration was beginning to enforce the act more energetically, and Adams speculated that if a recovery effort were made *and resisted,* it might "lead to an issue of blood between Federal officers & our people, that would

[15] Leonidas W. Spratt to Miles, February 12, 1859, and Daniel H. Hamilton to Miles, April 26, 1860, Miles Papers, SHC. Hamilton's opinion was ironic since he was Federal marshal for the Charleston District. But, as Trescot had earlier noted, there was irony in the very essence of the attack on the act of 1820, for it had been negotiated with Britain by President Monroe, with the concurrence of then Secretary of War John C. Calhoun! An act can be repealed, Trescot tartly concluded, but history could not. Trescot to Miles, February 8, 1859, Miles Papers, SHC.
[16] The fullest account of the incident is Tom Henderson Wells, *The Slave Ship Wanderer* (Athens, Ga., 1967).

be a *practical issue* and I should rejoice over it." For extremists such as Governor Adams, the goal was secession, whatever the means, whatever the cost.[17]

Nevertheless, even Adams was aware that the people of the South were far from united on the necessity or, indeed, the morality of reopening the foreign slave trade, whatever its utility as an instrument for disunion.[18] "The trouble is going to be with our own people," Adams feared. "Such a state of things would [be] disastrous and fatal to us. A quarrel on the subject of slavery would be the beginning of the end." But as Adams warmed to his subject, a still more profound fear emerged. The Governor wanted Chesnut to intervene with Buchanan, should the President attempt to recover the "Wanderer" Africans scattered across the cotton states, especially those in South Carolina and Georgia. For, Adams confessed, if a bloody clash erupted between white men over some aspect of slavery in the midst of the slaves, who could foresee the consequences?

Many of these in our cities and towns are now looking forward to the coming of their Messiah of deliverance with as much confidence as the Jews of old. Now if an effort on the part of the General Government to incarcerate one of our

[17] Adams to Chesnut, January 14, 1859, Chesnut-Miller-Manning Papers, SCHS. The renewed vigor in enforcing the Act of 1820 is demonstrated by the fact that between May 1852 and June 1859 only four slave ships were seized, while the number rose to sixteen in the much briefer period June 1859 to December 1860. See Robert R. Davis, Jr., "James Buchanan and the Suppression of the Slave Trade," *Pennsylvania History*, XXXIII (October 1966), 454–55.

[18] Opposition to reopening the trade had its source in political moderation, Negrophobia, and related matters. Writing from up-country Chester, James Hemphill lamented the continuing westward emigration of white farmers out of the district, and the movement of slave plantations in from the tidewater region. He utterly opposed importations of Africans. "If I had my choice," he wrote his brother, "I would prefer some more whites, and less blacks. I hope that is not treason," he half-jested, "but one hardly knows now what constitutes heterodoxy on the subject of the peculiar institution." James H. to William R. Hemphill, October 17, 1859, Hemphill Family Papers, DU. On the other hand, Presbyterian minister James H. Thornwell felt that most Southerners opposed the trade, not because it was immoral—"that not a man among us believes"—but because the illegal trade as it was then practiced was an organized "system of kidnapping and man-stealing, which is [as] abhorrent to the South as it is to the North." J. H. Thornwell, *The State of the Country* . . . (Columbia, S.C., 1861), p. 9.

citizens for having possession one of these ["Wanderer"] slaves would lead to a dissolution I say God speed the movement. But if the Government shall pursue such a course as to set our own people by the ears, God only knows the result.

The reopening of the foreign slave trade was obviously not the "practical issue" passionately sought by secessionists. It could not unite the South. It presented no clear threat to the security of slavery, nor any apparent violation of state's rights. The slave trade question offered tangential and dubious grounds upon which to lead a revolution, and agitation of the matter served only to divide and antagonize Southerners. "If this is the question on which the South must unite and break through the meshes which bind us," Barnwell Rhett convincingly wrote, "she is gone, and the days of the institution of slavery are numbered." A clearer, nation-wide issue was needed to destroy the Republic.[19]

$$- 4 -$$

The coming of 1860 found Southern spokesmen still divided in their counsels. The apparent failure of John Brown to advance visibly the cause of disunionism, or even to unite the slave states politically had generated confusion and distrust of public sentiment. In competing with their moderate opponents over the years, secessionists had confidently appealed to their own interpretation of the public mood to buttress their position. Radicals were sure that, in their hearts, the people desired the ultimate security of Southern nationalism; at the same time, their opponents were certain that the mass of citizens yearned for nothing more than an end to the tiresome and fruitless agitation of the sectional controversy, and were willing to rely upon the protec-

[19] *Mercury,* October 25, 1859. See also *Courier,* October 3, 1859, quoting the Unionville *Times;* and James L. Orr to James J. Pettigrew, April 20, 1857, Pettigrew Family Papers, NCArc. Valuable recent studies of the slave trade issue include Barton J. Bernstein, "Southern Politics and Attempts to Reopen the African Slave Trade," *Journal of Negro History,* LI (January 1966), 16–35; Ronald Takaki, "The Movement to Reopen the African Slave Trade in South Carolina," *South Carolina Historical Magazine,* LXVI (January 1965), 38–54, and Takaki, "A Pro-Slavery Crusade: The Movement to Reopen the African Slave Trade" (unpublished doctoral dissertation, the University of California, Berkeley, 1967).

tion of the Democratic party. This debate over the perplexing reality of a divided public opinion had become an urgent matter, for secessionists were groping towards a practical program to destroy the Union. William Porcher Miles was one of many who doubted that the Southern people were sufficiently aware of the dangers threatening their lives and institutions. In the midst of the speakership controversy he confessed to Memminger that he believed most Southerners "still continue to hope that a revulsion will take place in the Northern mind."[20]

Other secessionists were more optimistic. Robert Barnwell Rhett strongly dissented from Miles's "distrust of the people of the South." Speaking through his son, the radical leader blamed not the people, but the weak leadership of the Southern states, too concerned with the spoils and offices of party success to work vigorously for the formation of radical public sentiment. "It is my belief that the spirit of the people in the cotton states is higher than that of their public men," he wrote in a significant letter on January 29, "and that (at least in Alabama, Mississippi and Georgia—not to mention our own state) they would sustain them in a bold and decided course."[21]

But where was the leadership to focus this alleged spirit? The elected representatives of the South sitting in seats of power in Washington were too fainthearted for action, he wrote with contempt. And, according to Rhett, the reason for their timidity was obvious.

> So long as the Democratic Party, as a "National" organization, exists in power at the South, and so long as our public men trim their sails with an eye to either its favor or enmity, just so long need we hope for no southern action for our disenthrallment and security. The south must dissever itself from the rotten Northern element.[22]

Added to party spoils and loyalty was the subtle dilemma which existed for genuine disunionists who held national office. Trescot had already warned his friend Miles of the paradox of being a

[20] January 10, 1860, Christopher G. Memminger Papers, SHC.
[21] R. B. Rhett, Jr., to Miles, January 29, 1860, Miles Papers, SHC.
[22] *Ibid.*

United States representative to Congress and a secessionist at the same time. So long as Miles sat in Congress he was obliged to believe in the desirability and feasibility of Union. As a private citizen he, Trescot, could talk about disunion and such treasonable subjects. But for Miles to do so would be a violation of the tenure and the oaths of his office. Moreover, he continued, "You cannot create a viable third party—Calhoun backed by the whole state failed." Trescot concluded that the only course for an ardent Southern rights man in Congress was silence upon all questions of disunionism. Work pragmatically with the Democratic party, he advised Miles, for if he could not do so he must come home. There was no third course.[23]

However, politicians, even Southern patriots like Miles, did not always follow the dictates of logic, especially when this logic would oblige them to abandon their prestigious national offices. As a result, Rhett could correctly say that the development of an aggressive spirit and policy were handicapped by a perhaps unwitting obeisance to symbols of Union: the Democratic party and the offices of the Federal Government. What then was to be done to achieve revolution? First, Rhett expostulated in his letter of January 29, secessionists must accept the fact that a united South would never deliberately withdraw from the Union. "The idea is as absurd as it is unnecessary. Alabama and Mississippi are the only states, besides ours, at which there is ground to expect action. Georgia can do nothing (for [Alexander] Stephens, [Robert] Toombs and [Howell] Cobb) but would throw them overboard or drive them on in the event of an issue by other states." Nevertheless, Rhett was confident that secession could be accomplished if state's rights men in these few states would turn away from the allurements of party and national reputation. Disunion would forever elude Southern radicals if they persisted in trying to achieve essentially sectional goals through the national party. Rhett saw that this was a hopeless task, one that served to exacerbate schisms in the ranks of the slave states which already posed such formidable obstacles to disunion.

The *Mercury* editor was not satisfied to dismiss Miles's fears of a divided South merely because such division was inevitable.

[23] Trescot to Miles, February 8, 1859, Miles Papers, SHC.

Rhett scorned division, and his criticism provides insight into an important aspect of secession politics in South Carolina. Coming as Rhett and Miles did from the low country gentry, they held a frame of aristocratic political presumptions which played no little part in shaping the secession movement. Whether men argued that the people were insufficiently alert to the crisis, as did Miles, or that they were alert but confused by a lack of leadership, as Rhett believed, it is clear that the political attitude of such men was basically authoritarian. Whether the masses needed to be educated to their danger and then led, or merely roused to anticipated action by the proper signal, the end result would be the same. The secession movement was to be directed by a revolutionary elite which was identical with the traditional ruling class.

$$-5-$$

Under the strain of decision making, who could judge certainly if the leaders were creating moods and symbols to further their own covert purposes, or whether the politicians, in their earnest desire to retain power, were simply interpreting the desires of the masses? By 1860 the established upper class of South Carolina had enjoyed a position of special authority for generations, an authority which had been perpetuated by many factors and satisfied many needs. There was historical precedent and the persistence of an archaic but smooth-working governmental machine. There were the class insecurities of the low country gentry, urging them to preserve a system which offered the illusion of chivalry, quality, and ease, against the ugly pressure of a rising democratic up country. But above all there were the slaves toiling in the fields, inspiring to varying degrees in each Carolinian, regardless of class, a fear of insurrection, a fear of economic competition and dislocation, and a fear of social and sexual equality. These transcendent fears were a source of power, for because of them the people of South Carolina tended to look to their traditional leaders for direction, particularly in moments of crisis.

The gentry had preserved this position of leadership by remaining flexible in its membership and policies. This was not an aristocracy of blood, although a substantial and well-defined core of families had supplied numbers and leaders to it for generations.[24] Neither had South Carolina entirely escaped the democratization of political life which had been a significant force in America since before the Revolution. Rather, this was an open-ended aristocracy of kinship, talent, and style, where a man like James Hammond, "the son of a Massachusetts adventurer,"[25] could marry wisely, plant cotton and trade in slaves, learn the proper rhetoric, imbibe that necessary sense of knowing what was best for the masses, and wait expectantly for admission into the ruling circle.

> The Government of SoCa is that of an aristocracy [Hammond entered in his diary in 1850]. When a Colony many families arose in the Low Country who became very rich & were highly educated. They were real noblemen & ruled the Colony & the State—the latter until about thirty years ago & to a very great extent to the present moment.[26]

This aristocracy still survived in power because a man like James Hammond could, by external appearances and by his own instincts, become a part of it.

Patrician control of South Carolina embraced the governor's seat and judiciary, and to a remarkable extent the Assembly as well. By an almost sacred and inviolate "Compromise of 1808," a constitutional formula for over-representing the tidewater parishes and districts, "the great planters of the parishes and their satellites in the black belt counties of the piedmont . . . controlled the legislature, which completely dominated the state."[27] The legislature reserved to itself nearly all of the appointive and policy-making power. The people did elect the members of the General Assembly, but as Hammond remarked, the right to vote

[24] Rosser Howard Taylor, "The Gentry of Ante-Bellum South Carolina," *North Carolina Historical Review*, XVII (April 1940), 118.
[25] F. W. Pickens to Lucy Holcomb, December 6, 1857, Francis W. Pickens Papers, USC.
[26] James H. Hammond MS Diary, USC, December 25, 1850.
[27] William Joseph MacArthur, "Antebellum Politics in an Up Country County: National, State and Local Issues in Spartanburg County, South Carolina 1850–1860" (unpublished master's thesis, the University of South Carolina, 1966), p. 56.

was exercised "very negligently . . . from time immemorial."[28] He could have added that nominations of candidates in each state district remained within the purview of the local upper class. There were forces at work which could undermine the control of the gentry. New leaders representing farmers, mechanics, and merchants were emerging across the state. They were already challenging the assumption of unquestioned authority. In time they would reconstruct the political system of the state by instituting the direct election of the governor, of Presidential electors, of judges. There were men who even now doubted the wisdom of the system of rotten boroughs in the tidewater that was an integral part of the aristocratic machine. The point stressed here is less that the government of South Carolina was undemocratic on paper (that is, in its written constitution and statutes) than that the underlying political tenets of its main leaders, and its living political practices fostered magisterial, presumptive, aristocratic behavior by the gentry, and the appropriate corresponding responses by the masses.

This political system meshed perfectly with the needs of disunionists. Whether the people were more or less radical than their spokesmen, the present situation called for special leadership. What was needed was a kind of leadership that was so intensely motivated, so sure of the justice of its program, that it spurned the attraction of party spoils and expedient compromises, and ignored inevitable charges of overriding democratic procedures. The structure of politics in South Carolina was ideally suited to produce men with the proper benevolent authoritarian attitude towards the mass of citizens. With the nation preparing for the nominating conventions, and with the last chance for calm and deliberate Southern cooperation apparently gone, there occurred among the extremists of this state a critical coalescence of opinion. An air of terrible determination settled upon the minds of disunionists. The conservative revolution in defense of slavery had developed its vanguard.

What did it matter that, as Rhett had noted, the only states which could be counted on were Alabama and Mississippi. And what did it matter if the Southern people were confused and divided in their counsels?

[28] J. H. Hammond MS Diary, USC, December 25, 1850.

It is useless to talk about checking the North or dissolving the Union with unanimity and without division of the South [Rhett declared]. Those who are not prepared to face opposition at home are not fit for the crisis. The South must go through a trying ordeal before she will ever achieve her deliverance, and men having both nerve and self-sacrificing patriotism must head the movement and shape its course, *controlling and compelling their inferior contemporaries.* In my judgment there is now a feeling abroad throughout our borders that could be used successfully by a *few bold, strong men.*[29]

Rhett was confident that such a party could utterly destroy the spirit of Unionism and loyalty to the Democratic party in the key states of Alabama and Mississippi. Of course, if enough men did not throw off party attachment and rise to the emergency to "lead the van of revolution," there would be no secession. Still, Rhett considered it unfair for Miles to blame the Southern people for having an insufficient regard for their rights, when he believed they had never been given the opportunity to sustain a truly revolutionary movement. "So far from stimulating, I believe the public men of the South are restraining their people—are obstacles in the way of reform.[30]

— 6 —

If the goals were clear, difficulty remained concerning means. Here, too, Rhett saw the answer. It was common knowledge that William Lowndes Yancey, the Alabama radical leader, was entering the Democratic Presidential nominating convention in Charleston pledged to withdraw his delegation if an unyielding interpretation of the rights of slaveholders in the western public lands was not included in the national platform. For more than a decade Yancey had been waging a relentless battle within the Democratic party in defense of a broad right of slaveowners to retain their human property in the western territories. Yancey appeared to believe that both the Union and slavery could be

[29] R. B. Rhett, Jr., to Miles, January 29, 1860, Miles Papers, SHC. (Italics added.)
[30] *Ibid.*

preserved, so long as the Democratic party controlled the Federal Government, and the South controlled the party. The core of his plans for 1860 consisted of intimidating the party into endorsing his demand for the protection of the territorial rights of slavery by threatening a bolt of the Southern state delegates from the Democratic convention. The Alabama leader utterly failed in his campaign to persuade other Southern state legislatures to bind their Democratic party delegates to his scheme. After John Brown's raid, his plan was momentarily forgotten. But he was, if anything, even more determined. On January 14, 1860, the Charleston *Mercury* reported with evident satisfaction that the Alabama legislature had accepted Yancey's direction; the state delegation was bound to withdraw if a satisfactory platform and candidate were rejected by the Democratic party. At last a Southern rights movement had been inaugurated by a state other than South Carolina.[31]

The fact that the Democratic party was torn apart at Charleston, and that this disruption was an important step toward eventual secession, would suggest that Carolina radicals were allied with Yancey from the first. It appears instead that Rhett and others were never entirely convinced that his plan of calculated intimidation would succeed. A plan identical to this had failed in 1848. And South Carolina radicals, all of them heirs of Calhoun, shared their master's suspicion of national conventions. Ever since Yancey launched his scheme, Rhett had vacillated on whether or not to support it.[32] With other Carolina radicals, he

---

[31] Austin L. Venable, "The Conflict Between the Douglas and Yancey Forces in the Charleston Convention," *Journal of Southern History*, VIII (May 1942), 226–34; John Witherspoon DuBose, *The Life and Times of William Lowndes Yancey*, 2 volumes (New York, 1942), II, 442–48. A full outline of Yancey's program appeared in the *Mercury*, October 13, 1859.

[32] Rhett was apparently ready to back Yancey before the attack at Harpers Ferry, and hoped the Carolina legislature would endorse the plan, which offered the inducement of putting Alabama in the lead. Union with Yancey was shattered by Brown's raid and its aftermath; Rhett was convinced that any program that depended on deliberate joint action by the Southern states was doomed. In December he opened a vigorous attack on the convention itself, as a conglomeration of self-seeking politicians, devoid of principle, and he focused his efforts at the session of the Assembly on a vain attempt at holding the state out of the national convention. Yancey's victory in the Alabama legislature was doubtless instrumental in opening Rhett's eyes to

had serious reservations about Yancey's committment to disunionism. Indeed, as was mentioned at the outset of this chapter, the alienation of South Carolina radicals was complete. They were disgusted with the troublesome issue of slavery in the territories; they wanted nothing to do with the Democratic party platform and nomination; and they had little sympathy with Yancey's conditional Unionism.

Rhett analyzed this state of affairs, and with astonishing prescience he predicted the course of events in 1860. Perhaps Yancey really believed that his threat would yield control of the national convention to Southern radicals. Rhett, on the contrary, was convinced that states' rights men would be unable to dominate the convention. *And this was precisely what he wanted.* "Hence," he exulted to Miles, "the importance of obtaining the secession of the Alabama and Mississippi delegations on the issue of Squatter sovereignty and the construction of the Dred Scott decision. If they will but do it, the people will come up to the scratch, and the game will be ours." Once the Charleston convention was disrupted and the Democracy splintered, Rhett envisioned a true Southern party emerging, with pure Southern candidates and principles around which to rally. This would not be a party to achieve victory in the usual sense. Instead, this would be a party to "ensure the defeat of the double-faced 'National Democracy' so called—and make up the issue between the sections, with a resistance party already formed to meet the event of a Black Republican President elected by the North."

Here was the magic key to secession. The Republican party had played an important role in intensifying the very fears which would produce secession; now, perhaps fittingly, the long feared success of that party in the 1860 Presidential election could be the issue upon which disunion would be accomplished. Even before Harpers Ferry it was hardly necessary to debate further the threatening character of the party. With few exceptions, South Carolinians, whatever their political persuasion, were agreed that

---

the truly radical potential of the threatened bolt of delegates. See R. B. Rhett, Jr., to James Chesnut, October 17, 1859, Williams-Chesnut-Manning Papers, USC; *Mercury,* November 29, December 1–3, and 9, 1859; and above, p. 118.

the election of a "Black" Republican to the Presidency would be intolerable. Although no responsible Southern voices had been raised in 1856 for secession, the speeches of Seward, Lincoln, and others since then had convinced South Carolina that total and violent abolition was the central goal of the Republican party.[33] After John Brown's raid, the people of South Carolina became even more certain that the approaching presidential election would determine the fate of the nation. And whether or not one had despaired of preserving the Union, it was for the people of the North to decide the outcome. This was to be the meaning of the election of 1860.

> Should a Black Republican President be elected it is the necessary sequence of reason that a majority of the people of the country have endorsed his principles and raised a banner on which is enscribed—death to the institutions of the South. In that event it is my solemn judgement we can no longer with safety remain in the same confederacy.[34]

After Harpers Ferry, radicals grew increasingly willing to discuss publicly the gritty practical questions involved in such a decision. Why should the legal and constitutional election of a President be the basis for revolution; and how could that election unite the South? Barnwell legislator Alfred P. Aldrich answered these queries in an aggressive address to the South Carolina Institute Fair. He predicted that the election would not unite the whole South, and that Carolina alone would certainly not create that unity. But the real power of the section—the cotton states of the lower Southland—would be united by a Republican victory. Still, the question remained, how to justify secession. "There is but one answer," Aldrich declared, "the answer of necessity." The election of a Republican President would place the same spirit that had guided the hand of John Brown at the control of the national government. Aldrich called upon his audience to teach the people these truths, to educate them to the benefits of sepa-

[33] *Advertiser,* October 12, 1859, quoting the Orangeburg *Southron;* letter of Congressman John McQueen, September 24, 1859, quoted in the *Courier,* October 13, 1859.
[34] Speech of Thomas Y. Simons, quoted in the *Courier,* December 19, 1859.

rate nationalism. "Lectures, speeches, essays, these have their effect," anything to prepare the Southern mind to respond instantly to the election of a "Black" Republican in November 1860.[35]

Robert Barnwell Rhett merely hoped to precipitate these fears by making that election more certain. After decades of failure, Carolina extremists had come to depend upon the belief that no slave state, as Miles phrased it, "will endure the rule of a Black Republican President. That is what we must try and get them *committed to*. It is not the best—not the truest issue—but it seems at present the only *practical* issue that we can get the South to make."[36]

$-7-$

One fundamental question remained unanswered in the address by Aldrich, and this vexing problem lay at the heart of the coming upheaval at the national party conventions. South Carolina radicals believed that a victory of the Democratic party in 1860 was not worth fighting for. In part, this failure of confidence was a product of their undiluted desire for secession as the only final solution. But there was more to it than that. It had become increasingly obvious to many Carolinians that another victory by the Democratic party would be valueless; worse, that it would merely bring another four years of a surreptitious undermining of the rights of the South. Extremists such as former congressman James A. Woodward attacked the Northern Democracy as the perpetrator of those compromises which for the past thirty years had been vehicles for the implementation of free soil and abolitionist ideas. With Barnwell Rhett, Woodward believed that the National Democracy had become the South's enemy, by sapping the strength of state's rights radicalism, and creating disunity through its ready assistance to the abolitionists. Time and again the party had prevented direct aggression against the South, only to allow some precious ground to be lost to the antislavery forces in the false guise of compromise. The Democratic party had won the last two Presidential elections, Woodward granted, but what

[35] Speech of Alfred P. Aldrich, quoted in the *Courier*, November 19, 1859.
[36] Miles to Memminger, January 23, 1860, Memminger Papers, SHC.

security had this brought? He suggested that the past eight years had witnessed a deep corrosion of the Southern position. According to radicals, success by the Democratic party in 1860 offered no attraction, but would instead be another pyrrhic victory, to be followed by four more years of Northern aggression, and Southern apathy and division.

Only a Republican victory could at last draw the issue to a head. If only William Seward could be elected President, Woodward exclaimed, "if we could have a Lord North in the Presidency, some rash insulting act might be perpetrated that would alarm and unite the South." Otherwise he could not see how the course of events that had been going on for more than twoscore years, eating away at the security of slavery, would be halted.[37]

— 8 —

The self-conceived role for radical leadership in 1860 was not to create policy but to select techniques for implementing it. To look into the minds of South Carolina secessionists is to be impressed with a powerful sense of sectional patriotism, destiny, and confidence in the justice of their cause. But one cannot also avoid being struck with the insecurity, with the inevitable but thorough racism, and above all, with the compelling fear that their familiar and comfortable world was threatened by enemies from without and within. From the arrogant assurance of a William Henry Trescot to the irrational determination of an upcountry farmer, the self-delusive racial security of slavery was driving them all towards secession as the last hope against abolition.

To radicals, the logic of their position appeared inescapable. The underlying assumption, one which is easy to forget in the

[37] Letter of James A. Woodward, September 26, 1859, in the *Courier*, November 19, 1859. Woodward was careful to avoid supporting Rhett, however. "We should not aid in [Seward's] election," he noted, "—not make ourselves *justly* responsible for it. We should vote for any sound man that a sound party may offer. But I protest against our accepting any unsound man, 'the best that can be had' at the hands of the Charleston Convention, for the mere purpose of keeping Seward out of the presidency. Let us rather hope that he should be elected."

excitement and confusion of the conventions, was this: that whether or not the Democratic party remained united, and whichever party won the Presidential election in November, the abolition of slavery would surely be forced upon the Southern people in the foreseeable future if they remained in the Union. This assumption gave meaning to the thought and behavior of radicals in the spring, and to a majority of whites in the lower South in the fall and winter of 1860. By 1859, and particularly after the frightening attack by John Brown and the sympathetic reaction to it by the North (as proved by the fall elections and the speakership controversy), a considerable portion of the people of South Carolina were convinced that the Republican party would triumph in the Presidential contest. Correspondence in January and February reveals disunionists awaiting the event with an almost tangible sense of fatalism. Two generations of the growing consciousness of impending crisis had become an oppressive burden. Low country planter Robert Norton spoke for more than the parishes when he told his nephew J. D. B. DeBow of the "gloomy apprehensions" which prevailed concerning "our Political prospects, or rather our antagonisms with the abominable Abolitionists—I think our prospects are gloomy enough," Norton confessed, "& look forward with much anxiety, & very little hope, as to our future destiny . . . there never was a time," Norton wrote the Carolina-born publicist, "when we were more in jeopardy."[38]

The makers of radical policy felt considerable pressure to adopt a more aggressive policy than simply awaiting allegedly inevitable events. Some were urging an open alliance with the Yancey program, aimed at either capturing the Democracy for Southern radicals, or disrupting the party. Others, more moderate, counselled participation in the national convention to preserve the party and slavery in the Union. Despite this pressure, most Carolina disunionists appeared almost apathetic in the months preceding the April conventions. The correspondence of Christopher Memminger while serving his ill-fated commission to Virginia suggests some of the reasons for this surface apathy.

[38] Robert E. Norton to J. D. B. DeBow, March 12, 1860, J. D. B. DeBow Papers, DU.

Congressman William Boyce, for example, was convinced that "dismemberment" of the Union was a certainty, but he feared that the "Southern mind [was] not yet prepared for that event. . . . It will only be prepared when the majority of the Northern people elect a man like Seward." By late January and early February Memminger himself was beginning to feel that "we farther South will be compelled to act, and to drag after us these divided states," upon the election of a Republican President. "My visit here has convinced me that no co-operation in advance for secession can be had from Virginia," nor, it seemed, from the other slave states. While Memminger fondly wished that the Southern states could agree before November to sustain one another in joint secession, he was wise enough to see that too many variables stood in the way of planned revolution. "I think the Black Republicans will create an issue by giving us a new Candidate in place of Seward, and so I fear we can make up no issue in advance, but must await events."[39]

Not everyone was content with inaction. Beaufort planter William Lawton jokingly offered his friend Miles "from $100 to $500" to the Republican campaign fund if they could "bring about a plan to *drive, whip* or kick, two, three or more of the Southern States out of the Union."[40] In this same spirit of frustration, Rhett, spokesman for the most radical section of thought in South Carolina, had returned from opposition to the Charleston convention to private encouragement and preparation for Yancey's arrival. If the cotton states could be compelled to withdraw, Rhett and others reasoned, and a Southern party emerged to insure the disruption of the Democracy, the success of the Republicans would be assured.

Most of the political leaders of South Carolina were not na-

---

[39] William W. Boyce to Memminger, [January 4, 1860], Memminger Papers, SHC; Memminger to Miles, January 29, and February 6, 1860, Miles Papers, SHC. Miles was apparently persuaded by this logic. He further stipulated that South Carolina not begin the movement. "It is very certain that the withdrawal of any *single* State must break up the Union. However, I would much prefer to see Alabama or Mississippi lead off. Our State would certainly follow." Miles to Memminger, February 3, 1860, Memminger Papers, SHC.
[40] Lawton to Miles, March 18, 1860, Miles Papers, SHC.

tional party supporters, and the thought of destroying the Democracy did not frighten them. But there were powerful forces at work in the state during the spring which mitigated against the launching of an open, active campaign to join the Yancey camp. South Carolina radicals seemed confident that a Republican candidate—very likely Seward himself—would win the Presidential election in the fall. Most radicals seemed confident as well that whoever emerged as the candidate of the Democratic party, the election of a Republican was still certain. If, perchance, Yancey were successful, and the Charleston convention accepted his territorial slave code plank and nominated a conservative, even a Southern man, nothing would be altered. Carolina disunionists had grown so dependent on the conviction that the Republicans would be victorious in November that the possible nomination of a reasonable Democratic candidate did not alarm or interest them; it would simply constitute a fairer test of national sentiment on slavery, and unite the South on the eve of secession.

The sense of intransigence in the radical mind was overwhelming. To the traditional disinclination against participating in any national convention was added a special feeling of hatred toward the inevitable shuffling and compromising of the institution, and toward any meaningful contact at all with the North. Radicals feared that they or their more agreeable colleagues would be duped into accepting yet another tranquilizing compromise. This distrust of the moderation of fellow Southerners in part explains what was the strongest force working against a more active role for South Carolina prior to the conventions. The fear of putting the state into the lead has often appeared in this narrative. A passion for consensus and an anxious desire to avoid reopening old divisions in the state had prevented the legislature from advancing the state into alliance with Alabama in preparation for the convention and Presidential election. For disunionists, failure of the Memminger program only reinforced this dual fear of damaging their own position in the state, and the state's position in the South by an overly aggressive policy. For Rhett these apprehensions amounted almost to trauma. Thus the disunionists of South Carolina uncharacteristically but perhaps wisely "awaited events."

CHAPTER FIVE

Unionists on the Tightrope

The "policy" of masterly inactivity nearly proved fatal for radicalism. While disunionists mulled over their disruptive dreams, supporters of participation in the upcoming Democratic national convention—the "Convention party"—had been preparing to have the state properly represented there. These efforts were capped by success when the state party convened at Columbia in April 1860, and named a distinctly conservative slate of delegates. In their fear of reawakening old divisions, in their fear of failing again, the radicals of South Carolina presented their opponents with a victory by default.

— 1 —

The honorable tradition of Unionism in South Carolina extended back to the Nullification controversy and before, and many of those who graced the ranks of moderation in 1860 had had their political baptism in the struggles of the 1830's. Despite that triumph over Nullification, however, moderates remained on the defensive throughout the next decade, unable to advance into even tentative self-assurance. The years following the end of the Mexican War finally created conditions for the emergence of political moderation, Carolina-style. The period after 1848 was one of high excitement, division, and frustration. Under the leadership of the man who was for nearly two decades a virtual dictator of politics and public opinion, the state was advanced to the forefront of the Southern protest.[1] As John Caldwell Calhoun interpreted it, this was a protest against the decline of Southern power in the Union, and ultimately against symbolic and actual threats directed at slavery. Even the death of Calhoun in 1850 could not blunt the force of South Carolina's desire for a final judgment upon the security of slavery in the Union. Fear of secession, and the eventual rejection of that extreme solution by the other slave states divided South Carolinians, and compelled acceptance of the Compromise of 1850.[2] Public emotion, drawn to an almost painful tension for so very long, suddenly snapped, and state politics fell into disordered confusion. No man could pick up the mantle of Calhoun's personal domination.[3]

Out of this chaos there emerged the National Democrat movement, led from the first by Congressman James L. Orr of Anderson. This was a faction devoted to support of the Democracy, participation in the national convention, and greater attention to economic development outside the sphere of plantation and slaves. National Democrats also represented, to a lesser extent, the aspirations of the up-country districts for greater political representation and power. The movement tapped the same groups in the state—mechanics, farmers, merchants, in the pied-

[1] "While Mr. Calhoun lived, the only lesson either taught or comprehended, from the parish-schools to the Senate-Chamber, was to obey orders!" Alfred Huger to William Porcher Miles, June 1, 1860, William Porcher Miles Papers, SHC. See also William Henry Trescot, *Memorial of the Life of J. Johnston Pettigrew* (Charleston, 1870), pp. 27–28.

[2] Philip M. Hamer, *The Secession Movement in South Carolina, 1847–1852*, (Allentown, Pa., 1918); Chauncey S. Boucher, "The Secession and Co-Operation Movements in South Carolina, 1848–1852," *Washington University Studies*, V (1918); Chauncey S. Boucher, "South Carolina and the South on the Eve of Secession, 1852 to 1860," *Washington University Studies*, VI (1918); Harold S. Schultz, *Nationalism and Sectionalism in South Carolina, 1852–1860; A Study of the Movement for Southern Independence* (Durham, 1950).

[3] "Mr. Calhoun did all the thinking for the State & has died without appointing his Executor." Alfred Huger to W. P. Miles, May 7, [1860], Miles Papers, SHC.

mont and Charleston—who had opposed Nullification twenty years before, and secession in 1850. At last there arose the possibility of a genuine two-party system in a state whose politics, particularly in the tidewater parishes, had long resembled the aimless rancor of the colonial period, when competing cliques were tied to popular leaders, to public moods, or to nothing more than the desire for office. One historian has associated the movement with "the great forces of nationalism and democracy which were so powerfully moving the rest of the country," and has described opposition to it as the desire to preserve the "old order" in Carolina.[4]

Although there is considerable truth in this, the emotional basis of the faction led by Orr lay more in the question of Federal and interstate relations than in local issues. The internal struggle for more equitable political representation and a democratization of officeholding and elections was mainly a sectional dispute, which won little support from those supporters of Orr from the gentry, such as James Simons of Charleston, or Francis Pickens of Edgefield. Moreover, while the movement was principally identified with opposition to disunionism, the loyalty of Orr and his adherents to the preservation of slavery was unquestioned. Still, there was no doubting the earnest desire of this faction to align South Carolina in support of the National Democracy as the best hope for the protection of Southern rights in the Union. The "Nationals" won the first test of this reinvigorated brand of moderation in 1856 when, with the low country parishes largely abstaining, National Democrats succeeded for the first time in electing a

---

[4] Laura A. White, "The National Democrats in South Carolina, 1852 to 1860," *The South Atlantic Quarterly*, XXVIII (October 1929), 371–73. Since there was only one party in the state, with all politicians claiming to be Democrats, the "National Democrat" phrase is useful. It distinguishes these moderates who supported the Pierce and Buchanan Administrations, and the idea of a viable North-South national party, from their more radical opponents, who were members of the Democracy in name only. An analogy may be drawn between this "illogical" political system and the one-party structure of the post-Reconstruction South, in which all manner of political opinion felt obliged to remain confined within the catch-all Democratic party. See also Seymour Martin Lipset, "The Emergence of the One-party South—The Election of 1860," in *Political Man, The Social Bases of Politics* (New York, 1963), pp. 372–84.

delegation to represent South Carolina at the national party convention in Cincinnati.

Following the nomination and election of James Buchanan the forces of moderation were at their peak throughout the South. Symbolized by William Lowndes Yancey's endorsement of the party platform at the Cincinnati convention, National Democrats in all Southern states rose up in renewed strength to endorse the leadership of the national party. With South Carolina, perpetual black sheep of the flock, lending its support to the theme of security in the Union; with the leader of Carolina's moderates—James Orr—elected Speaker of the United States House of Representatives in 1856; with the Buchanan Administration backing such extremist demands as a pro-slavery constitution for Kansas and territorial acquisition; and with the Supreme Court casting its powerful weight in the balance through the Dred Scott decision, the safety of slavery in the Union apparently never was so secure.

— 2 —

This, then, was South Carolina's strongest faction of Unionists. Because they alone maintained organization and unity from the time of Buchanan's election to the invasion of Harpers Ferry, the "Nationals" appeared to represent the main sentiments of the people of Carolina. Given the new dispensation of the late 1850's, it was not surprising to see the moderate appeal begin to attract increasing popular support. It is essential to note, however, that the appearance of "moderation" in Carolina was by no means entirely due to the strength of true National Democrats. Other, peripheral groups of conditional Unionists slowly emerged during the Buchanan Administration to lend a tentative voice to the theme of security within the Union. The lethal quality of the condition of their support lay in the belief that slavery would be guaranteed by a predominant Democratic party.

Chief spokesman for this conditional Unionism was the state's new senator, James Hammond. The satisfying relations between the Southern states and the national administration had restored Hammond's confidence that the Union could endure. The Senator set forth his policy of Southern dominance most forcibly in a speech delivered at a political rally in his home district. Coming from a man whose radical credentials dated back to the Nullification era, the address at Barnwell Court House in October 1858 was a political bombshell.[5] In a private letter to another freshman representative of the state, Congressman William Porcher Miles, Hammond privately explained why he now felt Calhoun's dream of Southern rights, secure in the Union, could be realized. The South, he wrote, was economically independent and impregnable; Southern leaders had proved to all the world that the abolition crusade was nothing but a struggle for political power; and, most importantly, "these truths are accepted *in* the Union & the North is willing to accept our dictation if couched in decent terms & based on reason."[6]

The flaws in his analysis were to prove fatal. He was misled by the illusion that the South was united and could permanently control the policies of the Democratic party. He wanted desperately to believe that the antislavery crusade was nothing more than a disguised device for gaining simple *"power* & *spoils,"* and that it was backed by a small and declining number of Northerners.[7] Given these postulates, Hammond argued that secession was no longer necessary. "You ask," he wrote Miles, what protection the slave states have against a fixed Northern Majority.

> Why it is only a majority on the Slave question. I go for annihilating that & then we are the most powerful section on all other questions. If we can't pull it down. If the fanatics succeed in making a permanent sectional ascendancy, why then of course we must dissolve the Union and set up for ourselves. On Seward's platform they cant carry all New England & certainly nothing outside of it. Let us lie quiet, and allow them to fall into that trap. If they repudiate it, they split & are ruined.[8]

[5] *Speech of James H. Hammond Delivered at Barnwell C.H., October 29th, 1858* (Charleston, 1858).

[6] Hammond to Miles, November 23, 1858, Miles Papers, SHC.

[7] Hammond to B. F. Perry, April 9, 1858, Benjamin F. Perry Papers, Ala.Arc.

[8] Hammond to Miles, November 5, 1858, Miles Papers, SHC. See also Hammond to George DeRenne, November 20, 1858, George W. J. DeRenne Papers, DU; and William Gilmore Simms to W. P. Miles, December 28, [1857], Miles Papers, SHC.

Such an artful stance had great appeal to public opinion in the South, an appeal which transcended the more demanding position of National Democrats, one which attracted the overwhelming number of white Southerners who desired nothing more than the freedom to use and control their Negro property as peaceable Americans. This was the fundamental condition for the preservation of the Union in 1860.

— 3 —

As has been seen, the impact of the Harpers Ferry raid on political sentiment in the state was diverse. The effect upon moderate opinion, on balance, was to corrode that essential confidence in the reliability of Northerners, which was already none too strong. For unyielding National Democrats, the Brown raid only intensified the desire to bolster their party and secure the nomination and election of some conservative, preferably Southern leader. Clearly, the most effective contribution South Carolina "Nationals" could make to this grand and necessary goal was to have the state represented by a moderate slate at the Charleston convention. Disillusioned radicals rejected the attraction of a Democratic victory in November. But it was this hope which inspired thousands of National Democrats and other South Carolina moderates, who saw it as the last lawful, rational chance to avert both the election of a Republican President, and the secession crisis which now seemed more and more likely to follow that dreaded event. The practical effect of Harpers Ferry on persistent Unionists was to attach additional groups of citizens to the original core of National Democrats. This new enlarged faction was united ideologically by fear of secession and Republicanism, and a desire for the election of a conservative Democrat to the Presidency. Accordingly, the faction was united pragmatically by a willingness to work for the state's participation in the Charleston national convention. The amalgam of these disparate groups of moderates was the so-called Convention party.[9]

Certainly many Carolinians who had not previously supported the National Democrat movement and the idea of participating

[9] Charleston *Daily Courier,* November 16, 1859.

in the Charleston convention flocked to the banner of the Democracy in the fall and winter months following Harpers Ferry. Such a man was Charleston's well-known bookseller James McCarter. In a letter written to Miles in January, McCarter passionately expressed his lifelong affection for the Union, and anxiously called for "some way to escape from the evils of a dissolution." Moderates like McCarter were grasping for a demonstration of strength by the conservatives of the North. Now, as attention turned toward the Democratic national convention, Unionists began looking to the great confrontation as the arena for such a demonstration of Northern reliability. Southern radicals must silence their inflammatory words, and cooperate with Northern moderates, McCarter cautioned. "This element I have always considered as large enough to keep the Democratic party in power with the aid of the South," and without their aid the Union was lost. For Unionists and secessionists the election of 1860 was to have the same meaning.[10]

In like spirit the state's leading jurist, John Belton O'Neal, implored James Hammond to defend the rights of the South "in the Union and under the aegis of the Constitution." O'Neal was one of an anomalous breed of old-line Unionists in South Carolina. Brilliant, or only crotchety and verbose, like Charleston's James Louis Petigru or Alfred Huger, these men were the vestigial remains as much of the dead Federalists as of their erstwhile rivals, the state's rights Republicans. In the political hot house which was South Carolina, they combined emotional nationalism and attachment to the symbol of Union, cross-bred with state's rightism, fear and disdain for democracy and economic change, and, often, persistent doubts about the justice of slavery. These hybrids lived on in Carolina, tolerated as adornments, or merely ignored as irrelevant. In the past they had supplied some of the best minds, and first names, to the cause of political moderation, and now such men as O'Neal were eager to support the movement to participate in the national convention. Writing in mid-March, he expressed the dual hope that the source of all the troubles, "that mischievous faction the Abolitionists," would be crushed, and that the "suicidal policy" of those who counselled

[10] McCarter to Miles, January 15, 1860, Miles Papers, SHC.

abstinence from the convention would be rebuked. "Certainly no other end can be obtained [by Rhett's counsels] than to produce distractions and divisions among Southern men," O'Neal observed. Yet he rejoiced that Virginia had rejected the proposed conference of Southern states as a machination of "our restless uneasy Disunionists." What was left? Only that the Democratic convention would organize and select a good, conservative man.[11] Francis W. Pickens could not have agreed more. Replying to letters from George Sanders, Pickens scolded him for backing Stephen A. Douglas. "All I hope for is peace in our ranks, and a cordial harmony & union upon who-ever may be nominated," so long as he fairly received the two-thirds vote at Charleston. (Something Pickens believed Douglas would find impossible.) Rebuking Sanders for his morbid obstinacy, Pickens declared that the party would win if it could unite upon "some firm & *irreproachable* man . . . , for there is at bottom a great conservative feeling pervading the masses." It soon became evident that the Edgefield politician's motives were not entirely selfless. On February 6 he wrote to Buchanan, and in almost the same words he all but presented his name for the President's endorsement for the party's nomination as just the sort of Southerner who loved the Union and would fight for it. Such a man must be chosen, he told Buchanan, for only this could allay the plans of the fire-eaters to introduce new and divisive amendments to the Cincinnati platform, amendments which would split the party.[12]

Of all the disparate groups which found themselves working together in the convention movement, the most dissembling were radicals who called for the nomination of a conservative Southerner as a fair test of national sentiment on the security of slavery, in the full confidence of a Republican victory. Forthright disunionists, such as James Woodward, fervently desired the election of Seward, but turned away from taking any steps to, as he had said, "make ourselves *justly* responsible for it." But there were more conniving secessionists who contributed to the mo-

[11] O'Neal to Hammond, February 13, and March 17, 1860, James H. Hammond Papers, LC.
[12] Pickens to Sanders, October 24, 1859, Francis W. Pickens Papers, DU; Pickens to Buchanan, February 6, 1860, James Buchanan Papers, PaHS.

mentum of the convention movement, not as the way to influence or even capture control of the party, but to destroy the present Union. The most uncompromising statement of this attitude came in a report by "LEO," the Charleston *Daily Courier's* Washington correspondent.

> The Southern Members of Congress and other public men of the South who are here, speak very calmly and judiciously upon the subject of the political aspect of the country. They say that the Southern delegates at the Charleston Convention must agree upon a Southern man, and one of the most conservative of their men, as a candidate for the Presidency, so as to give the North no room for objection on that score, and then if an antislavery candidate be chose, it will not be the fault of the South, and *no responsibility will rest upon the South for the consequences.*[13]

The entire policy of Congressman William W. Boyce illustrated this sort of disingenuous prudence. He eschewed fire-eating oratory and support for such tangential issues as the foreign slave trade. He did not openly counsel participation in the convention, yet he asserted that the nomination was "due" the South, and that no "unsound" candidate should be accepted; more than once he put forth the name of Oregon's pro-slavery Senator Joseph P. Lane as a suitable Northern alternative. Boyce would hold the party together to maintain Southern unity, passively awaiting the verdict of the November election. A more aggressive variety of this attitude was presented by fellow Carolina Democrat James Farrow who believed that the national party could be maintained and could continue to protect slavery. As an erstwhile lieutenant of James L. Orr in the latter's piedmont Fifth District, Farrow was even prepared to believe that "if the question of Southern rights under the constitution on the subject of slavery was once fairly made before the Northern Masses . . . we could carry enough Northern votes to elect a National man." Farrow would appear to be the strongest kind of South Carolina National Democrat.[14]

[13] *Courier,* November 14, 1859. (Italics added.)
[14] Letter from William W. Boyce, September 26, 1859, in the *Courier,* October 13, 1859; *Courier,* November 10, 1859, quoting the Camden *Journal;*

On closer examination Farrow's brand of National Democracy blurs into Yanceyism. He would never accept Douglas, or any man from the North or South who espoused Douglas's popular sovereignty doctrine. He would not accept the conciliatory Cincinnati platform. The party must meet the Republican assault head-on, Farrow trumpeted, by declaring it unconstitutional either to abolish slavery on any federal soil, to interfere with the interstate slave trade or the operation of the Fugitive Slave Act, to deny admission to any state because it countenanced slavery, or to allow territorial legislatures to interfere with slavery in any way. If it were up to James Farrow, and those many South Carolinians who went into the convention movement with this doctrinaire predisposition, the Presidential election would be run on these issues alone. Let us "have a verdict on the single issue of the *rights of the South under the Constitution on the subject of slavery*," Farrow insisted of his correspondent James J. Pettigrew. "We have cried 'peace' long enough—our only chance now is *agitation*—war to the knife against the disorganizing principles of the Republicans." Long before November the people of South Carolina would come to look upon the Presidential election as a final verdict upon slavery.

$$-4-$$

Thus the political grouping which coalesced in the winter of 1859 was an uneasy alliance among many different fragments, including National Democrats with varying degrees of loyalty to the party: Hammond-style moderates who would support the party so long as it yielded to Southern dictation; Unionists who often had taken little part in politics, but who were moved by John Brown to support the Democracy; and a few essentially radical types who wanted the best possible candidate for the Presidency, confident that the "Black" Republicans would in any case triumph in November. This tenuous alliance, known as the

---

Boyce to Christopher Memminger, [January 4, 1860], Christopher G. Memminger Papers, SHC; James Farrow to James Johnston Pettigrew, February 15, 1860, Pettigrew Family Papers, NCArc.

Convention party, was to work together from December until April 1860, only to fall apart, along with the Democracy itself, at the Charleston convention. And the disintegration of both state and national parties was caused by the irreconcilable, unreasoning fear which so many Southerners felt about the security of their system of race control, a fear that stemmed from their distorted perception of the intentions of the Northern people.

It was perhaps inevitable that in this Presidential election year, an election which was to be given such dire meaning by the South, the Northern Democrat most hated by Carolinians should be the foremost candidate for the nomination. And it was a measure of the intensely precarious nature of conditional Unionism in the state that secessionists and moderates shared an identical hostility toward Stephen A. Douglas.

Enmity for the doughty senator from Illinois had been growing during the 1850's, as Douglas came to symbolize the alleged duplicity of Northern Democrats. In 1854 he had introduced a bill in Congress for the organization of the Nebraska Territory, and he became at once the leading advocate of the doctrine of popular sovereignty, the right of local territorial residents to decide for themselves the question of whether slavery was to be legalized or banned from their region. The Douglas bill, adopted as the Kansas-Nebraska Act, abrogated the Missouri Compromise Act of 1820, which had divided potential slave from free states in the western territories; because of Douglas's measure, many Southern radicals were convinced that slavery had been denied a constitutional right of free expansion into the West. Both the constitutional "right" and the issue of slavery expansion became points of vitriolic debate, a controversy that was only papered over by the ambiguous wording of the party platform adopted at Cincinnati in 1856. The question became explosive during Buchanan's first years in office, when the President sought to compel acceptance of a pro-slavery state constitution for Kansas, a decision which for most Northerners made a travesty of the idea of local freedom of choice. By 1859 the National Democracy was profoundly divided between supporters of Douglas and popular sovereignty, and those grimly determined to oppose the nomination of Douglas or any candidate in the 1860 convention who stood on that plank. Not surprisingly, the party division was to an important extent also a sectional one, although Douglas had Southern support outside of Carolina, and there were many opponents of the Illinois senator in the North.[15]

South Carolina radicals regarded the Democratic party itself with enmity, and they considered Stephen Douglas as the incarnation of hypocritical abolitionism. He was looked upon as the very man who had led the Democracy's covert assault upon slavery, the man who even sought to render the monumental Dred Scott decision a nullity. That was a measure of the advantage the South could hope to enjoy if Douglas, or anyone like him, were elected to the Presidency. As the respected Lexington planter and industrial promoter Paul Quattlebaum privately wrote just before the Charleston convention, "I have doubts about our success against that [Republican] party at the next election, and if we have to triumph with Douglas as a leader, success will be but little better than defeat." And Senator Hammond's son, Edward Spann, a state representative from Barnwell, even more definitely believed that "a union of the South is more desirable to us than any such Democratic victory, & defeat, where we unite on our nominee ardently, is preferable."[16]

If these comments by professed opponents of compromise suggest hostility toward Douglas, the attitude of so-called moderates in South Carolina is still more striking. These men shared the common perception of Douglas and popular sovereignty as a Trojan Horse for the eventual fulfillment of the antislavery crusade. Alfred Huger, a venerable defender of Union and slavery, believed that

---

[15] Austin L. Venable, "The Conflict Between the Douglas and Yancey Forces in the Charleston Convention," *Journal of Southern History*, VIII (May 1942), 226–41; John Witherspoon DuBose, *The Life and Times of William Lowndes Yancey*, 2 volumes (New York, 1942), II, 442–48.

[16] Paul Quattlebaum to James H. Hammond, April 18, 1860, Edward Spann Hammond to J. H. Hammond, April 21, 1860, Hammond Papers, LC. Not all Southern radicals were opposed to Douglas. Lawrence M. Keitt's articulate wife Sue Sparks Keitt told her father "I am in favor of Douglas because southern men can rule him and get what they want—and then he is in favor of taking Cuba and all those other southern enterprises. The only way the South can save herself is to spread south, get new territory, enlarge herself, and spread her institutions, and [then] cut loose from the North." Letter of [February 25, 1860], Lawrence M. Keitt Papers, DU.

if there be any difference so far as the South is concerned between the Squatter Sovereignty of Mr. Douglas and the "irrepresible conflict" of Mr. Seward, *that* "difference" is in my poor judgement, in favour of the latter! it is more natural, & it is farther off—the one is abolition "eo nomine" the other is abolition in an offensive disguise! and therefore the more alarming![17]

It was this perspective which placed Unionism in such an ambiguous position in South Carolina. To the moderate who would support the state's continued partnership with the National Democratic party was added the responsibility of dealing with the possible nomination of Douglas. By 1859, with Douglas the obvious front-running candidate, the strength of the Illinois leader was creating a formidable test of conscience for supporters of participation in the national convention.

Carolina "conservatives" sought to solve the problem by ignoring it. John Ashmore, a proper successor to Orr's piedmont congressional seat, admitted to Ben Perry that the nomination of Douglas would present a profound dilemma for "we of the convention party of the state." Like Huger, Ashmore could see nothing more in an election involving Douglas and Seward than a choice between evils. Ashmore, and virtually all South Carolina Unionists, believed that the unity of the Democratic party was prerequisite to the prevention of secession, but that that unity would be destroyed by the nomination of Douglas. The only way to avoid this dead end was to oppose Douglas and fight for the selection of a conservative Southern man, one such as Alabama Senator Benjamin Fitzpatrick, or Virginia Senator Robert M. T. Hunter, together with a platform that did not endorse popular sovereignty. For still more intransigent supporters of the Convention party the alternative was clear. If it was impossible to get a "Southern man with true State Rights principles" the election of a "Black" Republican like Seward might be preferable.[18]

[17] Alfred Huger to W. P. Miles, April 4, 1860, Miles Papers, SHC. Huger denied that any convention had the "power to make *me* distinguish between the stealing of our Slaves, & the expulsion of our People, with their property, from an unsettled territory."

[18] John Ashmore to B. F. Perry, November 22, 1859, and February 12, 1860, Perry Papers, Ala.Arc.; John E. Carew to W. P. Miles, February 28, 1859, Miles Papers, SHC.

— 5 —

Despite this common hostility toward Douglas, South Carolina radicals displayed an exaggerated apprehension that the Convention party—at the moment of decision—would accept both the Illinois senator and a popular sovereignty plank rather than see the Democracy split. They underestimated the obstinacy of their opponents. Time and events would continue to indicate the fundamental unwillingness to compromise of the people of South Carolina. Nevertheless, radicals persistently misrepresented National Democrats as potential "traitors" to the cause of Southern rights. That there was a chance for a real division of the state over acceptance of Douglas as the nominee was a source of growing consternation to Carolina radicals. Abbeville planter Edward Noble revealed his suspicions to Francis Pickens in August 1859.

> I think there is an evident design to bring the state to the support of *Douglass*. How successful will be the scheme I do not know. If the matter is pressed it will split the state into well defined parties, the up and down and out and out state rights and the National. I think the first will carry the day & hence I suppose the Douglass men will not be hasty in coming out. I think the Design is to feel a little the pulse of the state and to prepare it for his nomination.[19]

John Brown appeared to remove the need for such political soft stepping. Although Noble misunderstood the objectives of the Convention party, Harpers Ferry did give a powerful impetus to this movement to bring the state into the national convention. But he was not entirely misguided; there were a few National Democrats with sufficient courage and moderation to speak out in favor of Stephen Douglas. One of the rare public figures who did not falter under the burden of recognizing the preeminent candidacy of Douglas was Arthur Simkins, now an all but unremembered editor of the Edgefield *Advertiser*. Unlike most "Nationals," Simkins made no effort to blind himself to the imminency of a Douglas nomination, nor to avoid a public commit-

[19] Edward Noble to Pickens, August 10, 1859, Pickens Papers, DU.

ment on this question, in the hope that another man, less objectionable to South Carolinians, might be named at Charleston. Simkins supported Douglas as the outstanding Democrat in the nation even before the emotional watershed of Harpers Ferry. Benjamin F. Perry usually stands as the exemplar of Carolina Unionism. It will be revealing to follow the difficult journey of Arthur Simkins towards the secession crisis.

With Perry, Simkins was distraught by the news from Harpers Ferry, and for a moment his confidence fled. The raid, and the Northern expressions of sympathy for it, had "shocked the conservatism of the South and well nigh done away with all remaining attachment to this Union that yet burned on amongst us," he lamented. Disunion, "dreaded by many of us as the greatest evil that could befall the country," had been reawakened as a real possibility. The usually temperate editor excitedly called on the leaders of the state for action. Unless a change in the feeling of the Northern people was evidenced in the coming Presidential election, he believed that secession would inevitably follow.[20]

Deeply shaken as he was, traditional balance soon returned to the pages of the *Advertiser*. Nothing worked so sure a cure for Simkins as the contemplation of the twin demons that shaped his policies: fear of disunion, and fear of a Republican victory in the fall. Simkins spurned the resort to secession as a "dread experiment." Commenting on strictures levelled at him by more extreme editors, Simkins admitted that before 1852 the newspaper had been an ultra-secession advocate. The people voted that down, he replied, and times had changed. What was right then was no longer justified. Unlike many of his fellow South Carolinians, Simkins had moved toward Unionism during the 1850's. He was certain that Southerners were determined to fight for their rights in the Union until every possible compromise was exhausted. Constantly under attack by the generally more extreme Carolina press, Simkins answered threats with strong words of his own. When John Cunningham's Charleston *Evening News* warned that if the whole of the slave states refused to join in revolution, secession would be precipitated by "individual combinations" of Southern radicals in each state, the Edgefield

[20] Edgefield *Advertiser*, December 14, 1859, and January 4, 1860.

Unionist was livid. Did Cunningham threaten the nation with enforced revolution? Simkins asked. The Union was certainly to be preferred "to a reign of misrule, civil strife and bloodshed, which (constituted as our peculiar social system is) would assuredly bring destruction upon our section."[21] Like Benjamin F. Perry, James L. Orr, and the overwhelming majority of South Carolina's Unionists, Arthur Simkins fully accepted the predominant system of social attitudes that ruled the state. There was no line to be drawn between these men and their secessionist opponents on race, slavery, or general social conservatism. As a district, Edgefield sat astride the fall line, and the attitudes of its inhabitants reflected the divided loyalties of the middle range of districts across the state. Nevertheless, in 1860 only one of its five neighboring districts had a lower percentage of slaves in the total population than Edgefield's sixty percent. Thus, like a more prominent Edgefield leader of a later day, Ben Tillman, Simkins could never escape the primacy of race control as a fact of political life. Indeed, the editor waxed eloquent in the certainty that the hand of God himself was at work in the history of the South, blessing it with peace, with slavery, which was the basis of its social structure, and with economic prosperity. All of this, of course, was in contradistinction to the miseries of the North. Like the south-side Virginia protosociologist George Fitzhugh, whom he often quoted, Simkins liked to view the problems vexing the nation not as a sectional struggle founded in the slavery question, but as a struggle between different kinds of people. Infidels, freelovers, socialists, more-government men in the North were warring against Christian conservatives regardless of section. This "fact" made secession a monstrous error. Simkins entreated his fellow Carolinians not to allow hotspurs to push the state into disunion. The mass of Northerners still supported social conservatism, or so Simkins needed to believe.[22]

Nevertheless, when he looked up from Fitzhugh's gothic studies to view his Northern political opponents full face, he was plainly frightened. Republicans *were* abolitionists. Simkins claimed that

[21] *Ibid.*, January 25, February 8 and 15, 1860.
[22] *Ibid.*, December 14, 1859, and February 1, 1860.

Harpers Ferry had proved nothing; but the official words of the "Black" Republican party were more ominous. Reading from an official document which proclaimed the principles of the party, Simkins pointed to the real threat. "*'The integrity of the Union* [must be preserved] *against the conspiracy of the leaders of a sectional party to resist the majority principle,'*" the confident Republicans had declared. This, according to Simkins, was a threat to subjugate the Southern people to the horror of abolitionism, to destroy the prosperity—indeed, the social existence—of the South. Secession was certainly a "dread experiment," but one thing could drive Southerners to it: "self-preservation."[23]

Although he was the foremost National Democrat in Edgefield, and an ardent defender of the Convention party in the pages of the *Advertiser,* Simkins was very much aware of the precarious condition of Democratic party unity, and aware as well that an irreconcilable division of the national party would virtually insure the election of a Republican. By early spring the multiple threats against the Democracy had become so real that Simkins felt compelled to make the ultimate testament of Unionism: he was now prepared to accept the election of a "Black" Republican President, even Seward himself. Criticizing the arguments of extremists, he reasoned that emancipation would not be a necessary consequence of the election. Many hurdles would have to be surmounted before a Republican President could touch slavery itself. "The argument is a large presumption upon the unsoundness of the non-slaveholders of the South, upon the absolute cowardice of our section, . . . and more than all, we repeat, upon the almost miraculous mission of SEWARD." But Simkins, the loyal National Democrat, was not willing to concede defeat. The sure way to avoid both Seward's election and disunion was to breathe life into the faltering Democratic party, and to achieve victory in the fall. For Simkins, this was the only way to avoid impending "social, civil and servile war." Could the Republicans win in November, as they had in the Speakership contest, all because Democrats were unable to unite on one man to lead them? Simkins lampooned Rhett for demanding non-participation in the

[23] *Ibid.,* January 18 and 25, and February 15, 1860.

convention. "Are we to be Achilles in his tent?" he wondered. Clearly, Douglas was preferable to Seward.[24]

– 6 –

The convention movement was officially launched in December, with the publication of a list of thirty-seven members of the legislature who called for the state's representation at Charleston.[25] The legislature had generally opposed involvement in the national convention, and only reluctantly set Columbia as the place, and April 16 as the date for the convening of the State Democratic party.[26] Later, J. D. Pope, chairman of the Charleston delegation to the April 16 convention, wrote Ben Perry of efforts to move back the date of the meeting. The legislature "for certain reasons postponed" the state party meeting to April 16, Pope noted with annoyance, only one week before the national convention was to open in Charleston. "In the opinion of most of the delegation if not of all this day is too late," but attempts to change to an earlier time were abandoned because with so few pro-convention party newspapers, it was feared some district delegations in the state would never hear of the change. Such were the hazards of moderation in South Carolina.[27]

In response to the call from the thirty-seven legislators, moderate newspapers began to come out either for participation, or for a policy of forbearance towards those who wished to support the convention movement.[28] From all indications, the procedure followed in Edgefield to have the district represented at Columbia was typical. On January 4 the *Advertiser* printed a letter calling for all citizens to support a local election to select delegates to the April 16 Columbia state Democratic convention. On the same

[24] *Ibid.*, December 7, 1859, March 14, and February 15, 1860.
[25] Charleston *Mercury*, December 24, 1859. Forty-eight members had signed a similar call in 1855. See Schultz, *Nationalism and Sectionalism*, p. 211.
[26] William D. Porter to J. H. Hammond, April 12, 1860, Hammond Papers, LC.
[27] J. D. Pope to B. F. Perry, March 13, 1860, Perry Papers, Ala.Arc.
[28] For example, see the *Advertiser*, December 21, 1859, quoting the Spartanburg *Spartan; ibid.*, December 28, 1859, quoting the Newberry *Sun;* and *ibid.*, February 1, 1860, quoting the Laurens *Herald.*

page Simkins vigorously concurred, suggesting the day for the election. From then on, not a single issue of the weekly newspaper appeared without some spirited editorial, encouraging attendance at the local election. In January Simkins cited the need to support the Democratic party, which even then was fighting to oppose the election of John Sherman as House Speaker. As the election drew nearer, his words grew warmer. "It is important for the conservative up and middle country to be represented," he reasoned, "and to meet with the men of the parishes in this moment of crisis, poised as we are on the brink of revolution." Simkins's efforts were capped by a successful assembly of Edgefield moderates in late February. He chaired the courthouse meeting, and was among those selected by the voice ballot to go to Columbia; more importantly, he was able to say that only seven districts—five in the low country—had declined the opportunity to be represented at the capitol. The Convention party was on the verge of success in its drive to control the April 16 meeting.[29]

Charleston moderates were also busy. With a keen sense of urgency, National Democrats and other conservatives had joined hands to ensure that the city would be "properly represented" in the state party conclave. They were assisted in their labors by the fact that the national convention was to be held in that very place. Visiting Democrats were regularly feted, and after-dinner speeches, such as one by David Smalley of Vermont, Chairman of the National Executive Committee of the party, which "dwelt upon the coming and certain re-action throughout the North," were warmly applauded. More valuable were the carefully tuned arguments of experienced South Carolina Democrats. An important rally was held in Hibernian Hall in late February, with Charleston legislator Thomas Y. Simons delivering the main address. For those who were invoking Calhoun's words to oppose participation in the national convention, Simons noted that Calhoun had eagerly sought the Presidential nomination more than once. What did anti-conventionists want? he asked. To isolate the state with a "Chinese wall"? To make her a "San Marino repub-

[29] *Advertiser,* January 4, February 8 and 29, and March 7, 1860.

lic"? Simons denounced the extremists of his state, and called upon its citizens to support participation in the national convention, and union with the "conservative men of the North, who have shown their faith by their works."[30]

The effectiveness of the Convention party appeal was reflected in the frantic reaction of radicals. Taking their lead from editorials in the *Mercury*, disunionists condemned the movement as a mere "spoils party." After a visit to Charleston in March, William Lawton, a planter from Beaufort's Prince William Parish, dismissed the lofty motives professed by Simons and other moderates. "A good many of our Charleston folk are licking for office under the next President," Lawton wrote Porcher Miles, "however they may fancy themselves patriots & good Democrats. National Democracy at the South ought to be defined as *the scramble party*." Although Congressman Miles feared that his own seat was a target of the "Nationals," he may have realized that the main impulse behind the convention movement came out of the strong element of political moderation and Unionism which had been a part of Carolina life for generations.[31]

There is no denying that radicals were deeply frightened by the apparent momentum of the moderate faction. They were, of course, aware that many of their fellow citizens who favored participation in the Charleston convention were doing so in the belief "that this will be to all intents and purposes a Southern Convention—that is that the Southern States will control and will have a right to control the platform and the nomination." But what would happen if these hopes were proved false? And what of the more conservative portion of the pro-convention faction, the true National Democrats? With other radicals, William Henry Trescot feared that these men, led by Orr, would "take any can-

[30] William Henry Trescot to W. P. Miles, February 22, 1860, Miles Papers, SHC; *Speech in Favor of South Carolina being Represented in the Democratic Convention, delivered at a Meeting of the Citizens of Charleston, held in Hibernian Hall, February 26, 1860* (Charleston, 1860).

[31] William Lawton to W. P. Miles, March 18, 1860, Miles Papers, SHC. Many letters touched on the suspicion that the "Nationals" coveted Miles's position. William Gilmore Simms warned him against trusting certain Charleston politicos who were, "none of them, of the real States rights men, but rather of the mongrel faction who go for the Convention, and possibly for Douglas." Simms to Miles, April 9, 1860, Miles Papers, SHC.

didate of the Convention, Douglas not excepted and the Cincinnati Platform." Cautioning his friend about Orr and his followers, Trescot predicted that they would "carry the day" at the April 16 state party convention at Columbia. If a conservative delegation was named there to represent South Carolina at the national convention, the "Nationals" would "draw party lines in the state clearly and widely and should the Democratic Party triumph [the Unionist faction] will I feel sure be sustained by the new administration." The empty security of the past eight years would be perpetuated for another four.[32]

As for himself, Trescot was perplexed and pessimistic. An ardent secessionist nine years before, he had come to despair of ever seeing the birth of a Southern nation. Looking about him now, at the way Virginia had rejected the bid for a Southern conference, at Sam Houston's Unionist pronouncements, hearing the soft conservative words drifting through Charleston, he was disconsolate. "I believe all chance of Southern action separate or combined is idle," he confessed to Miles. Just the other night, William Aiken, perhaps the wealthiest man in South Carolina, had come up to him loudly singing the praises of Stephen Douglas, "as the only man who could save the party . . . , as the truest of men to the South and Southern interests, 'as true'—oh glorious climax 'as myself.' "[33]

Trescot's letters provide a valuable picture of the warped and hypersensitive perception shared by Carolina radicals. A patrician "by choice and marriage rather than by birth,"[34] with the autonomic fear typical of the low country gentry for anything that smacked of democracy, or which threatened to divide the state, Trescot declaimed against the convention movement. He refused to believe that the vote of South Carolina could in any way influence the outcome of the Charleston convention. According to him, Carolina had enjoyed an historically "distinct and independent influence" on American politics which was the "result of character rather than positive political strength." He would

[32] Trescot to Miles, February 22, 1860, Miles Papers, SHC.
[33] *Ibid.*
[34] Robert Nicholas Olsberg, "William Henry Trescot: The Crisis of 1860," (unpublished master's thesis, the University of South Carolina, 1967) p. 15.

not have opposed a genuine popular movement by all citizens to have the state represented at the national convention. But Trescot denied that the present Convention party was such a natural expression. To his eyes it was a radical democratic thrust, seeking not so much a moderate national policy for the state, as the disruption of traditional ruling cliques, a purge of officeholders, an alteration in the very basis of politics in South Carolina. So sensitive were tidewater radicals, so suspect was any voice coming out of the piedmont, that the convention movement was denounced as nothing but a veiled attempt to destroy the aristocracy in favor of democracy.[35]

By the end of March it was apparent even to Barnwell Rhett that the radicals' "policy" of passively condemning the purposes of the Convention party had created a power vacuum. Running largely unopposed in district and parish elections, moderates appeared certain to control the deliberations of the April 16 Columbia convention. As a result, Barnwell Rhett, Jr., was forced to tell Miles, "weak men will be sent to the Charleston Convention, untrammelled by any committments or instructions." Rhett was sure that "so far from encouraging Alabama & Mississippi to insist upon the repudiation of squatter sovereignty or to retire in case of failure, many of these delegates will strive to let down those states and defeat such action." By the time of the state convention, Rhett was convinced that a slate of delegates would be chosen who would undermine any move to disrupt the Charleston conclave. Perhaps they would stand firm against Douglas. But more important to radicals, "will they encourage Alabama to obey her instruction and secede from the convention when she fails to get a repudiation of Squatter Sovereignty? That is the question, and that, in my opinion, is just where they will fail." The Rhetts had reason to be concerned about the revolutionary ardor of the Alabama delegation and its leader, and they were eager to see the South Carolina contingent add its voice to the radical chorus at Charleston. Who could tell to what depths a delegation of the "Orr-Simons stripe" might fall?[36]

[35] Trescot to Miles, March 10, 1860, Miles Papers, SHC.
[36] R. B. Rhett, Jr., to Miles, March 28, and April 11, 1860, Miles Papers, SHC.

— 7 —

And so, on the eve of the state party convention, radicals again permitted themselves to become exercised over their inflated fears of Douglas support in South Carolina, fears which were directly related to the startling and misguided distrust they felt towards their Unionist opponents. From Washington, Miles frantically began writing letters to friends across the state with the single question: was there, could there be a faction of South Carolinians prepared to vote for Douglas? The answers ranged from incredulity to gloomy acknowledgments. Yes, there was such a faction in Charleston, wrote Federal Marshal Daniel Hamilton. They would show their faces more clearly throughout the state as the national convention approached. The Administration is surprised at the idea, Hamilton drily remarked, but the Administration had done nothing to propitiate South Carolina; it had taken the state for granted as safe. Now, Hamilton wrote, the National Democrats in Charleston were already apportioning the patronage they would grab under the "new administration."[37]

Not everyone agreed with Hamilton. Miles heard from Henry Gourdin, member of one of the most affluent families in the low country, a leading merchant in Charleston and Savannah, and a strong disunionist. Gourdin could not conceive that "Douglas should be countenanced or supported by any of our people." He confessed that he knew "little of the men in the interior of our State who have been thus far chosen delegates to Columbia, but [he did] know that our Legislature in Columbia in Decr. last was unanimous against Douglas, and I believe they fairly represented the sentiment of the State, whether Convention or anti-Convention." Gourdin was sure that Miles had been unduly alarmed by

[37] Letters to Miles from Robert Gourdin and Alfred Huger, April 4, 1860, Daniel H. Hamilton, April 4, 1860, and [April 7, 1860], Miles Papers, SHC. Miles was well aware of Buchanan's attitude toward South Carolina. Writing to Dr. Lewis R. Gibbes on April 9, he was compelled to say that he could find no Federal position for a relative of the doctor's. "These things are given to reward politicians and strengthen the Administration. *Our* State they do not care to give papp to because it cannot but act with the Administration against the Black Republicans." Lewis R. Gibbes Papers, LC.

false rumors circulated in Washington by Douglas men. Such rumors could shake timid men in the state, and could aid Douglas's effort everywhere "by creating the impression that he has supporters even in So. Carolina." Senator James Hammond heard much the same argument from William Dennison Porter, President of the Senate, who, like Gourdin, was certain that the 1859 legislature had overwhelmingly opposed Douglas.[38]

The weightiest of such verdicts came from Isaac William Hayne. A radical from the time of his graduation from South Carolina College over thirty years before, Hayne had served as Clerk of the Nullification Convention, and since 1848, as the state's Attorney General. Less well remembered than other members of his family, Isaac Hayne was in fact one of the most influential men in the state, and a charter member of the political group currently ruling Charleston politics.[39] In letters to Miles, and Senators Hammond and Chesnut written just before the Columbia convention, Hayne insisted that there was no organized movement, underground or otherwise, to carry the state for Douglas and the Cincinnati platform.

> All sorts of men, in a scattering way, have gone into the convention [he told Chesnut], and there is no definite understanding of any kind among them, but I have no fear of anything like a Douglas demonstration. On the contrary I expect a strong states rights declaration. The people are quiet at present, a great many men take part [in the convention movement], and those inclined to betray fear to rouse the people as they know Douglas to be odious and his doctrines an abomination.

[38] Henry Gourdin to Miles, April 5, 1860, Miles Papers, SHC; William D. Porter to Hammond, April 12, 1860, Hammond Papers, LC. The surviving letters received by Douglas held at the University of Chicago Library, and in the private possession of the Martin Douglas family, Greensboro, North Carolina, altogether number in the tens of thousands. For 1860 alone these collections contain hundreds of communications from supporters in all of the Southern states. Yet in the entire critical period from Harpers Ferry to December 1860 there are but *two* letters to Douglas from South Carolinians, J. M. Rutland, March 22, and J. Q. Smith, September 14, 1860; only the former is complimentary. Information on the Martin Douglas Collection was kindly supplied by Prof. Robert W. Johannsen.

[39] John Amasa May and Joan Reynolds Faunt, *South Carolina Secedes* (Columbia, 1960), pp. 155–56.

In short, there were Douglas supporters in South Carolina, "but when they get to Columbia they will forget they ever were so. It won't do." Hayne was also aware that there were men who were playing up to Douglas, thinking that he could never win the nomination, and believing that he would be compelled to throw his strength to a Southern candidate. "The *two thirds* rule," he assured Miles, "will save us from Douglass."[40]

Evidently Hayne's exact prediction of events did not persuade most radicals, for anxiety over the potential apostasy of the Convention party was reaching fever pitch by mid-April. And, as Trescot made clear, radical prospects at Charleston did indeed appear to be uncertain. Whether "Orr and his faction (the Convention party) are more Douglas men than we think," he told Hammond, was not the most important issue. The fact remained that if the people of South Carolina were faced with a choice between the Republican nominee and Stephen Douglas as the Democratic party's candidate, it was unlikely that they would be prepared deliberately to defeat Douglas and elect the Republican. To do so would imply that the people of the South were ready to submit to the presidency of a "Black" Republican in the confidence that the party would destroy itself in power ("a theory which . . . may after all turn out to be a mistake"); or that Carolinians were ready for immediate secession upon the inauguration of a Republican ("and this," Trescot noted, "I do not candidly believe the South is prepared for"). Could the citizens of South Carolina vote against a "man popularly chosen by representatives including the entire South"? More immediately, could the representatives of Carolina at the Charleston national convention refuse to accept the official nomination of Douglas? This was the dilemma which might compel support for the Illinois senator in the Presidential election, even though most South-

---

[40] Hayne to Miles, April 11 and 15, 1860, Miles Papers, SHC; Hayne to Hammond, April 15, 1860, Hammond Papers, LC; and Hayne to Senator James Chesnut, April 15, 1860, Chesnut-Miller-Manning Papers, SCHS. Carolina's own James Orr was one of those who harbored pretensions to the nomination. However, Orr did "not think it would be politic for my state to *vote for me* at the outset," for if Douglas were defeated, those who had opposed him in the balloting could never hope to receive his support. Orr to B. F. Perry, March 5, 1860, Perry Papers, Ala.Arc.

erners preferred one of their own to carry the party standard. This predicament had forced Congressman Ashmore, who had bitterly opposed Douglas as late as February, to acknowledge the possibility of his nomination and election. "If we have to take Douglas," he wrote Perry, "let it be with reluctance. It will I fear tear the South all to pieces. I can only support him in the event of a large portion of Southern States ratifying his nomination & as a choice between him & a Republican.—Such is the feeling of the large majority of our conservative Southern men."[41]

— 8 —

Radicals had convinced themselves that the Convention party was at once a bid for spoils, an attempt to undermine patrician political control, a "submissionist" scheme to divide the state, and prepare the way for acquiescence to a Republican victory, and an effort to transport the state into the Douglas camp. Since the movement began in the winter, radical leaders had made random efforts to discredit the moderates, or, belatedly, to capture control of the local district delegations to the April 16 convention. In March, for example, moderate John Hope, a legislator from Lexington, worriedly reported that disunionist Congressman Bonham was suddenly attempting to commit the district delegation to Yancey's extremist program. And at the courthouse meeting to select district representatives, General Paul Quattlebaum, the leading figure in Lexington, tried in vain to have the slate tied to an anti-Douglas plank.[42]

Hope, who was a long-time National Democrat, was astounded by the extent of popular support for the Convention party; so many who had repudiated the convention movement in 1856 were now loudest in proclaiming the need for participation. The danger was that too many of these men would prove to be unreliable Unionists. Nevertheless, from the outset, Carolina news-

[41] Trescot to Hammond, April 15, 1860, Hammond Papers, LC; Ashmore to Perry, March 10, 1860, Perry Papers, Ala.Arc. See also James Hammond to his brother Marcellus, March 9, 1860, and letters to Hammond from W. B. Hodgson, April 6, 1860, and Trescot, April 18, 1860, all in Hammond Papers, LC.
[42] John C. Hope to Hammond, March 10, 1860, Hammond Papers, LC.

papers eagerly debated the degree of popular support for the convention faction. A most striking statement in this controversy came just as the state Democratic party convened in Columbia. Franklin Gaillard's Columbia *South Carolinian* took the Charleston *Mercury* and *Evening News* to task for creating the impression that the people of South Carolina opposed participation at the Charleston national convention.

> In the up country and in Charleston the Convention party largely predominates. In the pine land belt of the interior, and in the parishes where there is a comparatively sparse [white] population, and where new ideas make slower progress, we readily assent that there the dicta of the *Mercury* is regarded as definitive of sound policy; but in the State [as a whole], the Convention party have the majority, and are every day gaining strength. The *Mercury* and the *News* represent the decrepit party of the State, and their determined non-action policy shows their decrepitude. The people of the State will not linger in the past with them.[43]

The spirit of radicalism in Carolina had been traumatized by the failure of secession nine years before. The state had drifted through the intervening years, confused, frustrated, divided, its new-found voice of moderation expressing more the tentative hopes than the grim beliefs of its people. Now, in the spring of 1860, the leaders of radical sentiment had reacted instinctively in abstaining from involvement in the convention movement. As a result, the groups that could control the politics of the state found themselves to be observers on the sidelines at the approach of the signally important state party convention. For those who could not stand idly by and see the state fail to back Yancey merely because a faction had gained control of the state party convention, there remained at this eleventh hour only the tactic of public denunciation.

> There is some talk here [Barnwell Rhett, Jr., wrote Miles on March 31st] of having a meeting—not to denounce the con-

[43] *Advertiser*, April 4, 1860; *ibid.*, April 25, 1860, quoting the Columbia *Daily South Carolinian*.

vention party—but to force them up on the issue of squatter sovereignty and to establish throughout the state a frigid sentiment of antagonism to this heresy. The object is to sustain Alabama and Mississippi by compelling these gentlemen to cooperate promptly and with cordiality, apparent, if not real.

The need for such a course seemed obvious. Not only was control of the April 16 meeting out of the hands of the radicals, but the public mood of Carolinians appeared disoriented and depressed. Daniel Hamilton laid the blame for this on the magnitude of events swirling about the nation. The citizens of the state "feel that So. Ca. is a small & a weak State, and as such that they will have but little voice in controlling the policy of this Country—everything appears gloomy and uncertain to them in the future."[44]

Wiser heads than Hamilton's knew that the ardent spirit of state's rights infused into every class of South Carolinian was hardly dead. The people did seem apathetic, but the reason was not discouragement. "The truth is," Isaac Hayne told Hammond, "that our *People* though still essentially *disunionist,* are sick of agitation. They don't mean that the State should move *alone,* and they have no confidence in their neighbours." What they want, Hayne correctly discerned, "is to be let alone until the time for real action has arrived." Rhett knew that this was exactly right. While he fumed at having failed to organize popular pressure upon the Columbia convention, the events of the next two weeks would show that he had learned his lesson well.[45]

[44] R. B. Rhett, Jr., to Miles, March 31, 1860, Daniel Hamilton to Miles, April 4, 1860, Miles Papers, SHC. See also *Mercury,* March 31, 1860; letters to Miles from Alfred Huger, April 4, 1860, John Cunningham, April 5, 1860, and A. O. Andrews, April 11, 1860, Miles Papers, SHC.

[45] Isaac W. Hayne to Hammond, April 15, 1860, Hammond Papers, LC; Hayne to James Chesnut, April 15, 1860, Chesnut-Miller-Manning Papers, SCHS; R. B. Rhett, Jr., to Miles, April 11, 1860, Miles Papers, SHC.

CHAPTER SIX

Secessionists and Unionists: the Last Confrontation

The Convention has been an Orr affair—Alabama resolutions rejected[.] Cincinnati Platform reaffirmed with Dred Scott decision uninterpreted. . . . Our friends justified a packed Jury trimming to keep in with Douglas.

Thus Rhett telegraphed the outcome of the long awaited state convention to Miles. There was no doubt that the moderate section of South Carolina had spoken at Columbia. National Democracy's leading Carolinian, James L. Orr, was elected president of the convention, and from his restrained and optimistic opening address to the final approval of platform recommendations, it was clear that the assembly well represented the spirit of political conservatism in the state. The convention endorsed Orr for the Presidency in the apparent hope that a Douglas-Orr ticket would prove attractive to the national convention, and named an anti-secessionist slate of delegates to Charleston. An effort to bind the delegation to the Yancey program was resoundingly defeated, and a resolution simply endorsing the slavery plank of the Cincinnati platform was accepted. After the Charleston debacle, Benjamin F. Perry testily remarked that this rejection of the Alabama platform in effect bound the delegation to remain in the national convention.[1]

[1] Telegram, Robert Barnwell Rhett, Jr., to William Porcher Miles, April 17,

Nonetheless, this was a conservative assembly only by the standards of South Carolina. The Columbia convention was not "submissionist." As Orr's introductory speech made clear, these moderate men hated and feared abolitionism, but they feared the implications of a Republican victory in November as much. "I am one of those who have believed, and who now believe, that this great Government . . . is yet worth preserving," declared Orr the Unionist. But, Orr the South Carolinian concluded, he would only oppose disunion so long as the nation could be "preserved in unison with our rights, with our interests and with our honor." For James Orr and his followers, the only prudent course lay in supporting the continuing rule of a "conservative" Democratic party. The leaders at Columbia specifically repudiated Douglas's version of popular sovereignty, and a resolution affirming South Carolina's intention to cooperate with the cotton states was only narrowly defeated by a vote of eighty-six to eighty-five. Despite the desultory public denunciation heaped upon the efforts of the April 16 convention by the *Mercury*, secessionists were not without hope. "On reconsideration," Barnwell Rhett, Jr., wired Miles, "so far so good."[2]

— 1 —

The South Carolina delegation found their familiar Charleston occupied by a troubled and quarrelsome collection of party poli-

1860, and letter of William Lawton to W. P. Miles, May 6, 1860, William Porcher Miles Papers, SHC; James H. Hammond to M. C. M. Hammond, April 22, 1860, James H. Hammond Papers, LC; "Territorial Resolution," [April 1860], Democratic Party Paper, USC; Edgefield *Advertiser*, April 25, 1860; letter from B. F. Perry to Franklin Gaillard, May 15, 1860, in *Advertiser*, May 23, 1860, quoting the (Columbia) *Daily South Carolinian;* Benjamin F. Perry, *Biographical Sketches of Eminent American Statesmen* (Philadelphia, 1887), pp. 186–87.

[2] *Proceedings of the Democratic State Convention of South Carolina, held at Columbia on the 16th and 17th of April, 1860 for the purpose of electing delegates to the Democratic National Convention, to meet in Charleston 23d April* (Columbia, 1860); Telegram, R. B. Rhett, Jr., to W. P. Miles, April 18, 1860, Miles Papers, SHC. See also Charles Edward Cauthen, *South Carolina Goes to War, 1860–1865* (Chapel Hill, 1950), pp. 15–16; Laura White, "The National Democrats in South Carolina, 1852 to 1860," *The South Atlantic Quarterly,* XXVIII (October 1929), 383–84; and Chauncey S. Boucher, "South Carolina and the South on the Eve of Secession, 1852 to 1860," *Washington University Studies,* VI (1918), 135–36.

ticians. The Democracy, the last major party with a claim to a truly national following, had been sliding towards a crisis of unity for more than a decade. It was the vexing slavery issue, that maker and breaker of parties, which lay at the root of the problem. The unity of the Democratic party was utterly dependent upon the desire of Northern moderates to keep hands off the constitutional rights of the South in their slave property; and dependent as well upon Southern confidence in the intentions of their Northern brethren. These conditions which had been preserved for generations, were becoming nearly impossible to maintain by 1860.

The immediate sources of dissension within the party, however, were more complex than pure sectionalism. As noted earlier, Senator Douglas—although the most popular Democrat nationally through most of the 1850's—had aroused the hostility of Southern extremists by his espousal of the popular sovereignty doctrine. His refusal in 1857 to countenance the pro-slavery Lecompton Kansas constitution promulgated by President Buchanan had widened the breach between Democrats. Opponents of his nomination now included the President and pro-Administration stalwarts in the North. On the other hand, Douglas's forthright stand on the Kansas question, and his subsequent defense of popular sovereignty in 1858 and 1859, made him a rallying point for Democrats, North and South, who opposed the policies of the Buchanan administration. Moderates saw in him a fair-minded leader who offered the best hope for victory against the Republicans. Southern supporters accepted his disavowals of abolitionist intentions, while many Northerners considered his position on the territorial issue a conciliatory way to prevent slavery expansion.[3] Were it not for the intractable and deadly animosity of Southern radicals and Administration stalwarts, it would appear that Douglas could have held the party together for a possible victory in November.

The mortal dangers posed by this bitter and uncompromising opposition were unfortunately intensified by attitudes within the Douglas camp itself. It was not clear that his backers were sufficiently aware of the extreme, almost paranoid, sensitivity of the

[3] See Robert W. Johannsen, "Douglas at Charleston," in Norman A. Graebner (ed.), *Politics and the Crisis of 1860* (Urbana, 1961), pp. 64–67.

Southern mind. Many of his proponents, and even Douglas himself, seemed perhaps willfully obtuse to the emotional content and implications of the issues involved. While recognizing the need for substantial support from the South to win the two-thirds majority required for a nomination, Douglas was hopeful that the ambiguous 1856 Cincinnati platform, as he interpreted it, could again serve as "party cement."[4] "We stand by the Cincinnati Platform according to its obvious meaning," he calmly wrote a Georgian in September 1859. "If this is not satisfactory to some of our Southern Friends we shall regret it but cannot avoid it." Douglas was convinced that he was right, and he would not change his opinions, "even to be President."[5] He may have been right, but he could never again placate the growing apprehension among Southerners that he was no better than the "blackest" Republican.

The recent fall and winter months had seen Southern racial fears inflamed by Harpers Ferry, and anxiety over the spectre of impending Republican rule enlarged by the Speakership controversy. In February radicals and Administration stalwarts progressed towards more extreme demands for Southern "rights," even to proposing a code for the positive protection of slavery in the territories. Despite these and other storm signals, the majority of Northern Democrats went ahead with their own inflexible plans to nominate a man who was totally unacceptable to a substantial portion of the party. Douglas's eager New York promoter George Sanders admitted to Francis Pickens that "the chances are that we will be defeated in 60," yet he obstinately refused to recognize the futility and danger of pushing the Senator's name. All of his "partizans are resolved that if Douglas is to be put aside that no Northern Lecompton [Administration] man shall receive the nomination. Of one thing you may be positive," Sanders correctly warned Pickens, "that if any Northern man receives the nomination it will be Douglas."[6]

[4] *Ibid.*
[5] Douglas to Henry K. McCoy, September 27, 1859, in *The Letters of Stephen A. Douglas,* edited by Robert W. Johannsen (Urbana, 1961), pp. 468–69; see also Johannsen, "Douglas at Charleston," pp. 65–66.
[6] Sanders to Pickens, June 12, 1859, Claude W. Unger MSS Collection, PaHS. See also the Charleston *Daily Courier,* October 5, 1859.

The President was no less adamant in defining his terms for the man who should succeed him. (A year or more earlier, he had irrevocably decided against seeking a second term.)[7] For Buchanan, as for most South Carolinians, Douglas and his faction were joined in perfidy with the hated Republicans. He believed that both groups seemed irrationally determined to upset the Dred Scott decision which had explicitly affirmed the right of slavery expansion into the western territories. "Seward & the Black Republicans resist this decision on the ground that Congress has the right to prohibit Slavery," the President lectured a supporter, "& Douglas & his followers resist it on the ground that a Territorial Legislature possesses this right." The former was an unwarranted inflation of Federal power, he explained, while the latter was simply erroneous, and both permitted interference with the illimitable right of slavery expansion. But Buchanan was confident that he saw the one light which could lead the nation out of this maze, and this was the same illumination that guided the hopes of National Democrats in South Carolina. "The issue in 1860, beyond all question will be between the Republicans who refuse to yield obedience to this decision [Dred Scott] & the Democrats who sustain it & in doing so will sustain the cause of law, property & order." And, Buchanan predicted, *On this issue we shall win.* If this was the sole basis upon which the Democratic party could unite and win the fall election, Stephen A. Douglas could win neither the nomination nor the Presidency.[8]

The "signals" coming into South Carolina from Northern and Southern leaders strongly seconded Buchanan's point of view. Even before Harpers Ferry many Southern Democrats were preparing to resist the nomination of Douglas, although it remained naggingly unclear just who would be the chosen candidate. From Miles's friend Muscoe Garnett, a tidewater Virginia congressman, he received an early promise that the Old Dominion would never cast its ballot for Douglas. "Virginia wants a Southern candidate," Garnett wrote in May 1859, "& her inclination will be very much

[7] Philip Shriver Klein, *President James Buchanan, A Biography* (University Park, Pa., 1962), p. 340.
[8] Buchanan to M. Johnson, September 19, 1858, James Buchanan Papers, NYHS.

determined by any strong outside demonstration that any particular man is the available person." Garnett was already promoting his own uncle and senator, Robert M. T. Hunter, and a few weeks later Hunter's colleague in the Senate James Murray Mason suggested that he had been seized by Presidential fever. But Mason saw more clearly than Garnett that the North was even then so "infected" with the doctrines of Douglas that any nomination would be impossible. "Your convention will break up," Mason advised Miles. More and more Southern politicians were being led by doctrine or expediency to conclude that the party and the Union could only be preserved by the nomination and election of a conservative Southern Democrat.[9]

Anti-Douglasites in the North tended to endorse this conclusion, and the news of John Brown's raid naturally spurred their efforts to appease the South. Few Northern conservatives failed to see the implications of Harpers Ferry for the coming national convention, and during the winter the incoming correspondence of South Carolinians was filled with plaintive disavowals of extremism. Nominate a capable Southern moderate and you shall have the next President, they cried. "Give us a *National man—*," New York business leader Charles Augustus Davis demanded of Miles, "and you will see that the *North* will rightly appreciate the object—we are *not all sectional.*"[10]

The schism between defenders of Douglas, and those unalterably opposed to him had worked its way deep into Northern state politics well before 1860; in such states as New York and Illinois the need to choose delegates to the Charleston national convention was sparking an enmity only intensified by Harpers Ferry. John Stryker, a member of the Administration side of the two opposing sets of New York state delegations to Charleston, provided a good

[9] Garnett to Miles, May 25, 1859, and Mason to Miles, July 1, 1859, Miles Papers, SHC. See also William M. Churchwell to F. W. Pickens, October 8, 1859, Pickens Papers, DU. Besides Hunter, who appeared to be the favorite of many South Carolina Democrats, some of the names mentioned as possible nominees were Alabama Senator Benjamin Fitzpatrick, Kentuckians James Guthrie and John C. Breckinridge, and, within Carolina, James Orr. This list, of course, only begins to mention the dozen or more eminently available men.

[10] Charles Augustus Davis to W. P. Miles, December 8, 1859, and March 22, 1860, Miles Papers, SHC.

example of the conciliatory mood of Northern Democrats opposed to Douglas. In a letter to John L. Manning, Stryker assured the former South Carolina governor that his delegation was eager to cooperate with their "state rights" friends in frustrating Douglas and nominating someone more acceptable to both. Douglas was backed by a strong vote from the Northwest, but, Stryker confided, "I do not think that his most intelligent friends have any expectation that he will be nominated unless he has Southern support which he seems now to lack." The differences which had split the New York delegations were more a product of personal animosities and struggles for power than of ideology, and in this letter Stryker perhaps unwittingly avowed a platform on slavery identical to that proposed by Douglas. Manning may have stumbled over this, but the Unionist planter doubtless welcomed Stryker's promise that New York Democrats conceded the nomination to the South. Stryker was, in fact, speaking for a delegation which was to be rejected by the national convention, but he well expressed the earnest intention of Administration supporters to stop Douglas and pacify radical Southern sentiment. If the South can present a candidate "with any degree of unanimity," Stryker concluded, "we are prepared to sustain him."[11]

Unfortunately, none of the events of the recent past—not John Brown's raid, the Speakership controversy, the call for a Southern conference—not even the genuine possibility of victory in November were sufficient to unite the Southern states on a mutually acceptable ticket prior to Charleston. In January Congressman Garnett was sure that despite Douglas's strong support he could not be nominated, as "It would break up the convention." "We shall have a hard fight with the Republicans," he told a supporter, "but we may, with the right candidate probably beat them." But who was the right man? In February Francis W. Pickens was warned by a Tennessee friend that the Democratic party was "derided, demoralized and distracted," and that its very existence depended upon the action of the Charleston convention. But still no man loomed above the mass of aspirants to arouse the respect and confidence of all sections. Three weeks

[11] John Stryker to John L. Manning, January 15, 1860, Chesnut-Miller-Manning Papers, SCHS.

later Pickens—still in a distant post as head of the American Mission in St. Petersburg—was reminded by George Sanders that Douglas remained the only significant candidate. "He will receive a majority on the first ballot," Sanders predicted, "& his chief opponents at Washington admit that if he receives a majority he must be nominated." In the face of such stubborn confidence Pickens, like many other Southerners, could only harbor the fragile hope that "as in the case of Mr. Polk and Genl Pierce, some man will be taken not now prominently mentioned."[12]

By late March the apparent disarray of Southern Democrats had worsened. Close to a dozen Presidential hopefuls were more or less in the field, and from the cacophony of voices coming out of Washington it was only clear that no one spoke for the South. By now reasonable men like Virginia's Garnett could do little to mask their desperation. With everyone else he was "anxious to know what course South Carolina will probably pursue in the Charleston convention." By raising these questions only a month before the convention, Garnett showed just how cloudy the future appeared to Southern politicians. "Will your state follow the Alabama line?" he asked John L. Manning.

Will she concur in what seems to be [the] wish of some who favour such a policy generally—that is, to make the nomination first, and the platform afterwards? For you will discern that many who would insist on an extreme resolution with a Northern candidate will be quite content with much more moderate counsels if the nominee is a sound Southern man. And then again, for whom will your State vote? Will Orr be in the field?

Garnett was certain that Virginia wanted a Southern candidate as a sign that the Northern Democracy was truly "conservative"

[12] Garnett to Samuel Downing, January 14, 1860, Samuel Downing Papers, LC; letters to Francis W. Pickens from William M. Churchwell, February 12, 1860, George N. Sanders, March 6, 1860, and John Thomson Mason, March 9, 1860, Francis W. Pickens Papers, DU. Sanders proclaimed that Douglas "could not be defeated unless large sums of money shall be used in absolute purchase of delegates." He underestimated the growing power of Southern nationalism. It was here that Sanders "offered" the Vice-Presidency to Pickens in exchange for Carolina's votes at the convention.

and prepared to accord control of the Federal Government to a Southerner. Garnett believed that such a nominee could more easily allay the divisions which ran through the ranks of Northern Democrats than would any Northerner identified with Douglas or the Administration. Democrats from the North will accept a Southern candidate, the Virginian promised, if the South could unite on the man. There was the rub. "Can such a union be effected? That is the only question for us, for once made, it is virtually a nomination."[13] The "union" was not effected, and a profoundly divided Democracy convened at Charleston in the last week of April 1860.

— 2 —

South Carolina's Unionist delegation nonetheless entered the convention grimly determined to reconcile party unity, national unity, and the essential "rights" of the South. The sixteen men dispatched to Charleston by the Columbia assembly perfectly represented the anti-secession party in Carolina.[14] They refused to join a caucus of the cotton states on the eve of the convention, a caucus which subsequently agreed to back the Alabama platform to the bitter end.[15] Despite the disconcerting radicalism emanating from the delegations of the lower South, Carolina's earnest moderates maintained a composure which agonized many

[13] Garnett to Manning, March 21, 1860, Chesnut-Miller-Manning Papers, SCHS.

[14] The delegation included such National Democrats as Edgefield's Arthur Simkins, James and Thomas Simons of Charleston, and Samuel McGowan of Abbeville; Benjamin H. Wilson of Georgetown, who had so vigorously opposed discussion of the Alabama platform in the state Senate the previous December; Franklin Gaillard, editor of the Columbia *Daily South Carolinian;* and, of course, Benjamin F. Perry.

[15] "Indications increase against Douglas," telegraphed a supporter. "Six [sic] southern states resolved last night to stand on Alabama platform and will bolt if he is nominated. . . . South not united on candidate yet but nearly solid against squatter sovereignty." James E. Harvey to George Harrington, April 21, 1860, Stephen A. Douglas Papers, UChic. The states involved in the caucus were Alabama, Georgia, Mississippi, Louisiana, Florida, Arkansas, and Texas. See Murat Halstead, *Caucuses of 1860. A History of the National Conventions of the Current Presidential Campaign* . . . (Columbus, Ohio, 1860), p. 8.

of their fellow citizens.[16] James L. Orr was there exchanging meaningful whispers in clouds of cigar smoke with Douglas's inescapable strategist George Sanders.[17] But even after Orr's ambitions ceased to guide the Carolina delegation, they continued to resist the call of extremism, turning instead to Virginia's R. M. T. Hunter as an acceptable Presidential alternative.

Yet on April 30 all but three men in the delegation rose, however reluctantly, and marched out of Institute Hall, and out of the Democratic party with the other bolting states.[18] Perhaps the only surprising feature was the extent of the secession. The spirit of Southern radicalism as embodied in the Alabama platform was certainly no secret to Douglas, and an insignificant withdrawal of some Gulf state delegates was even expected by him. Murat Halstead, a perceptive observer of all the national conventions, more than once had occasion to report the ebullient remark of a Douglasite, calling a bolt "Just the thing we want." It was believed that this expression of Southern extremism would galvanize Douglas sentiment, while it removed opposition votes from the convention. On the third day of the convention, April 25, C. P. Culver, who was acting as an aide to the Illinois senator in Charleston, confidently advised him that the irreconcilable opposition of the cotton states would not prevent the drafting of an acceptable platform; "one or two of these states" only might withdraw, he wrote Douglas. Two days later, with amendment proposals from

---

[16] "I am sorry to tell you that the So. Ca. Delegation in the Convention occupies a very contemptible position . . . they say that these gentlemen do not represent SoCa, that it merely represents a set of 'office seekers' who have gone into the Convention to gratify some end of their own. This is very humiliating, but I fear that it is true." Daniel Hamilton to W. P. Miles, April 26, 1860, Miles Papers, SHC. The "spoilsman" label was often used against National Democrats, and, indeed, as part of a general condemnation of the convention system and democratic politics in America by Carolina aristocrats. See James Johnston Pettigrew to Daniel M. Barringer, April 15, 1860, D. M. Barringer Papers, SHC; and Isaac W. Hayne to Charles C. Pinckney, III, April 23, 1860, Charles C. Pinckney, III, Papers, USC.

[17] Halstead, *Caucuses of 1860*, p. 10, presents a brilliant picture of Orr and Sanders.

[18] Perry and Lemuel Boozer of Lexington refused to leave the convention. Arthur Simkins "concurs with us in remaining here," Perry told the convention, "and would act with us if he were here, but he has been called home by the sickness of his family." Perry, *Biographical Sketches*, p. 150.

the majority (pro-slavery) and minority platform committees nearing a final verdict by the convention, George Sanders sent off a hurried letter to President Buchanan, urging him to rise above his deadly hatred of Douglas for the sake of party unity. Like most of the "Little Giant's" supporters, Sanders was confident that the Alabama platform demand for a territorial slave code would be rejected, and that Alabama and Mississippi would probably "retire"; Sanders was certain that this would bring Douglas close to the two-thirds majority, and he pleaded with Buchanan in vain to acquiesce in the impending success of his enemy. Again, on Saturday, April 28, Douglas's agent C. P. Culver assured his leader that the terrible clashes of the previous day, including a rousing speech by Yancey, were so many "safety valves" letting off pent-up emotion, and that the South as a whole had abandoned its opposition to the proposed minority platform (which declared against legislation for the positive protection of slavery in the territories). "Ala. & Miss. *say* they will withdraw," he confided, "Ga. in my opinion will remain." Thus, far from fearing the disastrous consequences of a major Southern withdrawal, Douglas and his partisans anticipated, welcomed, and perhaps encouraged a small bolt.[19]

Weeks before the convention Senator Hammond predicted that Douglas would never receive the nomination. "Over two years ago I told Douglas he had thrown away his present chances for the Presidency," he wrote William Gilmore Simms. "I have since told him so 20 times." Only the day before writing this letter, Hammond was approached by "the notorious Geo. Sanders" whose efforts, as usual, were directed to bargaining for Douglas votes. Hammond had informed Sanders that the nomination of the Illinois senator was impossible, that South Carolina would

[19] Halstead, *Caucuses of 1860*, p. 9, *et passim.*; C. P. Culver to Douglas, April 25 and 28, 1860, Douglas Papers, UChic; George Sanders to James Buchanan, April 27, 1860, James Buchanan Papers, PaHS. Daniel Hamilton, among other Carolinians, feared that this aggressive policy would win the nomination for Douglas. Hamilton to W. P. Miles, April 26, 1860, Miles Papers, SHC. The withdrawal of the Alabama delegation was immediately precipitated by a "very irritating" anti-Southern speech delivered by Michigan senator Charles E. Stuart. It was "exceedingly ill-timed, unless he intended to drive out the Gulf States, and he has been accused of entertaining such purpose." Halstead, *Caucuses of 1860*, p. 65.

never back him, and that there was almost literally no support for him in Carolina since his stand on the Kansas question. Looking squarely at the disturbing implications of a disruption in the Democratic party, Hammond personally thought Yancey a fool to "make an issue on such an abstraction as Squatter Sovereignty, but if it came up as a real question," he warned, "I should regard it as no less dangerous than abolitionism & fight it as fiercely."[20] Only two weeks after writing these words Hammond did see the convention faced with just this choice, and after three more troubled days, following the final rejection of the slave protection plank demanded by the cotton states, the greater part of the delegations from the lower South withdrew from the convention.[21]

"Outside pressure" had triumphed over the failing spirit of compromise. This pressure existed on many levels. There was the burden of more than a generation of rising sectional bitterness. There was the frustrated anger felt by Northern Democrats over their declining political strength stemming from their link with the slave states. There was the vitriolic hatred for Douglas which had created an unnatural alliance between Administration stalwarts and Southern extremists. Journeying to Charleston, many delegates must have been disconcerted by the estranged relations in Congress, where every day brought the danger of armed conflict between the members. "No two nations on earth are or ever were more distinctly separated & hostile that we are here," Senator Hammond wrote; and the scene in Washington seemed to mirror in microcosm the divisions rending the nation.[22] In Charleston there was a variety of influences calculated to inten-

[20] Hammond to Simms, April 8, 1860, Hammond Papers, LC.
[21] The full delegations from Alabama, Louisiana, Texas, Florida, and a majority from South Carolina, Arkansas, and Delaware withdrew. The next day, May 1, all but ten of the thirty-six delegates from Georgia joined the bolters. *Official Proceedings of the Democratic National Convention Held in 1860, at Charleston and Baltimore* (Cleveland, 1860), pp. 59–66. Charleston Democrat Nelson Mitchell informed Miles that it was not "anticipated by the Northern delegations that the secession would be so large, although the action of the Alabama members was a good deal talked of beforehand." May 1, 1860, Miles Papers, SHC.
[22] Hammond to M. C. M. Hammond, April 22, 1860, Hammond Papers, LC; also see Hammond to Francis Lieber, April 19, 1860, in Thomas S. Perry, *The Life and Letters of Francis Lieber* (Boston, 1882), pp. 310–11; and Hammond to Edmund Ruffin, April 16, 1860, Edmund Ruffin Papers, SHC.

sify the emotional pitch of the convention. Most subtle of all was the city itself, graceful, beautiful, the incarnation of Southern civilization, warped by sectional xenophobia. Many Northern Democrats came to the convention still seemingly unaware of the emotional chasm which had fallen between the sections because of Southern racial fears and anticipations, real and illusory, anxieties which made even these loyal allies in opposition to abolitionism suspect. "I am surprized at the bitterness of some of our Southern opponents," one bewildered Illinois delegate wrote Douglas. "They go so far as to call us abolitionists and say we had better stay at home and attend the Chicago [Republican] convention where we legitimately belong."[23]

Two weeks later Rhett described for Miles the consequences of these Southern fears.

I suppose you have heard and understood that the withdrawal of the South Carolina delegation was brought about by outside pressure and indignation expressed at the course of the Columbia Convention. Their spirit rose from the time they got to Charleston until they went out of the Convention. When they came, they had no more idea of going out than flying. They would not even go the Southern caucus. If they had not retired, they would have been mobbed, I believe.[24]

With skilled artistry Rhett and his cohorts had orchestrated the rising pitch of extremism in the city. Rhett did not create Southern intransigence, but the success of National Democrats in his own state had forced his hand, compelling him and other disunionists to use extra-political pressure to bring about the disruption of the party. The *Mercury* and the *Evening News* main-

[23] Murray McConnell to Douglas, April 22, 1860, Douglas Papers, UChic. Other letters to Douglas which illustrate this significant shift in the mood of Charleston during the convention are: J. J. Jones, April 20, John Clancey, [April 21], Charles E. Stuart and C. P. Culver, April 24, Samuel Hammond, April 27, and C. P. Culver, April 28, 1860, all in the Douglas Papers, UChic. See also Halstead, *Caucuses of 1860*, p. 60.

[24] Rhett to Miles, May 12, 1860, Miles Papers, SHC. Halstead described the holiday scene following the withdrawal (April 30). "There was a Fourth of July feeling in the public sentiment of the city. It was overwhelmingly in favor of the seceders. In all her history Charleston had never enjoyed herself so hugely." *Caucuses of 1860*, p. 76.

tained a steady barrage of propaganda, condemning Southerners for seeking any compromise with the North (while carefully avoiding any direct disunionist declarations). Every evening saw Southern rights meetings, caucuses, inflammatory speeches; every day saw the streets of Charleston, and the galleries of Institute Hall filled with more and more ardent radicals, as Northern delegates, their pockets emptied by the prolonged convention, left with their wives and friends. Examining the correspondence coming out of Charleston one can almost chart the fragmentation of pro-Douglas sentiment, and the intensification of a mood of uncompromising Southern extremism surrounding each delegate. As Ben Perry later observed, many delegates, especially South Carolina's moderates, were reluctant to bolt, but they were all awash in the swirling sea of emotionalism, and many fell victim to this pressure even while they were not aware of doing so.[25]

Thus did the intransigence of Administration stalwarts, the compulsive loyalty of Douglas supporters, and an open conspiracy of Southern radicals combine to destroy the Democratic party. "The last party, pretending to be a national party, is broken up," exulted the *Mercury*, "and the antagonism of the two sections of the Union has nothing to arrest its fierce collisions."[26]

— 3 —

This was a premature announcement of civil war. Not only did the withdrawal of the Southern delegations not spell disunion to all, but there was vigorous disagreement over whether the party itself was irreparably divided. Many Southerners who understood —whether with shock or joy—that the breach could never be healed, were merely convinced that the elected would be thrown into the House.[27] Many more, however, were not willing to see

[25] Charleston *Mercury*, April 16, 1860, and *ff.*, B. F. Perry to Franklin Gaillard, May 15, 1860, in *Advertiser*, May 23, 1860, quoting the (Columbia) *Daily South Carolinian*. See also William Lawton to W. P. Miles, May 6, 1860, Daniel Hamilton to W. P. Miles, April 28, 1860, Miles Papers, SHC.
[26] *Mercury*, May 3, 1860, p. 1.
[27] James Reid, Jr., to James Hammond, May 3, 1860, Hammond Papers, LC. Typical was William Porter's reaction. Porter predicted that the Southern convention would name its own platform and candidate, and the national convention would do likewise. "I think Douglas will be their man for they

the party destroyed, for it was obviously the last instrument of salvation from the Republicans. Like Virginia's Muscoe Garnett, Southern moderates were appalled at the outcome of the convention, and desired only to reunite both the South and the Democracy by returning to the adjourned national convention at Baltimore on June 18. And news that a number of senators and representatives from the Southern states had signed an address calling for a return to the national convention thoroughly depressed Rhett and his fellow secessionists.[28]

The performance of the "Constitutional Democratic" party had only worsened the fears of disunionists. The "retiring" delegates had adjourned to Saint Andrews Hall in Charleston, there to await either the rejection of Douglas and a triumphant return to the "rump" convention (according to Administration leaders), or the nomination of Douglas and the selection of a state's rights ticket of their own (according to Rhett). The adoption of a rule by the rump of the national convention requiring that any nomination be made by a two-thirds majority of the *original* membership prevented the naming of Douglas, and after fifty-seven ballots had proved this to everyone's satisfaction, the divided Democracy adjourned to meet again in Baltimore. The "retiring delegates," looking rather foolish at this turn of events, were compelled to adjourn as well, electing to meet again in Richmond on June 11.

There was a glaring lack of revolutionary zeal in the leadership of the seceders. It was probably known that Yancey had been persuaded to oppose the withdrawal of his delegation. With the

---

will probably supply the places of the seceders with men to suit their purposes. In all probability the question will get to the House; and . . . [*I*] am inclined to think it will be as much of a 'dead lock' there as in the convention; that the Senate will after all name the President." Porter to W. P. Miles, May 6, 1860, Miles Papers, SHC. Senator Hammond made an identical prediction. See the letter to his son Harry, April 27, 1860, Hammond Papers, LC; and to George W. J. DeRenne, April 27, 1860, George W. J. DeRenne Papers, DU.

[28] Muscoe Garnett to his mother, April 28, May 2 and 7, 1860, William Chisholm Papers, VaHS; letter and telegram, R. B. Rhett, Jr., to Miles, May 10, 1860, and Robert N. Gourdin to Miles, May 12, 1860, Miles Papers, SHC. The Southern Address is described in Allan Nevins, *The Emergence of Lincoln*, 2 volumes (New York, 1950), II, 263.

momentous vote on the party platform scheduled for the next morning, Administration leaders in Charleston met late Sunday night, April 29, in a desperate effort to hold the Gulf state delegations in the convention. The stalwarts, led by Senators John Slidell of Louisiana, James A. Bayard of Delaware, and Jesse D. Bright of Indiana, were at last frightened by the imminent destruction of the Democracy, confident that Douglas could be stopped, and hopeful the divisive issue of the security of slavery in the territories could be glossed over by a reiteration of the equivocal 1856 Cincinnati platform. After meeting with Slidell, Bayard, and Bright, a subdued Yancey evidently attempted to persuade the Alabama delegation to ignore the previous instructions of their legislature, and remain in the convention after their platform demands were rejected. This last-ditch appeal to unity and common sense was in vain.[29]

The moderating hand of the stalwarts was nevertheless felt within the seceders' convention. Senator Bayard was elected president of the conclave, and he successfully led resistance to making any nominations. Yancey acquiesced in this crucial decision, owning that it was caused by "timid & perhaps wise men in our councils, who were seriously opposed to a nomination here— or even a recommendation." From Rhett's point of view there was obviously "some want of nerve in the management of the seceders . . . and an evident want of leadership. Yancey is not capable in that way," Rhett admitted, "however great an orator and debater." The Charleston leader was not only disappointed over the fact that the seceders' convention had noncommittally adjourned, but also because it had selected Richmond for its next meeting and had not defined itself clearly as a purely Southern movement. "I expect the Richmond Convention to be virtually a Southern Convention," he wrote Miles, "though it should have

[29] John Witherspoon DuBose, *The Life and Times of William Lowndes Yancey*, 2 volumes (New York, 1942), II, 466–67; Nevins, *Emergence of Lincoln*, II, 226; Roy Franklin Nichols, *The Disruption of American Democracy* (New York, 1962), pp. 303–304. The account of Yancey's "conversion" is in the memoirs of Richard Taylor, son of President Zachary Taylor, and later a Confederate general. Taylor attended the meeting between Yancey and the "senatorial clique," and discussed it in *Destruction and Reconstruction: Personal Experiences of the Late War* (New York, 1879), p. 12.

been so in name and should have met at some city in the cotton states." Meanwhile, Hammond dubbed the "Charleston Secession under Bayard & Yancey—a fizzle."[30]

There is no doubt that the action of the seceding "Constitutional Democratic" convention, and the wave of confusion and apprehension which followed, generated suspicion among disunionists. Although Rhett was confident that the Southern Address calling for a return of the bolters to the national convention would fail "to carry the cotton state delegations to Richmond into the convention at Baltimore," the road to secession still looked uncertain to him.

> My fear is that Northern delegations, which were foolishly invited, and the outside pressure in the bad locality of Richmond may prevail to the extent of inducing the Richmond Convention to await the action at Baltimore instead of nominating their men and adjourning as they should do. Another apprehension I entertain is that, even if they nominate (Davis and Lane are probably the nominees), the nominees unless pledged beforehand to run the canvass through under all circumstances, may decline in case a compromise platform . . . is adopted at Baltimore and a man like Hunter be put upon it. Such a result would throw the seceders flat on their backs. . . . Promptness and firmness is wanted in the delegates from the cotton states at Richmond and candidates pledged to abide their action to the end. Without these the whole movement is likely to prove a failure,— The South Demoralised and Seward triumphant.

As for South Carolina, Rhett ended, "The state will present a united front."[31]

Rhett's perception failed him here. In fact, the state was not united behind the radical party. From the moment of the withdrawal Unionists raised their voices to condemn the entire move-

---

[30] James A. Bayard to Thomas Bayard, May 2, 1860, Thomas A. Bayard Papers, LC; William Lowndes Yancey to Clement C. Clay, May 4, 1860, Clement Clairborne Clay Papers, DU; R. B. Rhett, Jr., to W. P. Miles, May 10, 1860, Miles Papers, SHC; James Hammond to William Gilmore Simms, May 11, 1860, Hammond Papers, LC.
[31] R. B. Rhett, Jr., to Miles, May 12, 1860, Miles Papers, SHC.

ment as a giant step in the anticipated secessionist scheme. In letters justifying their opposition, Perry and Simkins minced no words in attacking the bolt as a deliberate effort to destroy the one remaining national party, the only institution left which could hope to hold the great sections together. The two Unionists differed on the acceptability of Douglas (Simkins still insisting that he was true to the basic interests of the South), but they agreed that the worst evil which could befall the slave states had been precipitated by the misguided zeal of Southern radicals: the disruption of the Democracy, the South divided into three contending parties, and the Presidential election handed to what Alfred Huger grimly called "Mr. Seward's Gang."[32]

Furthermore, South Carolina's moderates were appalled at the specific cause of the withdrawal. In a public letter explaining his action in the convention, Perry reviewed the resolutions of the Columbia state convention which had endorsed the Cincinnati slavery plank and the Dred Scott decision, and spurned the Alabama platform. Like the Administration stalwarts, Perry was convinced that such a platform could have been obtained at Charleston, with a Southern moderate to run upon it. Simkins was bolder. He not only endorsed the Douglas position, but he rejected the entire territorial issue as a sham, signifying nothing at all. He could see no dire threat to the South in popular sovereignty. Indeed, Simkins saw something ignoble in demanding special laws for the protection of slavery in the distant territories, while upholding it at home as right and strong. Simkins asked his neighbors whether they would insist upon congressional protection for slavery in territories where it would not and ought not go, and support a sectional candidate who would aid in electing the abolitionist Republicans at the risk of destroying the Union. Or, would they rather be content with the Cincinnati platform

[32] B. F. Perry to Franklin Gaillard, May 15, 1860, in the *Advertiser,* May 23, 1860, quoting the (Columbia) *Daily South Carolinian;* "Letter to the Democrats of Edgefield District," from Arthur Simkins, *Advertiser,* May 16, 1860; Alfred Huger to Miles, May 7, 1860, Miles Papers, SHC. See also John D. Ashmore to Henry Ashmore, May 13, 1860, in Rosser Howard Taylor (ed.), "Letters Dealing with the Secession Movement in South Carolina," *Furman University Faculty Studies Bulletin,* XVI (1934), 3–12; *Advertiser,* May 23, 1860, quoting the Newberry *Rising Sun.*

and the Dred Scott decision, unite under the banner of the Democracy, and defeat both Republicans and disunionists.[33]

Unfortunately, the people of South Carolina had devoted too much emotional energy to interpreting the issue of slavery in the territories as the "frontier" of the more dire question of abolition at home, to heed Simkins's plea. From the time of the American Revolution, Southerners had tenaciously defended the right to carry slaves into the West. Aside from the obvious economic motivation, there were other reasons for concern about slavery expansion. Many believed that the masses of blacks must be diffused across the continent to avert insurrection. Former President John Tyler, an opponent of secession in his native Virginia, nonetheless declared that his state would "never consent to have blacks cribbed and confined within prescribed and specified limits and thus be involved in all the consequences of a war of the races in 20 or 30 years."[34]

More important, perhaps, was the symbolic and actual political content of the territorial issue. It was long believed that the security of slavery depended upon a balance between slave and free states. The loss of this equality precipitated the secession crisis at the outset of the 1850's, and created a growing sense of insecurity through the remainder of the decade. Since the time of Calhoun the question of the rights of slaveholders in the trans-Mississippi West, however abstract the issue, was aggressively construed by Southern ultras as a question signifying the general protectiveness of the Constitution. Even before the egregious Mexican War, the rights of slavery in the territories had so often been proclaimed as the outermost ramparts against abolitionism, that the "rights" themselves came to lose independent meaning. Rather, for Southerners who accepted the extremist definition of the territorial issue (as most South Carolinians did) these rights had become symbols of their hypersensitive and inflexible defense of slavery. The rights of slavery in the territories may not

[33] *Advertiser*, May 9, 16, and 23, 1860. See also Henry William Ravenel MS Journal, USC, May 3 and 14, 1860; and the *Mercury*, February 28, 1860.
[34] John Tyler to ———, November 16, 1860, John Tyler Papers, LC. For the cogent objections of a Unionist, see the letter of John Belton O'Neall in the Newberry *Rising Sun*, June 20, 1860.

have offered *tangible* protection against abolitionism, but they gave the comforting appearance of strengthening slavery. And as Hammond observed in 1845, "whatever gives the world the opinion that we are stronger on the question gives us *real* strength."[35]

— 4 —

Debate over the territorial issue was only part of the controversy heating up in South Carolina. It soon became clear that the party battles during the secession crisis of a decade before had been reawakened by the bolt at Charleston. The nub of the disagreement was the membership of the state's delegation to the Charleston convention. Followers of Rhett wanted to retire that slate (although it had joined the bolt) because it was still composed of men who represented Unionism and National Democracy in Carolina. The same radical party which had always protested against representation at national conventions, and which had repudiated the claim that the "Nationals" truly represented the people of the state, now opposed sending the Charleston delegation on to Richmond. Radicals claimed that a new state of affairs now prevailed. The National Democracy had not delivered the compromises and guarantees promised. The Columbia convention of April 16 was again denounced by ultras as unrepresentative of political opinion in the state. The result of this perception of affairs was inevitable. The Rhett faction was already preparing to do battle with its opponents to ensure that a fresh slate of delegates to the Richmond convention was elected.

Opposed to Rhett was the rump of the Convention party. (A portion of those who had participated in the pre-Charleston movement welcomed the disintegration of the national party, and had now openly joined the radicals.) The official state Democratic party organization was not ready to have its own delegates

[35] W. N. DeSaussure to ———, March 6, 1850, Wilmot N. DeSaussure Papers, USC; Speech of Robert Barnwell Rhett, *Proceedings of the State Democratic Convention held at Columbia, S. C., May 30–31, 1860* (Columbia, 1860), pp. 82–83; James H. Hammond to Armistead Burt, March 18, 1845, Armistead Burt Papers, DU. See also Chaplain W. Morrison, *Democratic Politics and Sectionalism, The Wilmot Proviso Controversy* (Chapel Hill, 1967), pp. 52–74.

repudiated. "You will understand," Trescot explained, that as soon as the radical faction advocated participation at the Richmond convention

> every feeling of antagonism in the Convention party would be aroused—that they would not submit to the substitution in their places of men who, rightly or wrongly they believed had denounced them for doing what these gentlemen themselves proposed to do now. It is useless to argue that the Delegates to the Charleston Convention are functus officio—that the Richmond Convention is a new convention—that the State which would not go into the Charleston Convention *will* go into the Richmond Convention—that the conventions represent different conditions of public circumstances—all they *will* see is that they were willing in the face of violent and unjust denunciation to go into the convention and if a change of circumstances has produced a change in the state policy, they are entitled to the benefit of their advanced positions.[36]

Trescot had a more than passing interest in the controversy, for he was a junior member of a Charleston group which now set out to mollify both factions, and unify the state. They were eager to avoid a renewal of the bitter antagonisms which had torn the state apart a decade earlier; and, not incidentally, they were interested in gaining political power by taking command of the movement to represent the state at Richmond.[37]

Trescot, along with more significant leaders in this centrist effort, such as Isaac Hayne and Francis Richardson, sincerely believed that the predominant sentiment following the Charleston debacle was the desire for South Carolina to meet her sister Southern states at Richmond "in perfect good faith," and to unite with them in presenting an "ultimatum of southern principle on which they and the patriotisms of the North can act together."

---

[36] Trescot to Miles, May 8, 1860, Miles Papers, SHC.
[37] Robert Nicholas Olsberg, "William Henry Trescot: The Crisis of 1860," (unpublished master's thesis, the University of South Carolina, 1967) is an original, perceptive examination of the Charleston clique of political "managers." See also Andrew Gordon Magrath to J. H. Hammond, May 2, 1860, Hammond Papers, LC; and William D. Porter to Miles, May 6, 1860, Miles Papers, SHC.

Here at last was the chance for real state's rights cooperation, they said, and whatever the outcome it was worth this one last effort. Trescot believed that those who would represent South Carolina in this movement must be chosen in a spirit of warm unanimity; in order to achieve this, both the old convention men and the Rhett men must yield to the leadership of the "center." Radicals seemed inclined to go along with the policy of forbearance, in the confidence that public feeling was on their side. But Trescot was sorry to report that the state's National Democrats were reluctant to admit the wisdom of this new appeal, and to abandon their own original delegates and call a new convention. Theodore Barker, Chairman of the state party's Central Executive Committee had called a meeting of the committee and from conversations with him, Trescot believed that Barker intended simply to reassemble the old convention of April 16.

"Hayne & Co" were distressed. "To call the Columbia Convention together again," Trescot despairingly wrote Miles, "is simply to breed trouble for they are not *now* the representatives of the state and should they persist in so considering themselves, will force the nomination of another set of delegates." (This dual representation did occur in other cotton states that could agree neither to endorse nor repudiate the withdrawal of their delegations from the Charleston convention.) However, Trescot at last informed Miles that Barker had been persuaded to call primary meetings to elect an entirely new convention. Barker hoped that this would give "room for a fair expression of the whole sentiment of the state," in the confidence that the sentiment would be moderate. With secessionists, Unionists, and all shades in between equally confident of endorsement, the state party elections were called for the third week of May, with the new convention to assemble at Columbia on May 30.[38]

Both the National Democrats and the would-be Charleston centrists were to be disappointed. "Hayne & Co" moved at once to organize public meetings in the parishes. The key rally was held at Hibernian Hall in Charleston on the 18th, for those "who

[38] Trescot to Miles, May 8, 1860, Miles Papers, SHC. See also the (Columbia) *Daily South Carolinian*, May 6, 1860, in Dwight Lowell Dumond, ed., *Southern Editorials on Secession* (New York, 1931), pp. 73–74.

are in favor of the platform of principles recommended by the Majority of States in the Charleston Convention," and Trescot and Henry Lesesne, a state senator from the city, invited Miles, Hammond, and Chesnut to participate. Miles responded with alacrity, and his fire-eating address may have been an even stronger pill than Trescot cared to swallow. Although Trescot had begun to see the revolutionary potential of recent events, as a diplomat he encouraged Hammond to speak in order to "teach the South that its battle can be fought in the Union."[39] Hammond did not come to the rally. But his letter, read to the audience, was an effective blend of Unionism (the "broadest and perhaps truest goal"), support for the National Democracy, and an aggressive appeal for the unity of the cotton states. "In conclusion, permit me to say that I not only do not despair, but I entertain not a feeling of despondency. Come what may," Hammond counselled his constituents, "with our surplus productions of Cotton, Rice, Sugar, etc., and our substructure of black slaves, *we are safe.*"[40]

Similar meetings followed across the state, and it was soon apparent that the hopes of Barker and his "Nationals" would not be realized. The elections for a new convention were everywhere interpreted as a referendum on the character of the delegates named by the original Columbia convention, and the policy of restrained Unionism which those men represented. The old divisions in the state had reopened with a vengeance.

In the piedmont Perry and Orr worked for the reappointment of their original district representatives, while strongly seconding the call of the Congressional Address for a reunification of the Democratic party at Baltimore. Pendleton's John Ashmore urged Orr to go to Richmond, and, if the door were opened, to Baltimore as well, in order to make "one last final effort to save the

[39] Trescot to Hammond, and Lesesne to Hammond, May 12, 1860, Hammond Papers, LC; Trescot to Miles, Lesesne to Miles (letter), and Lesesne to Miles, Hammond and Chesnut (telegram), May 12, 1860, Miles Papers, SHC. See also Henry Gourdin to his son Robert, May 14, 1860, Gourdin-Young Papers, Emory. The elder Gourdin was helping to organize the Charleston rally, and regarded the Richmond convention as the "first movement toward a union of the Cotton States."

[40] *Mercury,* May 21, 1860; Charleston *Daily Courier,* May 18–21, 1860; *Advertiser,* May 30, 1860; William Gilmore Simms to Miles, May 21, 1860, Miles Papers, SHC.

country." If Orr would firmly declare that he would have "neither Douglasism for the Territories, nor [John] Brownism for the South," Ashmore predicted that Orr would be elected President. But in an earlier letter to Ben Perry, Ashmore showed far less optimism; the disintegration of his Unionism had begun. He believed that the endorsement of the original slate of state representatives would be an empty gesture, for most of that group, supposedly composed of "the safest & most able men . . . representing the moderate or conservative party in our state" nevertheless had abandoned the national party at Charleston and seconded the splinter Richmond convention. To condemn these men, and seek a still more moderate slate would doubtless drive them "into the Rhett & Yancey party . . . & weaken our forces, already weak enough, throughout the state." Ashmore could only hope that the party schism would be healed by the nomination of a mutually acceptable candidate at Baltimore.[41]

The piedmont was not entirely in favor of reunifying the Democracy. From northernmost Spartanburg, the leading newspaper echoed the sentiments of the *Mercury* in speaking against further cooperation with the apostate Northern Democracy. And with Arthur Simkins standing in unaccustomed silence on the sidelines, some of the more radical citizens of Edgefield took charge of affairs there, meeting first on May 7 to applaud the withdrawal of the Carolina delegation, and again on May 23 to appoint representatives to the second Columbia convention. On the eve of that assembly Simkins did come out with a strong attack upon the radical district meeting of the 23rd as "unrepresentative." He also scorned Hammond's invitation to isolate the lower South from its natural allies in the border slave states. If we fear that in time slaves will be drained from Virginia and the adjacent regions, the Edgefield editor warned, the same argument may someday be used against South Carolina. The logic of his position was lost on a good part of the state.[42] From Charles-

[41] Ashmore to Orr, May 25, 1860, Orr-Patterson Papers, SHC; Ashmore to Perry, May 13, 1860, Benjamin F. Perry Papers, Ala.Arc.
[42] Spartanburg *Spartan*, May 17, 1860; *Mercury*, May 23, 1860; *Advertiser*, May 9, 16, and 30, 1860; White, "National Democrats," 385–86; Cauthen, *South Carolina Goes to War*, pp. 19–21; Lillian Adele Kibler, *Benjamin F. Perry, South Carolina Unionist* (Durham, 1946), pp. 318–20. See also

ton to the smallest up-country village the campaign had called the latent radicalism and "that old submission spirit" back into battle.[43]

$$-5-$$

The convention, James Orr could have written, was a Rhett affair. Partly from abstentions, and partly from defeat, only fifty-two of the hundred sixty-one delegates to the April 16 convention were reelected to represent their districts again. Barnwell Rhett was chosen from St. John's, Colleton parish. "With his son, Barnwell, Jr., appointed from Charleston, and his brother, Edmund, from St. Helena, there was no doubt that Rhett was once again a factor in South Carolina politics."[44] An old disunionist, John H. Means, governor of the state during the 1851 secession crisis, was elected permanent chairman. The "Nationals" did not immediately concede defeat, however. They had vigorously contested the election of delegates to this convention, and had evidently come to Columbia in the full expectation of controlling the affair. The first test came in a clash over the method of electing the four at-large seats in the delegation to Richmond. Moderates sought to have these key men chosen by a committee based upon the six congressional districts; ostensibly this would have been democratic since the congressional representation more ac-

---

William W. Renwick to [Wade] Hampton, May 25, 1860, William W. Renwick Papers, USC; and Daniel Hamilton to W. P. Miles, May 29, 1860, Miles Papers, SHC.

[43] Former congressman Thomas D. Sumter described the political atmosphere in mid-May to Senator R. M. T. Hunter. All the districts now seemed interested and were actively participating in the canvass for delegates to the May 30 Columbia convention. There no longer was any division between convention and anti-convention men. "More than two thirds of our people have been heretofore opposed to Conventions," Sumter wrote, "but now they feel no hesitation in being represented at Richmond." Sumter to Hunter, May 14, 1860, in *Correspondence of Robert M. T. Hunter, 1826–1876*, edited by Charles Henry Ambler, American Historical Association, *Annual Report for the Year 1916*, 2 volumes (Washington, 1918), II, 327–28.

[44] Laura A. White, *Robert Barnwell Rhett: Father of Secession* (New York, 1931), p. 165. Hammond had declared that the Rhetts were "dead & ought to be dead as a political clique in So Ca." His pronouncement was premature. Hammond to Simms, April 3, 1860, Hammond Papers, LC.

curately reflected the larger white population of the piedmont districts. Instead, this plan, and Edmund Rhett's (to base the selection committee on state districts and parishes) was rejected in favor of electing each at-large delegate by a vote of the whole convention. This was to be decisive for the radicals, as the convention itself followed the unrepresentative system which obtained in the state House.[45]

National Democrats realized with a shock that control of the convention of their own party was threatened by the enemies of all they stood for. "The old Democratic ship in which conservative men had weathered many a storm of ridicule, abuse and opposition," wrote a startled Samuel McGowan, had fallen into the hands of those who had "thrown the most broadsides into that same craft." Under the advice of Theodore Barker, the "Nationals" had agreed not to reassemble the April 16 convention, but to act liberally and attempt to harmonize all sections of opinion, by broadening the base of the May convention. The election of district representatives to this meeting plainly indicated the corrosion of the Unionist position since the breakup at Charleston. And despite the disturbing imbalances in apportionment, the May convention was a wider reflection of sentiment in the state than the previous party conclave.[46]

Once these facts became apparent, radicals moved determinedly to ensure that the delegation to Richmond would include some of their own leaders. With their numbers in the convention increased by the full representation of the low country they succeeded only too well. Barnwell Rhett himself was elected by a vote of eighty-four to sixty-eight to lead the new delegation. His chief opponent on that ballot was not a National Democrat at all, but Isaac Hayne. So implacable was the hatred for Rhett, so completely would his election spell repudiation for the Unionist faction of the state that the original first nominee of the "Nationals,"

[45] This account of the May convention is drawn from the *Proceedings of the State Democratic Convention* (May); Isaac W. Hayne to Hammond, June 3, 1860, Hammond Papers, LC; Cauthen, *South Carolina Goes to War,* pp. 22–25; White, "National Democrats," 386–88; White, *Rhett,* pp. 165–168; Schultz, *Nationalism and Sectionalism,* pp. 217–19; and Boucher, "Eve of Secession," 137–39.
[46] *Proceedings of the State Democratic Convention* (May), pp. 51, 60.

James Simons, withdrew when Rhett was nominated. "Madness ruled the hour," Hayne later wrote Hammond. "Nobody seemed sane. Convention and Anti-convention men seemed to forget utterly that there was an enemy elsewhere or a purpose to be effected out of South Carolina." Hayne had vainly tried to moderate between the two factions by proposing that the four at-large delegates be shared equally, but he was spurned by both sides. Moments before the balloting Hayne's name was substituted for Simons's. "I was *sure* that Rhett's election would produce just the effect it has done," Hayne recalled, "and in the very faint hope that I might defeat him I consented to run. I withdrew afterwards to give a chance for a compromise. It was too late and Rhett's election fatal. So. Ca. stands now on the level with Alabama & Mississippi—if so high."[47]

Taking the defeat as a humiliating rejection of their leadership, the "Nationals" refused to vie for any of the remaining seats. Their language during and after the state convention demonstrated that they conceived of their opponents as pure secessionists, men who sought nothing less than the permanent disruption of the national party, and a dissolution of the Union to follow. No event could have revealed this to them so well as the election of Robert Barnwell Rhett to lead the delegation to Richmond. From the opening gavel moderate leaders had venomously denied the allegations of "editors of newspapers," and "filthy grogshop politicians" that they had only withdrawn from the Charleston convention under outside pressure "which we dared not resist." Theodore Barker and his party perhaps unwisely considered the Rhett-Hayne contest "as a test question," and interpreted the outcome as a condemnation of the Unionist faction of the state.[48]

National Democrats had taken enormous pride and no little courage in representing South Carolina at Charleston. William Preston, one of those delegates, reminded the delegates at the May convention that Democrats had come to Charleston expecting the Carolina delegation to be a set of fanatical disunionists. "They expected to find us rattling the bones of Calhoun, and shrieking out his hallowed name in the perpetration of mad

---

[47] *Ibid.*, p. 45; Hayne to Hammond, June 3, 1860, Hammond Papers, LC.
[48] *Proceedings of the State Democratic Convention* (May), pp. 53–56.

follies." Instead they found a slate of Unionists eager to cooperate for the good of the party and the nation. Preston and others strenuously denied that the aim of the bolt was for any other purpose than to reintegrate the national party on acceptable terms. Moderates looked upon the Richmond meeting as only a formal preliminary to a reunification at Baltimore. All of the other seceding states were sending their representatives to Baltimore, by way of Richmond. Preston warned that a disunionist involved in this process would find himself "most ridiculously out of fashion," as would anyone seeking to divide the cotton states of the lower South from the other slave states, and to bind them to a separate radical policy. Yet even the vitriolic Preston gave powerful evidence of the essential agreement of all South Carolinians. The whole national controversy was over slave labor, he declared, not a particular agricultural product. He rejected the phrase "Cotton is King" as a distortion of the true basis of the sectional crisis. "Slavery is our King; slavery is our Truth; slavery is our Divine Right," the Unionist declared. "The cotton plant might perish tomorrow, and yet slavery would be as necessary, as precious to us, as it is to-day." Preston believed the interests of the South were one, and would be guaranteed by the Democratic party. But the verdict of the state party convention suggested that confidence in this warranty was deteriorating.[49]

In the tense and hostile atmosphere created in South Carolina by the events at Columbia the charge was even made that (because of the over-representation of the parishes) a majority had lost control of affairs to a minority of the state's white population. This is doubtful.[50] Virginia's itinerant secessionist Edmund Ruffin

[49] *Ibid.*, pp. 56–59. See also Alfred Huger to W. P. Miles, June 1, 1860, Miles Papers, SHC; and *Advertiser*, June 6, 1860.

[50] Columbia editor Franklin Gaillard strongly asserted in the convention that the vote for Hayne represented a larger portion of the white population than the vote for Rhett, the former coming mainly from the districts, the latter from the parishes. Superficially, the Rhett-Hayne election seems a weak rod to measure class and sectional conflict. Hayne was not a National Democrat and had not supported the convention movement in the spring; few men had better credentials as a radical leader. Moreover, he himself was the leader of a political clique which had sponsored new elections for the convention in the hope of controlling the action of the state under a distinctly radical program. Before the balloting, Hayne declared himself to be a political "independent." Although he ostensibly was standing in for the moderate James Simons, votes unquestionably were cast for him which

did note in his diary that there seemed to be no more avowed disunionists at the Columbia convention than there were in his home state. Yet it is certain that Carolina supported the withdrawal of the delegation at Charleston, and would continue to support separate Southern action, especially while the Douglas majority persisted in the desire to nominate its man. It is also likely that a majority of the state's citizens opposed any "humiliating request for readmission to the Baltimore Convention." To be sure, the selection of Rhett was an unnecessary slap at those who had worked so hard to have the state participate in the national convention. Many who welcomed the radical spirit of the delegation to Richmond recognized that this personal factor injured the cause of unity in the state. "I knew Rhett had no popularity out of So Ca," Hammond later wrote Simms, "but I had no idea he was utterly *odious*. . . . When it was learned that he was chosen to the Richmond Con[vention] there burst forth at Washington such a wail (for there was grief in it) of indignant execration as I never knew any man to excite before[,] *Southern fire eaters loudest*." There is not the slightest question that South Carolina's new radical delegation to the Richmond convention favored secession and thought it inevitable, and hoped, with David Flavel Jamison, that their state could be "the leader to form a nucleus of the convention for radical action." Still, the persistent fear of dividing the state encouraged hypocrisy, and the new delegates muffled their radicalism, and publicly disavowed the charge that they were simply a vanguard for disunionism.[51]

---

in no way reflected opposition to aggressive state policy. Moreover, Rhett and Hayne were not the only candidates in the election for the first at-large seat, and even if Hayne were understood to be the conservative candidate, corrected census figures suggest that the bloc which voted for radical candidates represented a majority of the voting population. The Rhett-Hayne election did reveal sectionalism because of the presence of the arch-radical of the South. There was class and sectional conflict in South Carolina, and the insecurities of the tidewater did affect the pace of radical politics. But racial fears which were at the heart of the secession impulse consistently transcended the more "realistic" class anxieties. Credence to Gaillard's aspersions was given by Professor White in her "National Democrats," p. 387, and *Rhett*, p. 167. See *Proceedings of the State Democratic Convention* (May), pp. 45 and 71–72; Trescot to Miles, May 8, 1860, Miles Papers, SHC; and Cauthen, *South Carolina Goes to War*, p. 24, note.

[51] David Flavel Jamison to John Jenkins, June 8, 1860, D. F. Jamison

In estimating general public sentiment at this juncture, it seems safe to say that most of the anger stirred up across the state by the selection of a new slate of delegates arose not over principles but men. Senator Hammond received a thoughtful letter just after the convention from James Gillam, a prosperous farmer from Edgefield, who assured him that the current crisis was entirely beneficial for it had stirred the people out of their apathy into an uncommon unanimity of feeling. The excitement over the Columbia convention was insignificant because all factions were agreed on the fundamental issues; the only conflict seemed to be over who would lead the state in the movement begun at Charleston. Radicals should have shared the lead with the National Democrats, Gillam explained, but he understood that they had reason to believe that "many of the delegates had their minds fix'd on Baltimore instead of Richmond—which the fire-eaters could not tolerate, and chose rather to send men to Richmond which they regarded as more reliable." Gillam was encouraged to feel that the stand taken at Charleston had united the South and made slavery more secure. He hoped that all good men, North and South, would at last see the wisdom and absolute necessity of rebuking the mad Republicans. Perhaps it would be "too good to be true," the Edgefield farmer allowed, "but the best solution would be for the Baltimore convention to accept the [proslavery] majority platform and nominate a sound man to run upon it." This was the voice of Carolina moderation on the eve of the final Democratic party confrontations.[52]

Papers, DU; Hammond to Simms, July 10, 1860, Hammond Papers, LC. Governor Letcher of Virginia had a similar reaction. "I almost despaired," he told Senator Hunter, "when I saw in the papers, a day or two since, that Rhett was placed at the head of the South Carolina delegation, to the Richmond Convention. . . . I do not think it possible, that any party can survive the leadership, of two such politicians, as Rhett and Yancey. . . . Their purpose is the disorganization and overthrow of the Democratic party, and the country must see it, and understand it." Letcher to Hunter, June 6, 1860, in *Correspondence of Robert M. T. Hunter*, II, 331–32. See also Daniel Horlbeck to Miles, June 4, and Simms to Miles, [June 12, 1860], Miles Papers, SHC; John Ashmore to B. F. Perry, June 6, 1860, Perry Papers, Ala.Arc.; and Newberry *Rising Sun*, May 15, and June 6, 1860.

[52] James Gillam to Hammond, June 4, 1860, Hammond Papers, LC. See also Henry William Ravenel MS Journal, USC, June 1, 1860. As for Hayne himself, his bitter words after the state convention were mainly an expres-

— 6 —

In the end, the angry controversy in the state over the delegation to Richmond proved to be pointless. Rhett and his followers had won the right to drink the full cup of humiliation. The Richmond convention—its ranks and potential for action depleted by the spirit of the reunification appeal—met, only to adjourn humbly and await the chance to be readmitted to the Baltimore convention. Save for a few scattered radical delegates from the Gulf states, Yancey not included, South Carolina's delegation waited alone, impatiently, and more than a little comically, for the verdict of the national convention. That verdict was a foregone conclusion. Douglas's last minute letter to his floor leader offering to withdraw his name if party unity and "the principle of non Intervention" could only be maintained without his nomination was without effect. The Northwest was determined to have control of the party. As Murat Halstead startlingly phrased it, "The Democracy of the North-west rose out of the status of serfdom. There was servile insurrection, with attendant horrors, and Baltimore became a political St. Domingo."[53] Rejection of the bid by the Charleston bolters for readmission to the national convention at Baltimore was followed by a second bolt. With Rhett watching mutely from Richmond, the Southern delegations convened at Maryland Institute Hall in Baltimore to nominate John C. Breckinridge of Kentucky and Joseph Lane of Oregon for President and Vice-President on a pro-slavery platform. On June 26 members of these delegations met in Richmond with South Carolina, pointlessly reaffirmed the nominations, and adjourned *sine die*.[54]

---

sion of pique over the failure of his plans. He did not differ with Rhett over essentials, but he was justifiably concerned that he and his faction would divide the South, and alienate the loyalty of Carolina moderates. Hayne to Hammond, June 3, 1860, Hammond Papers, LC.

[53] Stephen A. Douglas to William A. Richardson, June 20, 1860, Stephen A. Douglas Papers, DU; Halstead, *Caucuses of 1860*, p. 229.

[54] Halstead, *Caucuses of 1860*, pp. 154–232; Emerson David Fite, *The Presidential Campaign of 1860* (New York, 1911), pp. 107–15; Dwight Lowell Dumond, *The Secession Movement, 1860–1861* (New York, 1931), p. 168; Schultz, *Nationalism and Sectionalism*, p. 219.

For Hammond, the events of the past six months had proved that the world had gone mad. Albert Gallatin Brown, a senator from Mississippi, had instigated the movement in Congress during the winter to pass special, unnecessary, codes for the protection of slavery in the territories—all to advance his own interests as a would-be Presidential candidate. Yancey, Hammond went on, in his ambition to be a senator, had persuaded the Alabama legislature to bind the state's delegation to Charleston to that same slave code position—resulting in the disruption of the national party. The Alabama radical then lost control of the movement, returned home, panicked, became a Unionist again, and went to Baltimore, begging to be readmitted to the convention. "It was silly enough to secede at Charleston on a very distant & improbable issue," Hammond wrote William Gilmore Simms a few days later,

> it would have been amusing if it had not been so mortifying to see the great leaders of this grand splurge so long before concocted, stand amazed & bewildered at their own success, with their fingers in their mouths utterly unable to lead an inch further; but then to see them sneak back to Baltimore, humbly entreat to be re-admitted in to the same convention with platform unchanged, & to be so scornfully rejected.[55]

And so the wheel turned, as Hammond saw it, each man blowing his own trumpet, seeking only his personal advancement, oblivious to the real needs of the party and the nation; and in the process stirring up in the masses the deepest fears and hatreds.

Hammond's descriptions of events is not entirely accurate. Nonetheless, it is clear that despite the fulminations of the National Democrats, Rhett did lead his radical entourage to Richmond determined to resist a reintegration of the party as the essential prerequisite to a Republican success in the fall. He may have grumbled at the minor role into which the state was finally cast. But victory was still his.

[55] J. H. Hammond to M. C. M. Hammond, July 4, 1860, and *id.* to W. G. Simms, July 10, 1860, Hammond Papers, LC.

PART THREE

CHAPTER SEVEN

Campaigning for Revolution

The campaign for the election of a President in 1860 was a curious affair. The people of South Carolina—who alone were unable directly to register their judgment—believed that the nation had been presented a rare opportunity in American political history, the chance to pass upon a clear and substantial issue: the fate of slavery and the Union. Not until the revitalizing hand of Reconstruction after the Civil War had democratized state policy did voters gain the right to cast their ballots in a Presidential election. In this most fateful of elections, with the power of decision out of their hands, and with that decision increasingly regarded as settled, South Carolinians turned inward to consider their fate. In this strangest of all campaigns, the citizens of Carolina prepared themselves for rebellion.

— 1 —

Abraham Lincoln, the sturdy frontiersman, the conservative, the peacemaker—from the very first this was not the view of the Republican candidate for President in 1860 held by the people of South Carolina. By the time of the party's national convention in Chicago, Robert Barnwell Rhett and Christopher Memminger were not alone in fearing that Republicans would abandon Seward. In a letter to Edmund Ruffin, Charleston scientist John Bachman expressed his suspicions that the Republicans would try to "lull us asleep a little while longer" by nominating another man. "They will probably get an ass into the presidential chair & get Seward to lead or drive him. . . . We will then see who will swallow black republicanism—nigger, tariff & all."[1] When Ruffin received this letter he had already learned that the party had selected "Lincoln of Illinois, inferior in ability & reputation to all." The Virginia disunionist was troubled by Seward's rejection at Chicago, for he believed the New York senator would have "made their success more probable."[2] But the meaning of the nomination seemed equally disturbing to those who did not welcome the prospect of a Republican President. In a letter to his wife, former governor John L. Manning eloquently voiced the anxieties of Carolina conservatives aroused by news of Lincoln's selection.

[The Republicans] have just overthrown their leader—their head and organization—their gifted and talented (altho he is a demagogue) leader; the man who gave their organization shape and effectiveness, the head as well as the soul of their party and the most gentlemanly of their whole fraternity—rudely—without warning—in the most violent and remorseless manner, they set him aside because he was a gentleman . . . and this was because he said that if he was elected President that no one should touch the rights of the South with his consent. And he had a will which would make his word good. In his place they have selected a wretched backwoodsman, who have [sic] cleverness indeed but no cultivation; who is a fanatic in his policy and an agrarian in his practice. Nothing but ruin can follow in his trail.[3]

Most South Carolinians had used Seward's words and ideas to

---

[1] Bachman wondered whether Virginia needed "another John Brown to wake her up to a sense of danger[.]" Bachman to Ruffin, May 23, 1860, Edmund Ruffin Papers, SHC. The Republican Party convention took place on May 16.

[2] Edmund Ruffin MS Diary, LC, May 21, 1860.

[3] M[anning] to his wife, May 29, 1860, Williams-Chesnut-Manning Papers, USC.

construct their image of the Republican party, and had convinced themselves over the past four years that he would be elected President in 1860. Still, there was little difficulty in putting Lincoln into the role as bearer of the vengeful sword of Northern abolitionism. When John Bachman read that Seward was not chosen at Chicago, he did not hesitate to brand Lincoln "the most dangerous of the two."[4] This was not the sophistry of a disunionist. Carolinians were not unfamiliar with Lincoln's words, especially those spoken during the Illinois senatorial campaign against Douglas in 1858. Even so moderate a newspaper as the Edgefield *Advertiser* declared that the speeches of that campaign had marked Lincoln as an ultra "Black" Republican of the worst stripe. The *Advertiser* even informed its readers that it was Lincoln, not Seward, who was the author of the hated "irrepressible conflict" doctrine. Months before Seward's address at Rochester, Lincoln had delivered his famous speech at Springfield, Illinois, accepting his party's nomination for the Senate. There he denied that the nation could permanently exist "half slave and half free"; there he predicted a national crisis over the slave question, a conflict, the *Advertiser* noted, which the North was fated to win.[5] This was the essence of Republican dogma. "[Lincoln] has openly proclaimed a war of extermination against the leading institutions of the Southern States. He says that there can be no peace so long as slavery has a foot hold in America." Thus, the *Advertiser* concluded, "The sectional issue between the North

---

[4] Bachman to Ruffin, May 28, 1860, Ruffin Papers, SHC.
[5] Lincoln stated, "Either the opponents of slavery will arrest the further spread of it, and place it where the public mind shall rest in the belief that it is in course of ultimate extinction; or its *advocates* will push it forward, till it shall become alike lawful in *all* the States, *old* as *well* as new—*North* as well as *South*." *The Collected Works of Abraham Lincoln,* edited by Roy P. Basler, 8 volumes (New Brunswick, 1953–1955), II, 461–62. The logic of foreign slave trade and territorial slave code advocates suggests that Lincoln's warning was not without substance. However, as Norman A. Graebner has pointed out, "Possessing no realistic formula for achieving the peaceful elimination of slavery against the South's determination to maintain it, neither Lincoln nor any other antislavery politician of the North could present to the nation any genuine alternative but civil war to indefinite coexistence with slavery." Norman A. Graebner, "The Politicians and Slavery," in Norman A. Graebner, ed., *Politics and the Crisis of 1860* (Urbana, 1961), p. 20.

and South is now as distinctly made up, as if SEWARD himself had been nominated."[6]

— 2 —

Whether from resignation or real approval, the Breckinridge and Lane ticket was promptly endorsed at local meetings throughout the state in early July. From its inception, their candidacy held a variety of meanings for South Carolina. For John Izard Middleton, a planter from tidewater Waccamaw, the nomination secured the division of the Democratic party. Middleton had been a member of the radical delegation to Richmond, and he was confident that the people of South Carolina approved "our course of masterly inactivity at Richmond," and would be ready to resist the "Black Republican rule" which that course had made inevitable. On the other hand, Arthur Simkins was not convinced that this was so. Is Breckinridge your leader, he asked the "Charleston seceders"? Simkins believed the addresses of the Kentuckian seemed to speak only of Unionism, and alliance with the Northern Democrats against the Republicans.[7]

South Carolina's unofficial poet laureate, William Gilmore Simms, a thoroughgoing defender of the South for thirty years, also questioned the supposedly dire implications of the Breckinridge candidacy. Simms doubted that disunion awaited the nation in December. Indeed, he actually hoped that Breckinridge would win the election if he, rather than John Bell the Whig, "Constitutional Union" candidate, received the votes of Northern conservatives. As Rhett had foreseen much earlier, however, the creation of a separate Southern Democratic party had greater significance than a slight possibility of winning the election. The very fact of a "radical" separatist pro-slavery ticket in the field contributed immeasurably to the creation of a united South, and

[6] Edgefield *Advertiser,* May 30, 1860.
[7] John Izard Middleton to Edmund Ruffin, July 10, 1860, Ruffin Papers, SHC; *Advertiser,* July 11, 1860. See also Daniel H. Hamilton to William Porcher Miles, June 28, 1860, William Porcher Miles Papers, SHC; and Miles to J. H. Hammond, July 10, 1860, James H. Hammond Papers, LC. Breckinridge repeatedly denied the charge that he was a disunionist. See Frank H. Heck, "John C. Breckinridge in the Crisis of 1860–1861," *Journal of Southern History,* XXI (August 1955), 316–46.

thus to secession. For a generation extremists had promulgated an intellectual rationale for Southern nationalism. Now at last the splinter Southern Democratic party provided an emotional vehicle for the realization of disunion. "No party, no confederacy can be held together by abstract principle simply," Simms had written Barnwell Rhett. "The great body of politicians & people require some symbols which they couple with principles, and which they finally receive as a substitute for it. These symbols," Simms noted with insight, "are our candidates for office." The election of a Republican to the Presidency, not the party split at Charleston, assured the secession of the lower South. But the Breckinridge-Lane candidacy aided the cause of radicalism, by adding fuel to the already superheated political atmosphere, by offering an undiluted pro-slavery alternative for voters and promoting separatist thinking among Southerners, and most important, by making the election of a Republican more certain. In striking first for the division of the National Democratic party, and establishing an independent ticket for the Southern people to support, a momentous step was taken toward secession.[8]

Of all the state's leaders, Senator James Hammond gave the most unconditional support to the new ticket. Like all South Carolina moderates, he was deeply shaken by the destruction of the national party. But unlike most, he did not despair of the Union. With his eye on the real enemy of the South, the Republicans, Hammond enthusiastically endorsed the idea of fusion with the Douglas slate in some of the Northern states. He repeatedly cautioned his Carolina friends to avoid public declarations of support for the ticket. Everywhere Breckinridge was fighting the label of disunionist, applied by his three opponents; and Hammond was painfully aware of the reputation held by South Carolina. "My opinion," he wrote Miles, "is that SoCa should be as quiescent as usual in the election & that every blow she or any of her people strike for B & L will damage them. I have reason to know that (*inter nous*) they *dread* the support of the Mercury & Rhett, & want SoCa to vote quietly as usual."[9] Nevertheless, some effort

---

[8] Simms to Miles, July 2 and 15, 1860, Miles Papers, SHC.
[9] Hammond to his brother Marcellus, June 4, 1860, *id.* to Simms, July 10, 1860, Hammond Papers, LC; Hammond to Miles, July 16, 1860, Miles Papers, SHC. And yet Hammond was keenly aware of Rhett's extraordinary

was made to engage the campaign assistance of Congressmen Miles and William Boyce for speaking tours in Pennsylvania and New Jersey.[10] More serious and successful solicitations were also made for funds to support the cause, and these won the support of such moderates as John L. Manning.[11] It should be noted that the irrepressible Rhett did not refrain from loudly proclaiming his support for Breckinridge as the only proper candidate for all true "Union-savers." ("Now this," Miles drily remarked, "was scarcely ingenuous.")[12] As late as October, despite signs of defeat all around them, Hammond, James Louis Petigru, and others had not abandoned hope.[13]

– 3 –

These were lonely voices. Even before the final collapse of efforts to reunite the Democratic party at Baltimore in June, Southern disunionists were assuring Edmund Ruffin that the

powers of observation. "How unfortunate that Cassandra came to preside over his birth," Hammond wrote Miles, "& make him say the wisest things, so out of time & place, that they are accounted by those who rule, mere foolishness."

[10] Isaac Ingalls Stevens (Chairman of the "National" Democratic Executive Committee) to Miles, July 18, 1860, and W. H. Trescot to Miles, July 27, 1860, Miles Papers, SHC; Miles to Hammond, August 5, 1860, Hammond Papers, LC.

[11] Draft of a letter of introduction for J. D. Hooper, member of the "National" Democratic Executive Committee, by John L. Manning, July 20, 1860, Chesnut-Miller-Manning Papers, SCHS; E. McBride to Miles, July 20, 1860, Miles Papers, SHC.

[12] Charleston *Mercury,* July 25, August 4, 10, 18, and 25, 1860; W. P. Miles to Hammond, August 5, 1860, Hammond Papers, LC. Miles believed that Rhett's dissembling Unionism was a bid "for the suffrages or at least the approbation of the more moderate of the State Rights men," in an effort to gain control of the state. See also Elizabeth Merritt, *James Henry Hammond, 1807–1864* (Baltimore, 1923), p. 137.

[13] Hammond to his brother Marcellus, August 30, 1860, Hammond Papers, LC; Simms to Miles, August 31, 1860, Miles Papers, SHC; James Louis Petigru to B. F. Perry, October 8, 1860, B. F. Perry Papers, Ala.Arc. On learning of Lincoln's election, Hammond confided to his diary, "I did think that Breckinridge would be elected. I supposed that the South was aroused enough, firm enough to unite & beat the Northern Black Republicans. . . . The South would not unite. It was foolish & corrupt enough to go off on Bell & Douglas, & we were beaten by a *Minority.*" James H. Hammond MS Diary, USC, November 7, 1860.

election of Lincoln was certain, and that the secession of the Southern states would definitely follow—so long as South Carolina took the lead. In early July, William Henry Trescot, then filling out a term as Assistant Secretary of State in the lame-duck Administration, reported from Washington that optimism was a rare commodity in party councils there. "The general expectation is defeat," he wrote Miles.[14] For the next two months the state's more radical leaders reiterated their complete confidence in the election of Lincoln. The only public message delivered over and over again in published letters and speeches by such men as Congressmen John McQueen, William Boyce, Lawrence M. Keitt, and Milledge Bonham, was that Lincoln would be elected, and that the state must secede upon that event.[15]

One of the most widely read of these declarations was a public letter from William Boyce. He went beyond a mere assertion of the "need" for secession, to delineate the "principles of the Republican party" which compelled every self-respecting South Carolinian to recognize the compulsion of disunion if Lincoln were elected. "The vital principle of this party," he explained on August 3, "is negro equality, the only logical *finale* of which is emancipation." Boyce traced the origins of the party to sectional competition for control of the Federal Government, and to the belief that majority rule was superior to state's rights. Boyce warned that the mute acceptance of Lincoln's election would destroy Southern civilization. Not at once, to be sure; party leaders were too sagacious for that. Federal patronage would in time build up an abolitionist party in the South itself. Those who believed in Negro equality would be rewarded with positions and power. A Republican party would grow up in the border states, and the Supreme Court would soon fall to Republican control. Slowly, inexorably, slavery would be ruthlessly crushed out. "If

[14] Edmund Ruffin MS Diary, LC, June 13, 14, 1860; Trescot to Miles, July 12, 1860, Miles Papers, SHC.
[15] Speech of John McQueen, July 4, 1860, in *Advertiser,* July 25, 1860; letter from William W. Boyce, August 3, in Charleston *Daily Courier,* August 8, 1860; Lawrence Keitt to Hammond, August 4, 1860, and Miles to Hammond, August 5, 1860, Hammond Papers, LC; Trescot to Miles, August 10, 1860, Miles Papers, SHC; Edmund Ruffin MS Diary, LC, August 11, 1860; Pickens *Keowee Courier,* September 1, 1860.

the South acquiesces in a Republican administration, I think the question of negro equality is settled against us, and emancipation only a question of time."[16]

Here were the words which were repeated day after day, in newspapers, in stump speeches, at Sunday barbecues and Sunday sermons, from soap boxes to pulpits, an unrelenting stream of emotional reinforcement from June to December. The people of South Carolina were not being brainwashed, at least in the usual meaning of that term. They were not being forcibly persuaded to give up basic political and social beliefs in favor of a contrasting set of attitudes. What was being accomplished, consciously or not, was the construction of a psychological set, a predisposition to perceive, interpret, and react to an external event in a predetermined fashion. The Presidential election canvass of 1860 was, as one historian has dubbed it, "A Campaign Like None Other."[17] In South Carolina it was not a campaign at all. Virtually no public figure in the state believed that anyone but Lincoln would win; indeed, for a considerable portion of opinion in the state, the splintering of the Democracy and the creation of an essentially Southern party was not done to win the election, but to lose it.

In effect, nearly everything that South Carolina's leaders (not simply politicians, but militia officers, newspaper editors, churchmen, educators, and respected merchants and planters in every district and parish) said and did in their public words and private correspondence contributed to the crystallization of a structure of interlocking emotional beliefs, beliefs that were logical within the framework of that peculiar society and its history. South Carolinians were preparing themselves to respond appropriately to the "inevitable" election of Abraham Lincoln.

There were three facets to this "set." The first, of course, was that a Republican victory was inescapable. This certainty flowed from two sources: the long-fated culmination of the conflict over slavery, and the unavoidable consequences of the disruption of the Democratic party. Intertwined with this was the second ele-

[16] *Courier*, August 8, 1860; *Advertiser*, August 15, 1860.
[17] Roy Franklin Nichols, *The Disruption of American Democracy* (New York, 1962), Chapter 18.

ment in the secession persuasion—the meaning of Lincoln's election. There was no need for Congressman Boyce to describe the principles of the Republican party to his fellow citizens. Those principles were ingrained in the hearts and minds of every man, woman and child from the hill country in the west to the Atlantic coast. Lincoln's election *meant* the ascendancy of abolitionists to national power—*meant* convulsive slave insurrection—*meant* emancipation of the Negro hordes with the political, social, and economic chaos that must follow the breaking of those bonds. The only possible way to avoid all of this was secession. Secession was the release from unthinkable catastrophe. It was not an escape from a vague apprehension of Northern industrialization, or the "modern world." Secession came to be understood by the people of South Carolina as the only practicable way to avoid a specific and terrible future: the erosion of white control over the Negro; and ultimately, the destruction of slavery.

There is no doubt that this concatenation of responses arose to meet the expected election of Lincoln. The process was given tremendous impetus by the collapse of the Democracy. Almost at once much of the earlier political divisions within the state miraculously disappeared. News of the nominations suddenly cut the ground away from National Democrats and other moderates whose last hope for defeating the Republicans lay in the unification of the Democratic party. By mid-July such leading spokesmen for moderation as John Ashmore, James Orr, Thomas Simons, and even Ben Perry had become deeply influenced by the secession persuasion. Save for Perry and a few others, the recent events at Baltimore and Richmond had finally obliterated the ranks of Union advocates.[18]

[18] Unionism was by no means wiped out among the citizens of the state, only its public advocacy. The "Nationals" appeared to abandon the field to their opponents after their virtual withdrawal from the May Columbia convention. Even before the final collapse at Baltimore, an ardent Camden Unionist complained to Perry that the tide of public opinion was running strongly for secession, because "the masses have not been touched" by the arguments of moderates. "The people need light upon the subject. Even the intelligent among them are ignorant of the true state of the *facts* about which such a clamor is raised. And this has arisen from their taking, for the most part, no newspapers but the Charleston Mercury & others of its school." Perry's correspondent, L. W. R. Blair, was himself writing articles for the

Ashmore advised Hammond on July 10 that he was now prepared to advocate secession in preference to "submission" to Republican rule. He still supported Breckinridge and Lane, "on the ground that it is one more effort to preserve the Constitution & the Union & is in fact a *National* & not a *sectional* movement." But, he admitted, "as I have no hopes whatever of success & believe that Lincoln & Hamlin will be elected I go for preparation first & dissolution afterwards on the first favorable opportunity." At that early date Ashmore was able to say that his up-country congressional district was "nearly unanimous for B & L." By the end of August that support had been transformed into disunionism. Union District was "red hot for separate state action," Ashmore told Hammond, and even in Spartanburg the citizens were "quiet, but looking to resistance of some kind as absolutely necessary in the event of Lincoln's election." And this, Ashmore sadly concluded, "I regard as certain."[19] Orr, Ashmore's political mentor, was no less influenced by the "new order of things" brought on by the dismemberment of the national party. That event had ended his lifelong hope of preserving the Union. As he admitted in a letter of July 23, and again in a much-publicized letter to the aged Jacksonian Amos Kendall, Lincoln's election was "inevitable." The Republican party stood for "open undisguised war

---

Camden *Journal,* and distributing copies of Perry's speeches in the surrounding piedmont districts to counter the "disunion sentiment so rife among us." A month later men such as Blair had become still more isolated. L. W. R. Blair to B. F. Perry, June 4 and 15, 1860, Benjamin F. Perry Papers, Ala.Arc. See also J. J. Knox to Perry, June 12, 1860, in *ibid.* A study of politics in Spartanburg District indicates that resistance to radicalism among the small farmers there was rendered ineffective by the lack of leaders to guide them. See William Joseph MacArthur, "Antebellum Politics in an Up Country County: National, State and Local Issues in Spartanburg County, South Carolina, 1850–1860," (unpublished master's thesis, the University of South Carolina, 1966) p. 78.

[19] Ashmore to Hammond, July 10, and August 30, 1860, Hammond Papers, LC. See also Ashmore to Miles, July 30, 1860, Miles Papers, SHC; Spartanburg *Spartan,* August 30, 1860. In his letter of August 30 to Hammond, Ashmore declared that the defeat of the Democracy was made inevitable by the events at Charleston. He could not "help but think that it was the aim & design of those who ruled the Charleston Convention to produce this very result." See also Henry William Ravenel's conversation with Richard Yeadon, editor of the Charleston *Courier,* on this same suspicion. H. W. Ravenel MS Journal, USC, October 25, 1860.

upon our social institutions. Secession is the only recourse to that," he concluded, "followed by demands for new terms in this union or the establishment of a new government.[20]

The state's foremost spokesman for the Union now stood more alone than ever before in his political life. Perry heard few public echoes as he continued strongly to denounce secession, and even his most powerful attacks seemed to aid the enemy, for his speeches and arguments were all premised on the certainty of Lincoln's election. He was simply shouting into the wind when he attempted to convince his fellow citizens that the election of Lincoln would "violate no Constitutional principle or provision of the Constitution." Perry was denounced as a hypocrite by those who recalled the tenor of his radical resolutions introduced in the state legislature the previous December. The Greenville lawyer replied that he had counselled disunion then only if it were proved that the entire North had adopted the "fiendish doctrines set forth in the addresses and resolutions at the John Brown sympathizing public meetings." He denied that the North had been "abolitionized" or that the election of Lincoln would prove any such thing. Perry had become disengaged from the mainstream of thought in South Carolina.[21]

[20] *Advertiser*, August 8, 1860, quoting the Anderson *Gazette; Advertiser*, October 3, 1860. Orr's letter to Kendall was widely reprinted until the very week of secession. Few names commanded such respect in the up-country districts. See the comment on it in the Camden *Weekly Journal*, August 7, 1860, and the Spartanburg *Exchange*, November 21, 1860. It is interesting to note that no man in the state was more feared by secessionists than Orr. As always, that fear involved not only the power to divide the state on disunion, but also to challenge the traditional political system. Miles, for example, was certain that "Orr and his friends" intended to "try and give the election of [Presidential] Electors to the people and perhaps if they succeed in that then to break down the Parish representation." Hammond apparently made a successful private appeal to Miles to "Let 'Orrism' & all that be dropped" in favor of mutual toleration. Orr's declaration for secession on July 23 appeared to quiet the anxieties of tidewater leaders. Miles to Hammond, July 10, 1860, Miles Papers, SHC; Hammond to Miles, July 16, 1860, Hammond Papers, LC.

[21] *Courier*, August 20, 24, and 29, 1860. See also, Benjamin F. Perry, *Biographical Sketches of Eminent American Statesmen . . .* (Philadelphia, 1887), pp. 171–85; Lillian Adele Kibler, *Benjamin F. Perry, South Carolina Unionist* (Durham, 1946), pp. 325–29. Nevertheless, from Charleston Robert N. Gourdin warned Miles, "You will find many here who endorse Major Perrys [*sic*] views." Gourdin to Miles, August 20, 1860, Miles Papers, SHC.

— 4 —

The only significant controversy which arose concerned the old questions of cooperation, and the specific mode of secession. Those who had been National Democrats became cooperationists in the summer. Orr and Ashmore, for example, adamantly refused to specify the time or the action that would precipitate the final act. "It is in my judgement unwise to specify *time* or *event* when the South should strike," Ashmore wrote fellow congressman Bonham, "for my fears now & always have been that we will be forced to do so before we are ready." As early as July, Ashmore was aware that there were plans afoot to launch the state onto the uncertain seas of separate secession. Orr was equally opposed to any action by South Carolina without the agreement of the other slave states. However, he gave clearer terms for consideration when he allowed that "If merely Ga, Ala and Miss agree to go out with us I will support it." By the end of August, Ashmore was on the defensive about the matter of waiting for Southern cooperation. Miles, Keitt, Boyce, and even Orr had been agitating the issue, pressing for a state-wide committment to secede at once upon Lincoln's election. "I have tried to avoid discussing it," Ashmore despaired, "taking the grounds of the Charleston Mercury once in my life, that there is no such issue before us, & its discussion is premature and ill advised."[22] But South Carolina radicals had been abandoned so often by the other slave states—twice within the past six months alone—that their determination to force a pledge for separate and immediate secession amounted to hysteria. Thus Miles wrote to Hammond in August:

> Lincoln will be elected President. What then? Ought our state Legislature when it meets in November to take any specific steps or should we wait for "cooperation"? Is there any hope for such "cooperation"? I feel very much inclined to

[22] Ashmore to Bonham, July 15, 1860, Milledge L. Bonham Papers, USC; Ashmore to Hammond, July 10, August 30, 1860, Hammond Papers, LC; letter of James L. Orr, July 23, 1860, in *Advertiser*, August 8, 1860, quoting the Anderson *Gazette*.

think that it is just as well to break up things generally, which any one state can at any time do. I am sick and disgusted with all the bluster and threats and manifestos and "Resolutions" which the South has for so many years been projecting and hurling with such force at the devoted heads of "our base oppressors." Let us act if we mean to act without talking. Let it be "a word and a blow"—but the blow first.[23]

— 5 —

For any Southerner who failed to see that the revolution was really coming, all illusions should have been gone by September. Carolina gentlemen began filtering back to their homes and plantations from the resorts where they had gone to escape the summer heat to find the public mind in a state of unusual, and rising, excitement. James Louis Petigru, the state's most distinguished, if politically inactive, Unionist, analyzed the situation, declared that "no possible issue could be more untenable than to make [Lincoln's] bare election a casus belli, without any overt act against the Constitution, or even the Dred Scott decision," and deduced that secession would not take place. "If our planter were in debt, or cotton was at 5 cents, as I have seen it," he reasoned, "such a thing might be likely; but our magnanimous countrymen are too comfortable for such exercise." His correspondent, Alfred Huger, was less sanguine. Huger was losing his faith that divine providence would preserve the Union. Elsewhere among the old Unionist clan, jurist John Belton O'Neal was frantically proclaiming secession to be "Revolution, exactly equal to that in '76," and denying that there was "any cause for that." The only public voice for Unionism to be heard above the radical din was that of Benjamin F. Perry. Yet even he was being condemned for giving the false impression that South Carolina would passively accept the election of Lincoln. The editor of the Sumter *Watchman* expressed the sentiments of many when he wondered whether the

[23] Miles to Hammond, August 5, 1860, Hammond Papers, LC. Other comments on the question of cooperative secession may be seen in the Newberry *Rising Sun*, August 8, 1860; the Yorkville *Enquirer*, August 30, 1860; and the Pickens *Keowee Courier*, October 20, 1860.

time had not come to silence this old gadfly's "obnoxious" remarks.[24]

The most thoughtful opposition to secession came not from old-line Unionists or National Democrats, but from Senator James Hammond. Isaac Hayne wrote the Senator on September 15 to complain about his silence. "It is said that you are opposed per se to any disunion movement based on Lincoln's election," and Hayne feared that failure to act in that event would demoralize the entire South. Hammond replied four days later in a letter of great length and insight. He deeply regretted that the whole cry of secession-upon-Lincoln's-election had been raised, for if the votes cast by the Southern people in the coming election showed an indisposition to support disunion, any move by South Carolina "would be the weakest, most impolitic and assuredly abortive" the state had ever made. Although he was prepared to support any action taken by the whole state, one thing was clear: South Carolina must not take the lead, for any movement starting with her would be doomed. Only if the election clearly indicated that the entire South was eager for resistance, should South Carolina take the lead.[25]

But what was the state of mind throughout the slave states? "To me it appears more strongly Union than at any time in ten years," the Senator exclaimed to Hayne. He referred to that dramatic moment in Washington when the news arrived that the convention at Charleston had collapsed. "That looked like a real beginning of the end and you should have seen how all the 'fire eaters' *blenched* and *shrank*. It was clear at once that all their big talk was bosh & many of them owned that they would be broken down if we went *too far*,—that is did any thing but talk." Hammond denied that there was any desire for disunion based on the Presidential election outside of South Carolina. There were many who would support secession if it became clear that the power

24 Petigru to Alfred Huger, September 5, 1860, James Louis Petigru Papers, LC; Alfred Huger to Joseph Holt, September 26, 1860, Joseph Holt Papers, LC; J. B. O'Neal to Hammond, September 22, 1860, Hammond Papers, LC; *Advertiser,* October 3, 1860, quoting the Sumter *Watchman.*
25 Isaac Hayne to Hammond, September 15, 1860, Hammond to Hayne, September 19, 1860, Hammond Papers, LC; see also Hammond to Milledge L. Bonham, October 3, 1860, Bonham Papers, USC.

of the Federal Government had permanently fallen into the hands of the Republicans. But if the state were to secede on the issue of Lincoln's election "she would have no more sympathy from the Southern states than she had in 1832, 42, 52 & 60." Not a single voice would be raised to answer the call of South Carolina, Hammond warned, not Yancey's, Jefferson Davis's or anyone else's.

Above all, Hammond was troubled by the continuing division of the Southern states. The invincible strength of a united South had long been the foundation of his policy. Even now, Hammond moaned, the South could control the Union, because she controlled the great rivers of the West. But that was gone. What was to be done now? First, Hammond repudiated the plan he had heard rumored to prevent the inauguration of Lincoln by force! This would not only result in the hanging of the fools who tried it, but in the destruction of the constitutionality of secession, and the demoralization of the entire South. "It would be a sad record for our descendants to look over," he reminded the long-time radical, Hayne, "that South Carolina, after resisting for over 30 years the aggressions of the General Government on the ground of their unconstitutionality, at last *rebelled against the Constitution herself.*" No, the proper last resort must be secession, "legally" executed through a state convention. In the meantime, Hammond suggested that the way to avoid premature action, before the attitude of the South was known, while preventing the demoralization of public opinion at home with inaction, was to have the legislature call for a general Southern convention.[26]

Less aggressive men, such as planter William Elliott and former governor R. F. W. Allston, shared Hammond's views. These low country leaders accepted the need for secession, but feared that the state would be isolated, or at best joined only by the Gulf states. Elliott foresaw that the states of the upper South would demand an *"overt act"* from the new Administration to push them into revolution. And even within those states, Allston noted that there were regions, like western Virginia, where there seemed to be no understanding of the "principles for which we contend and of the disastrous consequences which would flow from a triumph

[26] Hammond to Hayne, September 19, 1860, Hammond Papers, LC. See also Pickens *Keowee Courier*, October 20, 1860.

of the Seward party."[27] These planters were hardly alone in their sense of disquietude over the speed and manner of the impending withdrawal from the Union. A great many insisted upon that "overt act" before moving. Others simply cursed secession as a "truly insane plunge," and deliberately withdrew from the fracas to watch the demise of the Republic they loved from the sidelines.[28]

The spirit of the state as a whole, however, was rising rapidly towards a general and enthusiastic demand for secession, and that spirit would never tolerate another Southern convention. By late September Simms had become convinced that the state was "ripe for withdrawal, even though she goes alone." The supposed fire-eating congressman Lawrence Keitt still regretted the collapse of party unity at Charleston; but he accepted the "present condition of things as a *fact.*" His advice now was to arm the militia, call a state convention, retire the congressional delegation, and put South Carolina into the lead with a declaration of secession. Keitt understood why South Carolina could lead the movement, where others could not. "The absence of party spirit enable us to do so—" he told Miles, "and we should not deplore it. If we wait for Ala[bama] we will wait eternally." The state's radical leadership shared Hammond's fear of isolation. They wanted Alabama or Mississippi to initiate the movement, but they apprehended the dangers of waiting even more. Barnwell's Alfred Aldrich was opposed to holding a special state convention at all, believing that the legislature itself could break the Federal tie. He thought the need to "vote revolution" absurd.[29]

---

[27] William Elliott to Ralph Elliott, September 26, 1860, and n.d., Elliott-Gonzales Papers, SHC; Robert F. W. Allston to Benjamin Allston, October 6, 1860, R. F. W. Allston Papers, SCHS.

[28] John F. Hammond to his father, James H., October 16, 1860, Hammond Papers, LC; Jane North to Mrs. R. F. W. Allston, October 21, [1860], R. F. W. Allston Papers, SCHS; Mary Hort MS Journal, USC, October 21, 1860; James H. Hammond MS Journal, USC, October 22 and 23, 1860; Henry William Ravenel MS Journal, USC, October 25, 1860; John Berkeley Grimball to Elizabeth Grimball, November 1, 1860, John B. Grimball Papers, SHC; John H. Cornish MS Diary, SHC, November 8, 1860.

[29] Simms to Miles, September 28, [1860], and Lawrence Keitt to Miles, October 3, 1860, Miles Papers, SHC; A. P. Aldrich to Hammond, October 4, 1860, Hammond Papers, LC.

In effect, the people of South Carolina did vote for revolution on October 8. The general election for the state assembly produced a legislature disposed for secession at all cost. There was some effort during the fall campaign to test the radicalism of candidates, particularly in the upper districts where more aggressive leaders were conscious of the erstwhile Unionism of piedmont farmers. These elections exhibited little of the animosity which had characterized the division of the state in the secession movement of 1851. In the piedmont districts, as in the parishes, voters were not even being presented with genuine alternatives; the only tenable conservative position was opposition to separate secession (although many an up-country Unionist appeared to be running for office in the guise of a cooperationist). When the moment of decision came, these men proved to be poor friends of the Union. In general, the voters of South Carolina seemed inclined to choose established district leaders, or the more aggressive candidates, confident that there would be unanimity in the legislature on the basic issue.[30] To be sure, the problem of whether to secede at once, upon Lincoln's election, or await joint action still was unresolved. But the final question was settled on October 8. As Lawrence Keitt wrote Simms, the sentiment of the incoming legislature was "tremendously, out & out secession."[31]

— 6 —

The rest of the story has often been told.

On October 20 Rhett wrote his friend Edmund Ruffin, "The complexion of our legislature is good and I believe we are going to break up the Union, if Lincoln is elected. We wait however to give Alabama and Mississippi and Georgia every opportunity to lead."[32] Three days before this, Governor William Gist secretly

[30] *Courier*, October 8–11, 1860; *Advertiser*, August 22 and 29, 1860; York-ville *Enquirer*, October 4, 1860; Chauncey S. Boucher, "South Carolina and the South on the Eve of Secession, 1852 to 1860," *Washington University Studies*, VI (1918), 141–42.
[31] Simms to Hammond, October 16, 1860, Hammond Papers, LC. See also Simms to James Lawson, October 16, [1860], in *The Letters of William Gilmore Simms*, edited by Mary C. Simms Oliphant, Alfred Taylor Odell, and T. C. Duncan Eaves, 5 volumes (Columbia, 1955), IV, 247–50.
[32] R. B. Rhett to Ruffin, October 20, 1860, Ruffin Papers, SHC.

dispatched his brother, aptly named States Rights Gist, with a letter to the governors of the states mentioned by Rhett, as well as to Florida, Louisiana, and North Carolina. Gist spelled out the reluctance of his state to move first, and assured the Southern governors that she would cooperate in a joint secession with any other state. The replies would have unsettled those who hoped for cooperation. While all of the chief executives except North Carolina's John Ellis and Louisiana's Thomas Moore were convinced that their people were ready to join in the secession attempt, none of them were prepared to take the lead; Gist must have been particularly irked by the letter from Albert B. Moore. The Alabama governor now explained that the state convention which had been required in the event of the election of a Republican by the January legislature would not take place until February 1861 at the earliest.[33] For thirty years the Southern states had trembled at the violent words and acts of South Carolina. Now some of them, at least, looked to her for leadership.

On October 12 Gist issued the official call to convene the legislature, and prepared the members for more arduous duty than simply choosing the Breckinridge Presidential electors. With South Carolina in a high state of excitement the General Assembly came together on November 5 to hear the Governor request a special continuation of the session, once the electors were named. Gist wanted the legislature to wait in Columbia for confirmation of Lincoln's election, and once that was an accomplished fact, to call for a secession convention. Gist assured the Assembly that "the long desired cooperation of the other states, having similar institutions" was near at hand.[34] Franklin J. Moses recalled that the new legislature was composed of many more young, inexperienced and radical men than in previous years, and they welcomed these fiery words from Gist. "The vast majority favored separate State action," Moses wrote, believing that prompt action by South Carolina would carry other states with it. South Caro-

---

[33] Gist's letter, and the replies received to it are in John G. Nicolay and John Hay, *Abraham Lincoln, A History,* 10 volumes (New York, 1890), II, 306–14.

[34] *Mercury,* October 16, 1860; Message No. 1 of Governor William H. Gist, November 5, 1860, William H. Gist Papers, USC.

linians were fortified in this belief by a mass of "signals" flooding the state from Southerners and Northerners. In addition, by the end of October it was generally known that most of the important early state elections in the North had been won by Republicans. Their success in Pennsylvania, the home state of President Buchanan, was particularly cited as conclusive proof that "LINCOLN will carry every Northern and Western free state, which is sufficient to elect him."[35]

Nevertheless, there was still division in the legislature. As the frightening time for decision rushed toward them, calmer voices were heard counselling caution and delay. Hammond, whose advice had been solicited by the leaders of the Assembly on November 5, gave a lengthy reply two days later, substantially reiterating his earlier objections to seceding "because Mr. Lincoln has been elected President, when his election has been . . . entirely constitutional." Perhaps such an appeal was "best calculated for the comprehension of the masses. But to the world at large and to posterity we shall, if we adopt it, place ourselves in a false position." He had full confidence that the new Administration would provide the essential "overt act" soon enough, but for the present he pleaded with the legislature to forbear from separate secession, and to insist upon the joint action of at least two more states.[36]

Another mollifying voice was that of William Henry Trescot, who occupied the peculiar position of being the only South Carolinian in an official capacity in Washington at the time. Convinced of the inevitability of secession, but fearful of damaging prospects for Southern unity, or isolating the state, Trescot's message, in numerous letters to his influential friends at home, was procrastination. On November 1 he told Rhett that Howell Cobb, then

[35] [Franklin J. Moses, Jr.], "How South Carolina Seceded, by the Private Secretary of Gov. Pickens of South Carolina," *The Nickell Magazine,* (December 1897), 345–47; William Nelson to W. P. Miles, October 8, [1860], Miles Papers, SHC, W. H. Trescot to Hammond, October 14, 1860, Hammond Papers, LC; Pickens *Keowee Courier,* October 20, 1860. On these early Northern state elections, see Allan Nevins, *The Emergence of Lincoln,* 2 volumes (New York, 1950), II, 311–12.
[36] Alfred P. Aldrich, *et al.,* to James H. Hammond, November 6, 1860, and Hammond to same, November 8, 1860, Hammond Papers, LC; and rough draft of his reply, in Hammond Papers, USC.

Buchanan's Secretary of the Treasury, and a powerful and respected Georgian, opposed the secession of South Carolina prior to the inauguration of Lincoln. Cobb was said to believe that such a delay would better unite the South, allow the current cotton crop to be harvested and sold, and avoid any collision of authority with an Administration which had been friendly to the South. Trescot wrote more imploringly in the same vein to Miles on the 8th. The legislature was then debating the timing of the proposed convention. "All that I am anxious about is just that every effort shall be made to induce Georgia to take the lead in this move. Give her all the glory, take her men and her measures to secure that joint action. . . . If that fails," Trescot ended, "I suppose we must 'go it alone.'" When Cobb's reasoning was ignored by South Carolina (when it was decided to call for a state convention in December), he privately expressed dismay. "It looks as if they were afraid that the blood of the people will cool down."[37]

There were elements in the legislature receptive to counsels of delay. Former National Democrats and other moderates joined with uneasy cooperationists to argue for consultation and joint action with the other cotton states. Bills were introduced in the House and Senate to the effect, setting dates as late as January 15 for the convening of the special assembly.[38] Radicals met these tactics with sharp words, demanding an early date for the proposed state convention. Rhett prepared a letter for the *Mercury* signed "Now" denouncing those who were seeking a later call for the convention. The first rule of revolutions was to avoid leaving excessive "time for re-action on the part of the people."

Now, why do we not take a lesson from the past & call a convention of the people of this State *at once*—Why do we wait for forty days, or the 17th Decr to do what can be done with

---

[37] Trescot to Rhett, November 1, 1860, W. H. Trescot Papers, LC; Trescot to Miles, November 8, 1860, Miles Papers, SHC; Howell Cobb to "My Judge," November 11, 1860, Howell Cobb Papers, NYHS.
[38] Charles Edward Cauthen, *South Carolina Goes to War, 1860–1865* (Chapel Hill, 1950), pp. 54–55. See also Henry W. Conner to James Conner, October 28, 1860, in *The Letters of General James Conner*, edited by Mary Conner Moffett (Columbia, 1950), pp. 22–23.

so much more advantage to ourselves *now* . . . why do we pause in so vital a cause when all are, or ought to be ready to resent our injuries & daily insults, saying nothing of our increasing risks of internal domestic discontent, which the North will be heaping upon us, by hordes of emissaries pouring in & no law to prevent their ingress . . . will not delay cool the ardor of our people, who incensed now would resist promptly?[39]

Indeed, David Hoke, a representative from Greenville, remarked that Rhett's urgings for an early call for elections and convention were designed to "make a speedy work of the whole matter and that too before two parties can be formed in South Carolina."[40] As Charles Cauthen has noted, until late in the session it was likely that the election for the special convention would be put off until January. The prospect suddenly appeared for a disintegration in that "gratifying unanimity" which had been so long a-borning.[41]

Although there was no longer a realistic possibility for division over secession, fate was already intervening to inspire the legislature into a greater sense of alacrity. On November 7, as soon as the election of Lincoln was established, the highest Federal officials in the state, District Judge Andrew Gordon Magrath, and District Attorney James Conner, announced that they had resigned their commissions. News of Lincoln's election had been received throughout the state with much public excitement and

[39] R. B. Rhett, draft of unsigned letter to the Editor of the *Mercury*, November 10, 1860, Robert Barnwell Rhett Papers, SHC. Counsels of delay were heard again before the convening of the secession convention in December. Porcher Miles turned the argument of cooperationists on its head when he urged his radical colleague Robert Gourdin to avoid delaying the secession of the state "*a day*. It is not on our account alone, but all our best friends in the entire South urge it upon us as the step best calculated to advance the great cause of the South in all their States. They tell us that *any delay*, under any pretext will demoralize them at home—while it will answer no possible good purpose." Miles to Gourdin, December 10, 1860, Gourdin-Young Papers, Emory.
[40] David Hoke to W. A. McDaniel, November 8, 1860, in Rosser Howard Taylor, ed., "Letters Dealing with the Secession Movement in South Carolina," *Furman University Faculty Studies Bulletin*, XVI (1934), 3–12.
[41] Cauthen, *South Carolina Goes to War*, p. 57; *Advertiser*, November 7, 1860, quoting the Camden *Journal*.

a general sense of resolution. These resignations now signalled a wave of enthusiastic, spontaneous celebration. Three days later, upon hearing an erroneous report that Georgia senator Robert Toombs had resigned, Senator James Chesnut announced his own resignation from Congress.[42] Perhaps the most influential incident of all was a large public meeting in Charleston on the night of November 9, at which a number of Georgia politicians and railroad enthusiasts "pledged their state" to follow South Carolina out of the Union. The city was aflame with excitement. "A monster meeting was held last night in Institute Hall," wrote one observer.

It was plain, from a brief glance, that the respectable citizens of Charleston were there. The speakers were persons of note. They, one after another, in burning phrase, counselled immediate secession, declared the Union was even now dissolved. As they uttered their fierce words, the multitudes rose from their seats, waved their hats in the air, and thundered forth resounding cheers.[43]

Who could resist such an appeal? James Louis Petigru, returning to his beloved city that day, sorrowfully wrote his daughter, "Nearly the last hope of safety is cut off by the last news from Georgia, implying the consent of the majority to follow Carolina."[44] It was fitting that a revolution conceived in fear and executed in passion was sealed by this mass action, and these "fierce words."

A delegation sent by the Charleston rally arrived by train on the afternoon of the 10th, and later that night the House and Senate unanimously agreed to hold the special election on December 6, and the convention on December 17. William D. Porter, President of the state Senate, wrote Hammond to tell him that his conservative letter of November 8 had been suppressed; the spirit

---

[42] Andrew Gordon Magrath to James Buchanan, November 7, 1860, and James Conner to James Buchanan, November 7, 1860, Attorney General Papers, National Archives; Chesnut to Hammond, November 10, 1860, Hammond Papers, LC; *Mercury,* November 8, 1860.

[43] J. W. Claxton to "My Dear Mr. Jones," November 10, 1860, Bonham Papers, USC.

[44] J. L. Petigru to Sue Petigru King, November 10, 1860, J. L. Petigru Papers, LC.

of the legislature had radically changed since that time, Porter explained, and it was now necessary above all else to establish the unbroken unity of South Carolina before the South and the world. "The City [Charleston], which is most exposed & must bear the brunt in great part, is clamorous for secession," he wrote; and "in the State I think no one can resist the current. We are too far committed." In response Hammond, who had "thought Magrath & all those fellows were great asses for resigning," submitted his own resignation. "People are wild," he roared. "The scenes of the French Revolution are being enacted already."[45]

Hammond exaggerated. The cheering throngs which greeted the news of the legislature's action were not expressing a feeling of mindless hatred or anguished frustration. They were moved by the politics of fear and the urge for catharsis. "Disabuse your mind of the notion that there is any party, or body of men, in S. C. not willing for secession," Simms told a New York friend. "The fact is that it is a complete landsturm, a general rising of the people, and the politicians are far behind them. . . . The people will not suffer the politicians any longer."[46] Simms also exaggerated. There were some, perhaps many, who looked on in stunned silence, grieving at the approaching catastrophe. But even these conservatives could see the roots of the revolution, even as they doubted the need for it. So Alfred Huger, septuagenarian, bemoaned the passing of the old order.

> Mr. Seward with all his sagacity has not appreciated the feelings or the natures of those he has treated as the enemies of the Civilized World! Nor does he at the moment dream of the deep indignation he has first cruelly provoked and then more cruelly ridiculed! The consequences rest upon such men as himself, not upon those he has outraged, invaded, murdered and poisoned by his emissaries during the past eventful year.[47]

[45] Cauthen, *Carolina Goes to War*, pp. 57–61; Yorkville *Enquirer*, November 15, 1860; William D. Porter to Hammond, November 11, 1860, Hammond to Marcellus Hammond, November 12, 1860, Hammond Papers, LC.
[46] Simms to James Lawson, [c. November 10, 1860], in *Simms Letters*, IV, 260–62.
[47] Huger to Joseph Holt, November 12, 1860, Joseph Holt Papers, LC.

CHAPTER EIGHT

The Radical Persuasion

South Carolina did not retreat from the precipice. With a quickening momentum her people—fused into an intense unity they had never achieved before or since—rushed forward to grasp that security which she would never know. Yet this was never a perfect unity, nor was it easily achieved. South Carolinians were not political freaks, devoid of the social and economic divisions that characterized the rest of the South and the nation. No group knew better than ardent secessionists how real was the potential for the reemergence of political factionalism. The startling degree of unanimity for secession in December could not hide the fact that beneath that smooth surface lay years, even decades, of unrelenting sectional and class antagonism. The shallow quarrel over cooperationism which dominated public discussion now was only a dim reflection of this struggle. In these last months and weeks the radical persuasion had to overcome a persistent fear of division at home, an uncertainty, a recriminatory self-doubting that drew its strength from a multiplicity of anxieties, real and imagined.

— 1 —

In its broadest terms the debate that raged among the people of South Carolina from midsummer to the declaration of the

Ordinance of Secession in December concerned the necessity for that final solution. The unsettling image of the possible consequences of disunion has already been suggested. Who could know for certain whether this was the right course? Who could prove that slavery would not be safer in the present Union? This fear was unquestionably a potent source of conservatism, and a still more obvious motive for cooperationists who opposed separate secession. "How it is in the great cities I know not," wrote one sensitive man, "but in this little inland town [Chester] all is confusion and excitement; . . . thinking men ask where is this to end? are we drifting on ruin? . . . a few months ago, great, prosperous & powerful and what now? internal dessentions [sic] tear us asunder." He understood the reasons for the controversy. "The parents will not let its southern children enjoy that heritage which they themselves bequeathed to them." Yet the magnitude of events swirling about him seemed too much to bear. "I am nearly crazy," he exclaimed, "all this is beyond my control or comprehension . . . if So Ca goes out alone we are ruined, [but] if other states follow we may make a prosperous Southern Confederacy."[1]

Everyone in South Carolina was compelled to turn these troubling thoughts over in his mind, and each individual naturally interpreted the crisis according to his own predilections. For ultra-conservative Colleton planter David Gavin the turmoil gripping the nation stemmed from the granting of the suffrage to the general populace. Even the secession effort, which he thought necessary, would come to no good because of the influence of the "masses" in it. Disunion was justified "because the Gen. government and Northern States will not protect our slave property," Gavin noted in his diary, yet he had no confidence that slavery would be any safer in an independent confederacy. Unshaken Unionists shared the belief that the future held only the promise of anarchy.[2] These anxieties could not be shaken off. A Columbia woman described the atmosphere there only three days before the opening of the secession convention.

[1] Charles Holst to Isabella A. R. Woodruff, November 18, 1860, I. A. R. Woodruff Papers, DU.
[2] David Gavin MS Diary, SHC, December 6, 1860. See also Meta Morris Grimball MS Diary, SHC, December 15, 1860; and Jane Petigru North to Jane Caroline Pettigrew, December 20, 1860, Pettigrew Family Papers, SHC.

It is with heavy sorrow that they see themselves so near the success of a scheme that has been the offspring of many years trials and tribulations. There are but few voices that do not falter—few eyes that are not dimmed as day after day passes. . . . Men seem quite aware that they are moving towards self destruction. . . . And after all is it mistaken?[3]

Perhaps she projected too much of her own sadness into her picture of the convention delegates, but radicals were not warring against ghosts in their unrelenting effort to demonstrate the legitimacy of secession, and the unity of the state.[4] Yet the blurring effect of personal interpretation beclouds any attempt to estimate with precision the strength of Unionism across the social and physical strata of South Carolina. Excellent examples of this occur in the correspondence of Hammond and Simms. On November 2 the Carolina senator received a letter from the Reverend F. Asbury Mord, who described himself as a Unionist, and was a native of Hammond's own Barnwell district. Writing from Charlotte, North Carolina, Mord told of his recent travels across the "Upper Districts of South Carolina" which proved to him that the majority there was "far from believing that we reap only misfortune & injury in the Union & that prosperity & blessing is to be had only in South Carolina setting up for herself." Only three days later, Simms described his own recent "journey of 200 miles in our State, on its Northern border," and reported that "excitement is great and concentrated." Legal and extra-legal volunteer militia companies were drilling everywhere, and the state representatives of those piedmont districts, "fresh from the people," were redhot for secession.[5]

There were other sources of concern for radical leaders than anxiety over secession itself, or over sectional division. One of the most disturbing questions for planters and their defenders was

---

[3] Sally Baxter Hampton to "Mr. Ruggles," December 14, 1860, Sally Baxter Hampton Papers, USC.

[4] See, for example, the Edgefield *Advertiser*, September 26, 1860, quoting the Darlington *Southerner*; and A. G. Baskin to ———, October 27, 1860, Chesnut-Miller-Manning Papers, SCHS.

[5] Mord to Hammond, November 2, 1860, James H. Hammond Papers, LC; Simms to James Lawson, [November 5, 1860], in *The Letters of William Gilmore Simms*, edited by Mary C. Simms Oliphant, Alfred Taylor Odell, and T. C. Duncan Eaves, 5 volumes (Columbia, 1955), IV, 256–59.

the loyalty of non-slaveholders. The underlying threat posed by Hinton Rowan Helper's *Impending Crisis of the South* was the disintegration of the alliance between all classes of whites in support of slavery as a system of race control. The whole movement for Southern "rights" and finally for Southern nationalism (as every contemporary knew) was in defense of slavery. The situation was made more complex by the belief—propagandized by Republicans and Southern Unionists—that the secession movement was created and controlled by the slaveholding gentry, the "aristocracy," for the sole purpose of protecting their economic and political control over up-country non-slaveholders. The history of South Carolina to 1860 provided ample evidence of the up country's desire for a more equitable distribution of power, and opposition to extremism may easily be correlated to the sectional division of the state—farming piedmont and mercantile Charleston *versus* the plantation low and middle country.

Suspicions about the reliability of the majority of whites, who were not slaveholders, had a long tradition in the state. During the controversy over reopening the foreign slave trade, apprehension over this group became especially keen. The slave trade issue was one which divided whites more perfectly than any other racial question. It would seem that additional cheaper slaves would have benefitted the planters more than any other class, while an influx of fresh Africans in a state which already had the highest concentration of blacks would only have aroused fear and enmity among those unable or unwilling to purchase slaves. Writing from Edgefield in the summer of 1859, the Reverend B. E. Habersham predicted a terrible clash on the issue. "I think the opposition among the working classes in the towns & up country must soon show itself," he told Benjamin Yancey, "and then who shall say where the end will be?" The attack at Harpers Ferry intensified a feeling among many in the gentry that non-slaveholders constituted the weakest link in the armor of white solidarity. The timorous Daniel Hamilton gave an inkling of how deep those uncertainties lay:

Forming a Southern Confederacy can only be effected calmly, quietly, and while we have the strength and ability to choose what our position shall be—not when "we have been driven to the wall,"and the option is given us of Abolition or War— And if we are to judge by the past, when matters have reached that position, think you that 360,000 Slaveholders will dictate terms for 3,000,000 of non-slaveholders at the South— I fear not, I mistrust our own people more than I fear all of the efforts of the Abolitionists.[6]

Hamilton spoke more sharply than most, but the debate over the potential danger continued throughout 1860. Newspaper editors, for example, vociferously argued whether slaves ought to be permitted to move freely into craft occupations as hired labor. The controversy over the "freedom" enjoyed by free and slave blacks which had flared up after Harpers Ferry had not waned, but instead had grown hotter. The Camden *Journal* condemned the practice of hiring out slaves because it struck at the livelihood of the very groups that would provide physical defense if slavery were openly attacked! More to the point, newspapers in the piedmont were replete with articles and editorials denouncing the abolitionist intentions of the Republican party, and repeating time and time again that non-slaveholders had as dear an interest in the preservation of the institution as the wealthiest planter on the coast. "The whole end and aim of the [Republican party] is to bring the negro into equality, contact, and rivalry with the laboring white," wrote "Pickens" in the local *Keowee Courier;* while the Camden *Weekly Journal* reaffirmed that abolition would uproot the very "constitution of Southern society . . . and the line of demarcation which is now so clearly drawn, would be obliterated, and the races would flow together." By late November, with the great adventure at hand, the question of support for slavery and secession was no longer academic, and speakers and writers openly alluded to the argument that the South harbored its own assassin in the person of the non-slaveholder.[7]

6 Habersham to Yancey, June 14, 1859, Benjamin Cudworth Yancey Papers, SHC; Hamilton to W. P. Miles, February 2, 1860, William Porcher Miles Papers, SHC.
7 *Advertiser*, January 18, 1860, quoting the Camden *Journal; Keowee Courier*, November 3, 1860; Camden *Weekly Journal*, November 6, 1860. There were frequent calls for broadening the base of slave ownership. "A MINUTE MAN" proposed that every slaveowner sell at least one to persons who did not own a slave, thus making personal *"interest* supply the deficiency

Similar fears and charges abounded concerning the political posture of businessmen. For generations past this group, mainly centered in Charleston and engaged in commerce and banking, had cast its weight on the side of the Union and against extremism. To a greater extent than other elements in the state, businessmen had remained in touch with the world beyond the borders of South Carolina, and had preserved a greater sense of perspective and equilibrium, which made them potent opponents of political hysteria. They should also have been more aware of the financial upheaval that could accompany disunion. It was apparent weeks before secession was consummated that the troubled state of politics in the nation had already disrupted the delicate balances of credit. In October merchant-planter Henry Gourdin was informed that Savannah banks were refusing to discount drafts on New York banks, save to the very wealthy. Following Lincoln's election the financial situation worsened, with more and more banks in commercial centers suspending the payment of specie in anticipation of a political and possibly military convulsion. The "realistic" economic argument against disunion was perhaps never so persuasively stated as in a private letter from Benjamin Blossom & Son, a New York mercantile house, to Daniel Jordan, a Camden merchant, planter, and state legislator. "We are Union men," they wrote him,

> We believe we are right & you wrong—very wrong—Your only safety for your property is in the Union—the value of your property depends on this—& you will yet see it—Your position & protection before the World is *in* the Union—You will yet see this. . . . You seem not to realize what you have to go through—with your landed & negro property depreciated 50 pr cent—& all trade & commerce killed for no one knows how long—with outside foes & possible trouble with your negroes

of patriotism." *Advertiser,* November 28, 1860. For further selected discussion of this much-debated issue, see the Spartanburg *Spartan,* January 26, 1860; the speech of William Gregg (the state's foremost industrial promoter) in defense of slavery and secession, in the *Advertiser,* November 14, 1860; and an example of the many Grand Jury Presentments which demanded legislation against the practice of hiring out slaves, in Presentments for Kershaw District, December 3, 1860, SCArc.

—& the certainty that in less than one year after peaceable
separation the two sections would drift into war—unless terms
were made & a re-union arranged.

Most important of all, the New York merchants pointed out, "The
credit of the South as of yourself here is based on the supposed
stable value of land & negroes & crops etc," which had all declined
because of the secession threat. "The maintenance of the Union
alone will cause return of confidence & recovery of prices."[8]
The cogency of such warnings, however, appeared to be lost on
the state's business community. In fact, Miles enthused, "Charleston which in consequence of its mercantile interests it was feared
might hold back and prove lukewarm has led the van in the movement for secession." Despite the heady predictions of unparalleled
prosperity issued by Southern nationalists, it was apparent that
pecuniary interests played only a slight part in motivating businessmen. Rather, the same forces which were operating to excite
the rest of the populace into revolution were now carrying these
erstwhile conservatives toward the brink. A great many merchants
were themselves owners of city slaves or even plantations, for
reasons of social status or profit, and the election of Lincoln had
much the same meaning to them as it had to any other South
Carolinian; they were just as determined to maintain absolute
white supremacy against the self-conceived threat of abolition,
and they shared with their fellow citizens the same intense love
for their state. Moreover, the Charleston mercantile establishment existed in large measure to serve the needs of planter families and their multitudinous slaves. The profit of the former depended upon the well-being of the latter, and as satellites of
plantation slavery their primary interest was to defend the institution in what was believed to be its hour of greatest peril.[9]

[8] George McB. Smith to Henry Gourdin, October 22, 1860, Henry Gourdin
Papers, LC; Jacob Schirmer MS Diary, SCHS, November 7, 17 and 23,
1860; E. H. Rodgers and Company to O. M. Dantzler, November 20, 1860,
O. M. Dantzler Papers, Calhoun County Historical Commission; Benjamin
Blossom & Son to Daniel W. Jordan, December 8, 1860, D. W. Jordan
Papers, DU.
[9] W. P. Miles to Muscoe Garnett, November 13, 1860, William Chisolm
Papers, VaHS; McCarter MS Journal, LC, pp. 16–20. The Journal is an
otherwise unidentified copy of a personal recollection for the period October

Also noteworthy is the fact that Carolina business and political leaders—for all the public rhetoric about "colonial" exploitation by the Northeast, and the evils of capitalism—did not regard Northern businessmen as their enemies. The frank character of the message from Benjamin Blossom & Son to Daniel Jordan was not atypical, but more common were letters from merchants and industrialists proclaiming their support for slavery and the Southern states, and denouncing the moral excesses of the Republicans. At the approach of the Presidential election it was frequently mentioned by South Carolina leaders that the votes of commercial centers such as New York City and Philadelphia, and the towns and cities of New England were expected to go against Lincoln, but, as William Elliott wrote, "the fanatical spirit of the interior districts" would nevertheless push those states into the Republican column.[10] Both Lawrence Keitt and textile mill founder William Gregg had looked particularly to state elections in Connecticut, since few other states had prospered as much on Southern commerce. Even there, Keitt observed, "capital carried the cities for us—but fanaticism carried the rural districts." South Carolinians were not preparing to secede from one of the few groups in Northern society they considered trustworthy, nor were they to secede because of an antipathy for capitalism. Planters were prosperous, the commercial class had joined the revolution, and a Camden editor correctly noted, "there are few slaveholders who are not, to a considerable extent, capitalists."[11]

It should have been no surprise to hear the state's business leaders adding their voices to the general chorus. What did sur-

---

to December 1860, written by a Charleston businessman. Internal evidence suggests the author of this valuable account was the book merchant James J. McCarter.

[10] William Elliott to his wife, September 18, 1860, Derby & Jackson [New York Publishers] to William Elliott, December 28, 1860, and William Elliott to his son Ralph, n.d. [October 1860], all in Elliott-Gonzales Papers, SHC; D. W. Lee to Thomas Green Clemson, November 13, 1860, Thomas Green Clemson Papers, Clemson; F. W. Byrdsall to J. H. Hammond, November 20, 1860, Hammond Papers, LC; Samuel Gourdin to Henry Gourdin, December 10, 1860, Gourdin Papers, LC.

[11] Keitt to J. H. Hammond, October 23, 1860, Hammond Papers, LC; Speech of William Gregg, in *Advertiser,* November 14, 1860; Camden *Weekly Journal,* November 6, 1860.

prise and delight secessionists was the extent of the enthusiasm. "So unanimous is public sentiment," wrote planter William Grimball, "that in the city of Charleston[,] formerly from its commercial interests the most union loving and conservative portion of the State, no other candidates will present themselves to the people" in the coming special convention election than outright disunionists. Of course, after doing battle with these moderates for thirty years, some secessionists doubted until the last that the remarkable degree of unanimity would last. Frank DeBow, who matched his brother James in devotion to the cause, was startled by the unbroken appearance of radicalism in Charleston after Lincoln's election. "I think there are too many flags hung out," he wrote, "too much unnecessary show—it looks more like excitement than real solid substance. I am afraid that many of those who hang out flags are afraid their fidelity will be doubted."[12]

While there was certainly some truth in DeBow's suspicions, there is even more evidence to suggest the "real solid substance" of the radicalization of the business community. After the Presidential election and the action of the legislature there were frequent references by former moderates to the fact that the political divisions of the past were no longer either relevant or tolerable, and that there was now "but one party [including] the men of property," The people of Charleston were impressing themselves and the whole state with their zeal. "The merchants & their clerks, the lawyers, the mechanics & all classes of business men, after working all day for money to support their families, drill nearly half the night in order to be able to defend them," wrote one visitor to the city. As substantial and gratifying was the financial support forthcoming from the state's banks. On the day the legislature in Columbia was ratifying the call for a December state convention, secessionist William Lawton reported to Miles his success in gaining pledges of support from key bankers in Charleston. "I determined to make the effort first, at our own Board [The Merchant's Bank of Charleston], so as to feel its temper, [and] the response was beyond my anticipation." Funds

12 William Grimball to "Elizabeth," November 13, 1860, John Berkeley Grimball Papers, SHC; Franklin to J. D. B. DeBow, November 19, 1860, James D. B. DeBow Papers, DU.

were allocated in support of state mobilization, and Lawton was confident that other banks would follow suit. *"All here for our cause."* Much the same response occurred in the state capital, as the *Tri-Weekly Southern Guardian* reported that the directors of the Columbia Exchange Bank had voted unanimously to purchase a large share of the bonds being issued "for the purpose of arming the State." The radical persuasion had done its work. As early as September, Arthur Simkins could declare it "a cause of congratulation to know that from the mountains to the seaboard, inclusive of the mercantile and moneyed interests of the State, South Carolina awaits events with a calm preparation of spirit to meet the danger she may not be able to avert."[13]

— 2 —

Fear of secession, state sectionalism, non-slaveholders, merchants—these were only some of the potentially divisive factors apprehended by South Carolina secessionists. For this reason they were unrelenting in their efforts to establish an irresistible motion towards disunion. The half-conscious propaganda efforts of the summer and early fall were more and more regarded as inadequate as the impending election of Lincoln had grown closer. Radicals began to see the need for a more organized method of remaining in touch with the other slave states, and, more importantly, of reinforcing the crisis atmosphere building towards the election of a "Black" Republican. These desires became formalized in the "1860 Association."

The organization grew out of secret discussions among Charleston leaders in late September.[14] Supported by "some of the wealthiest, most influential men in the state, such as the Lowndes, Hey-

[13] Meta Morris Grimball to ———, November 18, [1860], Grimball Papers, DU; Edward Laight Wells to Thomas L. Wells, December 6, [1860], in *Mason Smith Family Letters, 1860–1868,* edited by Daniel E. Huger Smith, Alice R. Smith and Arney R. Childs (Columbia, 1950), pp. 3–4; William Lawton to W. P. Miles, November 13, 1860, Miles Papers, SHC; Columbia *Tri-Weekly Southern Guardian,* November 26, 1860; *Advertiser,* September 26, 1860. As will be seen, Simkins himself had been radicalized during the summer.
[14] Isaac Hayne to Hammond, September 15, 1860, Hammond Papers, LC; Simms to Miles, September 28, [1860], Miles Papers, SHC.

wards, Middletons and Aikens,"[15] the group quickly assumed a formal structure, with a president, William D. Porter, and an executive committee, chaired by Robert N. Gourdin. By the end of October the "1860 Association" had emerged as the most aggressive publisher of secessionist pamphlets in the South, and the center of agitation for military and psychological preparation for disunion. According to a public letter issued by Gourdin in November, the objects of the association were to organize committees of correspondence throughout the South, to distribute literature in the Southern states "designed to awaken them to a conviction of their danger and to urge the necessity of resisting Northern and Federal aggression," and to provide information on the military condition of the state for the use of the legislature. The association feared the possibility of Northern conciliation and, Gourdin concluded, "it is necessary to defeat it." William Tennant, Jr., secretary and treasurer of the group, made their propaganda goals clearer when he told Congressman Bonham that the main object was to unite Southerners for secession "through the publishing of strong and incendiary pamphlets that will stir the sleeping South out of the lethargy fostered by the poison called love of Union," and to prepare the Southern states for defense against the "contemplated emergencies of Lincoln's election."[16]

The publications of the association were a powerful expression of the disunion argument, and, widely distributed as they were, certainly contributed to the goals set by Gourdin and Tennant.[17] Among the best known were two pamphlets by John Townsend, an Edisto Island planter, who had opposed Nullification in 1833 and secession in 1851.[18] Townsend wrote to Milledge Bonham in

[15] C. Fitzimmons to Hammond, October 19, 1860, Hammond Papers, USC.
[16] Robert N. Gourdin, "Public Letter from the 1860 Association," November 19, 1860, Archibald Rutledge Papers, SHC; William Tennant, Jr., to M. L. Bonham, October 16, 1860, Milledge L. Bonham Papers, USC.
[17] Over 166,000 pamphlets were distributed by late November. Cauthen, *South Carolina Goes to War*, p. 35.
[18] Tract No. 1 of the Association was Townsend's *The South Alone Should Govern the South. And African Slavery Should Be Controlled by those Only Who are Friendly to It* (Charleston, 1860); Tract No. 4 was Townsend's *The Doom of Slavery in the Union: Its Safety Out of It; An Address to the Edisto Island Vigilant Association, October 29, 1860* (Charleston, 1860).

October, asking permission to join the association, and to publish his own articles as part of the program. The private thoughts he expressed to Bonham differed from the tone of his pamphlets only on the question of means; before the election of Lincoln, Townsend still believed that cooperative secession was the best way to protect the South. But there was no discrepancy in Townsend's public and private comments on the reasons for disunion. "Submission to the rule of a party who have openly declared themselves our enemies and that they intend to destroy our property and (what is worse that they intend to degrade us and our families to an equality with our slaves), *submission* I say," he repeated to Bonham, "under such circumstances is a thought to be entertained not for a moment." A majority of the citizens of South Carolina would choose the perils of separate state action to acquiescence to a Republican administration.[19] Other material published by the "1860 Association" dealt specifically with those elements in Southern society which were deemed weakest for the coming revolution. Endless pictures were drawn of the inevitability of abolition at the hands of the Federal Government, and of the awful consequences of the destruction of slavery, in terms of its physical threat, the pecuniary loss, the "reign" of Negro idleness and crime, and ultimately, of political, social, and sexual equality with the white race. The hopes and fears of Southern Unionists and merchants were lambasted, and the most potent source for division, the up-country non-slaveholder, came in for special attention.[20] Rhett, a contributor and sponsor of the association, admitted that the Southern border states were not a prime target of their labors. He told Edmund Ruffin that the slave states outside of the lower South could "only be managed by the course pursued at Charleston & Richmond & Baltimore in the conventions." And what was that course? "They must be made to choose between the North & South and then they will

See also Simms to Hammond, October 9, [1860], Hammond Papers, LC; *Simms Letters*, IV, 246–47, note.
[19] J[ohn] Townsend to M. L. Bonham, October 16, 1860, Bonham Papers, USC.
[20] [James Dunwoody Brownson DeBow], *The Interest in Slavery of the Southern Non-Slaveholder* (Charleston, 1860). The publications of the Association are described in Cauthen, *South Carolina Goes to War*, pp. 34–43.

redeem themselves but not before." In fact, the approach of the "1860 Association" towards the attitude of the people of the cotton states was similar. Its efforts were aimed at broadening and intensifying the campaign begun during the summer to compel the South to choose secession as the only alternative to submission to Lincoln.[21]

$-3-$

Skillful and effective as the "1860 Association" doubtless was, the most powerful force at work in South Carolina contributing to the remarkable unanimity of sentiment in December was not the asseverations of her leaders, but the basic fear of the Negro. The reemergence of a profusion of news stories detailing the activities of suspected abolitionists in the South during the summer campaign has often been noted. The correlation between many of the newspapers that most readily printed such tales, and support for the Breckinridge candidacy was accepted as part of the evidence for an interpretation of secession which emphasized the irrationality and pointlessness of disunionism. This school of thought also tended to see the existence of a conservative conspiracy at work to subvert the wishes of an essentially Unionist majority. One historian, for example, entitled his discussion of Southern fears of insurrection in 1860 "The Uses of Emotionalism."[22] There is little doubt that terrible stories of black unrest, and abolitionist infiltration were seized upon by advocates of disunion without regard for their veracity. And the reason was that there was no more

[21] R. B. Rhett to Ruffin, October 20, 1860, Edmund Ruffin Papers, SHC. See also E. C. Anderson (September 30, 1860) and John Richardson (December 14, 1860) to Robert N. Gourdin concerning the "1860 Association," Gourdin-Young Papers, Emory. Gourdin also led a special fund appeal in mid-November to support the continued publication of Rhett's Charleston *Mercury*. R. N. Gourdin, *et al.*, to O. M. Dantzler, November 13, 1860, O. M. Dantzler Papers, Calhoun County Historical Commission.

[22] Ollinger Crenshaw, *The Slave States in the Presidential Election of 1860* (Baltimore, 1945), Chapter 5. Until recent years the distinguished work of Avery O. Craven provided the best statement of this interpretation. In particular, see his *The Coming of the Civil War* (New York, 1942), and *The Growth of Southern Nationalism, 1848–1861*, Volume VI of Wendell Holmes Stephenson and E. Merton Coulter (eds.), *A History of the South* (Baton Rouge, 1953).

potent weapon with which to prove the perfidy of Northerners and the disadvantages and dangers of remaining in the Union; such stories merely played upon the Southern fear of the Negro, they did not create it. The fear-of-insurrection-abolition syndrome was the *core* of the secession persuasion, not its vehicle. The multiplicity of news items reporting incendiary activities of slaves and abolitionists was not the fabrication of a segment of the Southern elite, but a natural result and expression of the anxiety which existed in the mind of the entire white population.[23]

The apprehension over declining subordination among South Carolina Negroes which had been excited by the attack at Harpers Ferry did not abate in 1860. In January, for example, abolition agents were still in danger of falling victim to vigilance lynching in Pendleton. February saw the sea island of St. Helena criss-crossed by extra patrols, as the island was distressed by rumors of the discovery of Sharp's rifles and meddlesome abolitionists. Letters from Yorkville in March told of troubling numbers of slaves running away from farms in the piedmont district. An April news item frantically reported the discovery of an obviously fictitious "bloody conspiracy against the peace and safety" of Kingstree and Williamsburg district "by a band of Northern Abolitionists headed by the Northern teachers that were some time driven from their midst under most suspicious circumstances." In May the tiny village of Elmsville in tidewater Colleton district was disturbed by suspected slave arson. As the Democracy approached final disruption in June, newspapers and correspondence reported a growing number of public meetings called to organize volunteer patrol and militia companies, and to inspire old ones to renewed activity. These were dangerous times, an officer told his company of Edgefield Riflemen, for some "John Pike Brown the Second may be in our midst aiding and counseling

---

[23] It was no secret that reports concerning slave unrest were exaggerated. The Edgefield Vigilant Society declared, "That while we do not doubt that the rumors of evil are in some instances exaggerated, and while we apprehend no immediate insecurity from the nature of our peculiar domestic institution we believe that the great duty of the freemen of the South is to guard at the outset against any development that may tend to weaken that institution in the eyes either of its friends or its enemies." *Advertiser*, September 19, 1860.

and urging our slaves to an immediate and bloody insurrection."[24] Still hoping for the impossible reunification of the Democratic party, Arthur Simkins's language in the *Advertiser* had become very blunt. Southerners must be made to see that the true enemy was the Republican party.

> Men of the South! think of your threatened firesides, your menaced wives and daughters, and beware of this useless strife. . . . We should remember that the social system upon which the wealth and power of the South depend, is yet comparatively a new one. We believe it to be the best ever devised. But it has enemies by the thousands and hundreds all over Christendom.[25]

Through the hot summer months, reports of fiendish, extensive conspiracies, even in distant Texas, increased in number, alongside details of vigilance justice meted out closer to home.[26] The peace and quiet which had only recently returned to St. Helena was suddenly broken in July by the murder of an overseer by his slaves. In Newberry a special committee was established in mid-August to reinforce vagrancy patrol laws in the wake of evidence of "tampering" with local blacks.[27] Political propagandizing in the state more and more assumed a military character, as militia and volunteer companies began to muster, drill, and patrol with greater regularity. Political leaders increasingly adopted military reviews and drills to exhort the local populace to prepare themselves spiritually and physically for the election of Lincoln, and to strengthen community defense against invasion by sus-

---

[24] John D. Ashmore to his brother, January 12, 1860, in Taylor, "Letters Dealing with the Secession Movement"; E. I. Wallace to J. D. B. DeBow, February 10, 1860, J. D. B. DeBow Papers, DU; Micah Jenkins to John Jenkins, March 19, 1860, John Jenkins Papers, USC; *Advertiser*, April 25, 1860, quoting the Clarendon *Banner;* David Gavin MS Diary, SHC, May 2, 1860; speech of Thomas G. Bacon, June 4, in the *Advertiser*, June 13, 1860.

[25] *Advertiser*, June 23, 1860.

[26] Information on the frightening insurrection panic in northern Texas appeared frequently in the *Courier, Mercury,* and *Advertiser* from early August on. John Townsend also reprinted letters from the region in *The Doom of Slavery*, pp. 34–38.

[27] E. I. Wallace to J. D. B. DeBow, July 22, 1860, DeBow Papers, DU; *Advertiser*, August 22, 1860.

pected abolition emissaries. Many who expressed the belief that the people seemed utterly apathetic regarding the fateful political canvass, were unconscious of the militaristic context of political persuasion going on, or of the political implications of the increasing popular participation in vigilance and regular military operations. It was in part on the dusty regimental fields outside of Edgefield Court House, and Georgetown, and Spartanburg, and dozens of similar unassuming spots, that the conversion of nonbelievers and the emotional preparation of all for the election of Lincoln was accomplished.[28]

By September most spokesmen for moderation in South Carolina had experienced the conversion to disunionism. Arthur Simkins was virtually compelled to abandon his stand for Douglas following the Senator's famous speech at Norfolk, Virginia on August 25. In answer to a question submitted from the audience, Douglas vigorously invoked the name of Andrew Jackson to repudiate the idea of a peaceable acquiesence to secession. With other Unionists, Simkins had been forced to retreat to progressively narrower grounds by the action of the North.[29] But it was not Douglas's nationalism alone which destroyed Simkins's earlier position. A review of his newspaper during the summer and fall reveals a rising spirit of extremism throughout the latter half of the year. He became a leader in the movement to promote vigilance committees and more aggressive patrols of neighborhood plantations. He printed more fear-of-insurrection news items. Finally, in late September he was ready to stand alongside Ashmore in prefering the dangerous solution of separate state secession to permitting the abolition of what the piedmont congressman had termed "that institution which was the life-blood and heart of our social system."[30]

[28] *Advertiser,* March 21, July 18, and August 15, 1860; Camden *Weekly Journal,* August 7, 1860; Yorkville *Enquirer,* August 16, 1860; Spartanburg *Spartan,* August 30, 1860; Anderson *Intelligencer,* August 11, 1860; Benjamin A. Allston to Henrietta Simons, July 6, 1860, R. F. W. Allston Papers, SCHS; Benjamin Allston to James Johnston Pettigrew, July 8, 1860, Pettigrew Family Papers, SHC; William C. Round MS Diary, in Louis Round Wilson Papers, SHC, August 19, 1860.
[29] *Advertiser* August–October 1860, See also Allan Nevins, *The Emergence of Lincoln,* 2 volumes (New York, 1950), II, 293–94.
[30] *Advertiser,* September 26, 1860; *ibid.,* November 7, 1860, quoting the

It was the implacable fear of losing total control over the Negroes, combined with the energetic mobilization of political sentiment going on all over the state that was converting men like Arthur Simkins to radicalism.

For those who had sensed the flush of panic which swept across a region experiencing a real or rumored sample of slave unrest, there was no need for special sermons or political exhortation over the meaning of Lincoln's election. Congressman Lawrence M. Keitt could claim such a personal visitation, for in February his brother was horribly murdered by slaves while sick in bed on his plantation in Florida. Keitt was "relieved" to learn that the tragedy had not been committed by the house servants, but by field hands; he also claimed to be satisfied by the news that one of the accused blacks had been dragged out of jail by the townspeople and hanged on the spot. Nevertheless, Keitt was deeply shaken by the murder.[31] The rumors of slave insubordination, the reports of abolitionist emissaries being caught and whipped, the details of vigilance committees and militia patrols organizing and increasing their activities which multiplied in the latter half of

Anderson *Intelligencer.* A similar case was that of James Johnston Pettigrew. He came to Charleston over a decade before with a pronounced disgust for South Carolina radicalism. Life in his adopted home worked a subtle change in his outlook, but he remained the outstanding opponent of slave trade advocates in the state, and a supporter of the national Democracy. Following the disruption of the party in June his pessimism increased, and by late October he was telling his brother William that Lincoln's election would necessitate revolution. "You know I am no fire-eater," Pettigrew wrote, "but I must sincerely assure you that in my opinion the continuance of the present form of the Constitution under a settled anti-slavery rule is a consummation to be avoided by all means short of destruction." See Pettigrew to ———, April 14, 1849, and [June] 29, 1849, *id.* to James Johnston Pettigrew, January 1, 185[5], and *id.* to William Pettigrew, August 16, and October 24, 1860, all in Pettigrew Family Papers, SHC; and *id.* to Daniel Moreau Barringer, April 15, 1860, D. M. Barringer Papers, SHC.

[31] Robert Barnwell Rhett telegraphed the news to Miles, n.d., Miles Papers, SHC. See also Lawrence Keitt to Susan Sparks, February 29, 1860, L. M. Keitt Papers, DU; George Bryan to Miles, February 24, 1860, Miles Papers, SHC. Keitt's animosity towards the Republican party was deepened when he read in the Orangeburg *Southron* of May 21 that his brother's home district had been marked by John Brown on his map of Florida. See Elmer Don Herd, Jr., "Chapters from the Life of a Southern Chevalier: Lawrence Massilon Keitt's Congressional Years, 1853–1860," (unpublished master's thesis, the University of South Carolina, 1958) p. 164.

the year—all of these events, coupled with the impending election of a Republican President, drove Keitt toward hysteria.

> If Lincoln is elected—[he wrote James Hammond] what then? I am in earnest. I'd cut loose through fire and blood if nescessary [sic]—See—poison in the wells in Texas and fire for the Houses in Alabama—Our Negroes are being enlisted in politics—With poison and fire how can we stand it? I confess this new feature alarms me more than even everything in the past. If Northern men get access to our negros [sic] to advise poison and the torch we must prevent it at every hazard. The future will not "down" because we are blind.[32]

— 4 —

Just as the spontaneous propaganda movement of the summer was complemented by the organization of the "1860 Association," the sudden sprouting of militia and patrol efforts received formal recognition and direction from an agency founded at about the same time. The constitution of the "Minute Men for the Defence of Southern Rights" was drafted in Columbia on October 7. The justification was clearly set forth: the election of a "Black Republican President will be a virtual subversion of the constitution of the United States, and . . . submission to such a result must end in the destruction of our property and the ruin of our land." Practically, it was an organization to promote the formation of volunteer infantry and cavalry companies throughout the state.[33]

[32] Keitt to Hammond, September 10, 1860, Hammond Papers, LC. See also Allan MacFarlane to Robert N. Gourdin, October 18, 1860, Gourdin-Young Papers, Emory.
[33] Minute Men Association Paper, USC; E. J. Arthur to Langdon Cheves, October 8, 1860, Cheves Family Papers, SCHS; Henry William Ravenel MS Journal, USC, October 22 and 30, 1860; Robert F. W. Allston to his son Charles, November 8, 1860, R. F. W. Allston Papers, SCHS. On October 9 Hammond was informed by G. D. Tillman that a secret society called "Minute Men" was being formed, preparing "to march at a minute's notice to Washington for the purpose of preventing Lincoln's inauguration in case of his election." Tillman claimed that ex-Governor James Adams, Francis W. Pickens, and Robert Barnwell Rhett were the organizers, and that the association aimed at thwarting Hammond's reelection to the Senate. This doubtless is the source of Hammond's repeated references to a secret plan to forcibly prevent Lincoln's inauguration. There is no evidence of the veracity

The need for such an independent military organization arose from the inefficiency of the decrepit militia structure in South Carolina. "Minute Men" companies functioned in a similar manner to their official, but increasingly ineffective, models.[34] They provided a system for molding volunteer companies to be used at the call of the governor; they were also a military arm to assist the burgeoning number of vigilance committees in their work of patrolling plantations, apprehending suspicious whites, and examining them before self-constituted vigilance society juries. A network of extra-legal slave law enforcement bodies and militia had sprung up almost spontaneously on soil which had often proved fertile for such growth in the past.[35]

Many of those who called for the formation of these militia and patrol groups denied any intention to commit the local citizenry to separate secession. As one "Minute Man" explained, the only aim was to prepare the minds, arms, and estates of the people of South Carolina for a defense against the domination of "mongrel tyrants who mean . . . to reduce you and your wives and your daughters on a level with the very slaves you buy and sell." The political implication of such warnings was never subtle. After the election of Lincoln, proponents of militia and vigilance organization more frankly admitted that secession was their ultimate goal. No matter how effective local surveillance could be, Carolinians

---

of Tillman's charges. G. D. Tillman to Hammond, October 9, 1860, Hammond Papers, LC.

[34] On the organization of vigilance patrols and societies and "Minute Men" companies in typical communities, see the Edgefield *Advertiser*, September 19, October 17, 31, and November 7, 1860; Spartanburg *Spartan*, October 11, 1860; James H. Hammond MS Plantation Journal, USC, November 10, 1860; Branchville Vigilant Association MS Journal, USC; G. Allen Wardlaw to Samuel McGowan, December 2, 1860, Samuel McGowan Papers, USC; John S. Ryan to ———, December 4, 1860, John S. Ryan Papers, USC. It is interesting to note that William Gregg organized a "Minute Man" company in his cotton mill town Graniteville on November 9, 1860 (*Advertiser*, November 14, 1860).

[35] For descriptions of the cursory and abusive justice administered by these extra-legal agencies, see David Gavin MS Diary, SHC, October 29, and December 31, 1860; *Advertiser*, November 28, and December 12, 1860; H. Milton Blake to Samuel McGowan, December 1, 1860, Samuel McGowan Papers, USC; Jeanette Holst to Isabella Woodruff, December 16, 1860, and January 6, 1861, Woodruff Papers, DU.

were convinced that slave unrest would never be quelled until the federal tie with the "abolitionized" North was broken. The present commotion in national politics inevitably "works its way down to the slave population," the Yorkville *Enquirer* explained, "they gather fom one another vague rumors about an abolitionist being elected who is going to set them free," and the result was an intolerable state of recalcitrance.[35]

During the final six weeks, from the action of the legislature to the declaration of secession, the pitch of excitement in the state rose to an incredible level, and with it rose the fear of slave insurrection. The centuries-old pattern of frightened men denying fear, of white Southerners rejecting the notion that one's own blacks could be anything but "naturally" tranquil, save for outside agitators, persisted. On the day that Charleston learned of Lincoln's election Jane Pettigrew, niece of James Louis Petigru, warned her husband that "The negroes are all of opinion that Lincoln is to come here to free them," but she adamantly assured him that "they are perfectly quiet & *nothing* is apprehended from them." Yet Charleston was alive with anxious vigilance patrols, drilling militia, and ceaseless rumors and evidences of black unrest. Writing at the same time from his plantation north of the city, Henry William Ravenel described the great "alarm among the people of servile insurrection." Ravenel refused to believe that there could be a general, concerted insurrection because of the lack of communication between plantations; and, of course, "the attachment of slaves to their masters is too strong to permit a suspicion of such a design." Nevertheless, "there should be

---

[35] *Advertiser*, October 31, 1860; Yorkville *Enquirer*, November 22, 1860. A good example of the process occurred in Limestone Springs, Spartanburg District. A vigilance association was formed in September to patrol the locale. In early November two volunteer militia companies were organized, and addressed an appeal to the governor. "This Section of our Dist. (& indeed we might add, our whole Dist.) is far behind the Central & Coast Dists. in the doctrine of "States Rights,"—& more especially, in that of "Separate action" on the part of our State. We are endeavoring to arouse our Sec to a sense of our true position." For this reason, they concluded, "we set about organizing a Com[pany] of Min[ute] men." "Limestone Southern Rights Guards" to Gov. W. H. Gist, November 12, 1860, Muster Rolls, South Carolina Confederate Organizations, National Archives; Spartanburg *Spartan*, November 22, 1860.

much vigilance & police regulations . . . to keep off all suspicious & designing persons."[36]

The same dynamic operated day after day: reports of slave insurrections coming in from North Carolina, St. Petersburg, Florida, everywhere and nowhere; communities panicking; no one disputing that the Negroes of Charleston, or Camden, or every other town believed "that this election decides their freedom";[37] letters from militia officers unable to organize the men in their neighborhoods into companies for the service of the governor, because "They dread more danger at home than abroad and will not on that account, leave their families."[38] These many apprehensions and alarms seemed justified time and again by the revelation of abolitionist (or more likely, restless slave) activity from Charleston to Pickens. South Carolinians were to spend many uneasy Christmas eves in the next few years, and the celebration in 1860 was no exception. Letters written by a farmer's wife in Abbeville district described how the holiday was spent there. "I am happy to inform you that christmas has come and gone and we are still on the troubled waves of existence," she wrote. "The men have been very vigilant indeed, parties of them have patroled nearly the whole night every night during the week." A suspected abolitionist was captured early in the week, and soon after news came of "an alarming plot" discovered in a nearby village. "Five negroes are to be hung, twenty white men

[36] Jane Pettigrew to Charles Pettigrew, November 7, 1860, Pettigrew Family Papers, SHC; Henry William Ravenel MS Journal, USC, November 8, 1860. On the other hand, it was very generally understood that the slaves were aware of the wave of fear sweeping across the South, and more specifically, aware that insurrections were said to be occurring in many localities. The editor of the Laurens *Herald* (September 7, 1860) believed that "Cuffee" had learned of these things happening even in far-off Texas, for " 'Nigger news' is proverbial for its swiftness and exaggeration." And the Richland Grand Jury cited those "recent disturbances in Texas, and of their possible recurrence here," to support its demand for expanded patrol and militia legislation. Grand Jury Presentments, Richland District, Fall Term, 1860 (October 31), SCArc.

[37] Jane Pettigrew to Charles Pettigrew, November 7, 1860, Pettigrew Family Papers, SHC; Mary W. Milling to James S. Milling, November 23, 1860, James S. Milling Papers, SHC.

[38] Alex C. Haskell to Charles W. Hutson, [December 1860], Charles W. Hutson Papers, SHC.

implicated all *southern born*, the poor white *trash* who have associated with negroes and are jealous of the higher classes and think insurection [*sic*] will place all on a footing and they get some plunder in the bargain."[39] Still, Caroline Gilman, wife of Unitarian minister Samuel Gilman, calmly told her daughters that there was no alarm among slaveholders, that no one avoided returning to his plantation, that the "customary Christmas revels" would go on, and that slaves would dance and sing as before. In his final annual message President Buchanan alluded to "fire & poison" being carried into the South by Northerners. "Without interference from them," Mrs. Gilman assured her daughters, "there is no apprehension, but if a planter knew that his slaves were tampered with by incendiaries the case would be altered."[40] To be sure, not every South Carolinian accepted this comforting thesis. As the danger of insurrection seemed to come closer, many frantic appeals for better vigilance by "our District police" were accompanied by criticism of the "general confidence in the integrity of our slave population. . . . The experience of other sections demonstrates that this confidence may easily be misplaced."[41] On the whole, however, South Carolinians continued to believe what they wanted to believe, and trusted in the fidelity of their bondsmen in accordance with their idealized vision of race relations long after that faith proved to be a dubious warrant of conduct.

— 5 —

The recurrence of apparently self-contradictory lines of belief or behavior was nowhere more obvious than in the coexistence of

[39] "Sister," to "Julia," December 30, [1860], Lalla Pelot Papers, DU.
[40] Caroline Gilman to her daughters, December 16, 1860, Caroline Howard Gilman Papers, SCHS. See also [James Warley Miles], *The Relation Between the Races at the South* (Charleston, 1861), p. 14.
[41] Yorkville *Enquirer*, September 20, 1860. "Proof" of the precarious state of race controls might be no farther away than a Bible. The Newberry *Rising Sun* (August 29, 1860) noticed a case involving a group of runaway slaves apprehended, all of whom could read. "In the bible of one of them marks and references were found which leads conclusively to the belief that he had been misapplying the true meaning of certain passages of the scripture," indicating the "evil consequences" of permitting slaves to read even Holy Writ.

the militarism which pervaded the entire state, with the wide-spread confidence that there would be no coercion by the Federal Government following secession. The question of the interminable agreements, real and imagined, which were struck within the Buchanan Administration, or of whether the President was guilty of treason, stupidity, or rather a wise masterly inactivity, has been fully treated.[42] What is indisputable is that the overwhelming majority of South Carolinians believed in the imminence of a peaceable acquiescence by the North to the secession of the state.

They had good reason to think so. The correspondence of all the state's leaders was replete with letters from Northern con-servatives giving assurances that there would be no attempt to restrain the secession movement by force if their erring sister states chose disunion.[43] Immediately after the act of disunion was ratified these disclaimers continued to pour in, often, like Boston's Charles Eliot Norton, giving congratulations and approval, or, like Thomas Bell, an Illinois farmer, pledging their support in putting down "this ungodly howling of Mr. Lincoln's Nigar Equality."[44] Similar disavowals of hostility before secession were daily repeated by such future copperhead newspapers as the New York *Herald*. And, of course, there was the famous, and since disputed offer by Horace Greeley's antislavery New York *Tribune* to let the slave states "depart in peace"; however ambiguous the

[42] The involved history of the relations between Buchanan, his cabinet, and representatives of South Carolina is set forth lucidly by Roy Franklin Nichols, *The Disruption of American Democracy* (New York, 1962), chapters 20 and 21; and Robert Nicholas Olsberg, "William Henry Trescot: The Crisis of 1860," (unpublished master's thesis, the University of South Carolina) pp. 45–82.

[43] For example, see the numerous letters from Northern conservatives in the papers of William Porcher Miles, November-January 1861; J. F. Hammond to his father, James, October 16, 1860, F. W. Byrdsall to J. H. Hammond, November 20, 1860, in Hammond Papers, LC; John Dix, *et al*, to the peo-ple of the Southern states, November 10, 1860, Manton Marble Papers, LC; and letters to Henry Gourdin from J. T. Welsman, December 12, 1860 and Richard Lathers, December 19, 1860, Gourdin Papers, LC.

[44] Charles Eliot Norton to W. P. Miles, December 22, 1860, Miles Papers, SHC; Thomas Bell to Francis W. Pickens, January 15, 1861, F. W. Pickens Papers, DU. See also James Gibbes to Pickens, January 6, 1861, in Pickens-Bonham Papers, LC; and J. S. Potter to Pickens, March 30, 1861, E. M. Law Papers, SHC.

"offer," it was promptly seized upon by Carolina editors to demonstrate the probability of Northern acquiescence to secession.[45]

There were more dependable guarantees than these. Northern
Democrats, who had been fuming at the Presidential election defeat which could have been averted, began speaking many
thoughtless words to the South at the approach of secession, assuring against any support for military repression. Ohio congressman Clement Vallandigham gained considerable notoriety by his
opposition to the war for the Union, but even before the secession
of South Carolina he was loud in his promise that he would never
cast a vote to maintain a civil war; and Vallandigham was only
the most vocal of a significant number of Northern Democrats
who considered coercion a more heinous crime than secession.[46]

Pledges of non-interference came from the very highest political
circles as well. In early October James Hammond's son reported a
conversation with Joseph Lane, in which the Oregon Senator and
Vice-Presidential candidate expressed the remarkable opinion that
"he would not be surprised, and wished to see a Minister Pleni-
potentiary" from an independent South Carolina coming to Washington within a month. "[Lane] desired me confidentially to say
to you: let South Carolina sustain her honor in this crisis, maintain firmly all her constitutional rights, and by prompt action
secure the cooperation of an immense body of sympathizers at
the North." Hammond's son, a cadet at West Point where Lane
was paying a visit, was now convinced, as he had not been before,
that the best time for secession was during the Buchanan Administration. The President will "take no action until the matters
are fairly discussed in Congress," young Hammond accurately

[45] New York *Herald*, November-December 1860; Laurens *Herald*, November 30, 1860; Yorkville *Enquirer*, November 22, 1860. Greeley's sincerity in
offering peaceable secession is debated by David M. Potter, "Horace Greeley and Peaceable Secession," *Journal of Southern History*, VII (May 1941),
145–59; and Thomas N. Bonner, "Horace Greeley and the Secession Movement," *Mississippi Valley Historical Review*, XXXVIII (December 1952),
425–44.
[46] Vallandigham to Editor, Cincinnati *Enquirer*, November 10, 1860, Clement L. Vallandigham Papers, SHC. See also *The Record of Hon. C. L. Vallandigham on Abolition, the Union, and the Civil War* (Columbus, Ohio,
1863); and James L. Vallandigham, *A Life of Clement L. Vallandigham*
(Baltimore, 1872).

predicted, and "it leaves ample space for the Seceders to organize themselves and for all parties to come to a clear understanding." This kind of reasoning played an important part in the decision to strike before the end of the year.[47]

Such critical assurances continued right up to the moment of secession. On December 19, Congressman Bonham reported from Washington that Andrew Johnson had just delivered a combative speech denouncing the secession movement and promising not simply to crush the rebellion, but to reconstruct any state which attempted secession. According to Bonham, Johnson had declared that South Carolina would be "forced back as a conquered province." But Joe Lane spoke for more of his party colleagues when he rebuked Johnson and swore that "he & other Northern democrats will be there to meet Johnson & the invaders with their bloody flags."[48] More interesting than Lane's militance were the sincere and quiet efforts of those Democrats, North and South, who considered disunion inevitable, to help make the disruption nonviolent. Typical perhaps were men like Thomas Caute Reynolds, a Missouri politician who, on December 15 wrote this remarkable message to William Porcher Miles from Washington:

I think I told you yesterday that I had made endeavors to induce Senator Douglas to declare against coercion; in consequence of reports that he would soon make a speech in favor of it, some of the Mo. delegation requested me to see him again, and accordingly Mr. Rust of Ark. & I had an interview of four hours with him today. Without going into any detail or stating what views may have been advanced by any party to the interview, I can only say that my hope of a peaceable acquiescence of the Government in the secession of S. C.—since I presume that event inevitable—has considerably increased. I therefore write this to urge you to advocate the propriety of so arranging the secession movement that there shall be no collision with the federal government, even in the slightest particular, until *ample* time has been given it to consider its situation and hear from the tobacco (or border

---

[47] J. F. Hammond to his father, James, October 20, 1860, Hammond Papers, LC.
[48] Milledge Bonham to Miles, December 19, 1860, Miles Papers, SHC.

slave) states. The Legislature of Mo. meets on the 31st inst, a week before that of Virginia; and while our State has still a strong desire to maintain the union, I feel confident that the voice of her Legislature will be decided for the maintenance of peace so long as possible.—The main danger to it at present, would arise from any hasty attempt of S. C. to resume her sovereignty over the U.S. property within her borders.[49]

Whatever the final verdict history renders on the role played by Buchanan in the secession crisis, one thing cannot be doubted: the people of South Carolina, from those in the highest echelon of the state to the great body of citizens, believed that a mutual agreement had been reached between state and national authorities which would protect them from any military action to thwart secession. To be sure, South Carolina had contributed her own share of bluster in an effort to prevent coercion. On November 24, for example, Barnwell Rhett sent a letter to Buchanan asserting that the state would unquestionably leave the Union in the near future, and that it was in the hands of the President alone "to make the event peaceful or bloody. *If you send any more troops into Charleston Bay,*" Rhett warned, "*it will be bloody.*" Having thus tried to intimidate the President, Rhett sweetly concluded that his intention was simply to "inform," not to "direct," his judgment.[50]

A more reliable source of reassurance for Carolina politicians was the steady stream of messages from William Henry Trescot, the state's lone representative in Washington, virtually guaranteeing that Buchanan could not move against South Carolina without destroying his cabinet, and affirming in the most unequivocal terms the fact that the President pledged positively to avoid the use of force.[51] On the latter point, Buchanan had already em-

---

[49] Thomas Caute Reynolds to Miles, December 15, 1860, Miles Papers, SHC. See also N. J. Eaton to Reynolds, January 1, 1861, Thomas C. Reynolds Papers, NYHS. Reynolds was a native of South Carolina, and served as wartime lieutenant governor and governor-in-exile for the pro-Confederate Missouri state administration.

[50] R. B. Rhett to James Buchanan, November 24, 1860, Buchanan Papers, PaHS.

[51] For examples of the message Trescot was transmitting to the leaders of the state, see Trescot to Miles, n.d. [December], Miles Papers, SHC; *id.* to

ployed his annual message to the nation on December 3 to deny the power of the executive to resist a secession.[52] Moreover, the complicity of members of the cabinet in the secession movement, supplying guns and moral support, was an open secret, and at least as early as November 12, Governor Gist was authorizing frankly secessionist militia companies to organize under the Federal militia law, with federally supplied weapons.[53] But above all there was the formal agreement struck between Buchanan and a delegation of South Carolina congressmen in early December, by which (however the President thought he understood it) the leaders of the state confidently assumed that the Federal Government had acceded to the secession of South Carolina, at least until such time, as Buchanan himself noted, as "Commissioners had been appointed to meet with the Federal Government in relation to the public property & until the decision was known. I informed them," the President concluded in a memorandum of his conversation with the South Carolina delegation, "that if they (the forts) were assailed this would put them completely in the wrong & making [sic] them the authors of the Civil war."[54] It is

Robert N. Gourdin, November 17, 1860, Robert N. Gourdin Papers, DU; *id.* to [James Louis Petigru], December 14, 1860, Pettigrew Family Papers, SHC; *id.*, "Views Presented to Gen. [Lewis] Cass and the President," undated MS draft, Trescot Papers, USC. Governor Gist had asked Trescot to remain in the capitol as his agent. William Gist to F. W. Pickens, June 7, 1861, Law Papers, SHC.

[52] Philip Shriver Klein, *President James Buchanan, A Biography* (University Park, Pa., 1962), p. 362. The editor of the Columbia *Daily South Carolinian* believed that Buchanan's message had opened the door to a peaceful dissolution of the Union. *Spartan,* December 13, 1860, quoting the Columbia *Daily South Carolinian.*

[53] John G. Nicolay and John Hay, *Abraham Lincoln, A History,* 10 volumes (New York, 1890), II, 319–27; "Limestone Southern Rights Guards" to Governor W. H. Gist, November 12, 1860, Muster Rolls, South Carolina Confederate Organizations, National Archives; and letter from Samuel Y. Tripper and J. M. Harleston, Officers, Vigilant Rifles Company, to W. P. Miles, December 10, 1860, asking for assistance in obtaining arms from the Charleston Federal arsenal, Miles Papers, SHC.

[54] Congressmen McQueen, Miles, Bonham, Boyce, and Keitt to James Buchanan, December 9, 1860, and memorandum by Buchanan, dated December 10, written on the reverse side of this letter, evidently returned to Miles by the President, Miles Papers, SHC. The agreement read,

"In compliance with our Statement to you yesterday, we now express

true that this course of action was consistent with Buchanan's delineation of his executive authority, by which he was constitutionally impotent to arrest the secession of an errant state. According to the President, Congress alone had the authority to arbitrate the case. But one may speculate on the consequences of a less compromising stand before the declaration of secession. Civil war was delayed under the Buchanan interregnum. Yet secession was unquestionably hastened by what he said, and did not say.[55]

In the end the controversial issue of peaceable acquiescence to secession, like the motivation behind disunion itself, can only be understood as it was perceived by South Carolinians. The question of coercion was a significant one for them. As late as the convening of the state legislature at the moment of Lincoln's election there remained opposition to disunion, and still more, a reluctance to have the state secede hastily and alone. If the people were being asked to endorse an act of revolution, it was important to know whether or not that act would bring down the powerful arm of the nation to end it. The "signals" emanating from the North, from public meetings of conservative appeasers,

---

to you our strong convictions that neither the constituted authorities nor any body of the people of South Carolina will either attack or molest the U.S. Forts in the harbour of Charleston previously to the action of the convention, and we hope and believe not until an offer has been made through an accredited Representative to negotiate for an amicable arrangement of all matters between the State and the Federal Government, provided that no reinforcement shall be sent into those Forts & their relative military status remains as at present."

In his memorandum, Buchanan objected to the word "provided" as implying a binding agreement "which I would never make." Nevertheless his words and deeds were in accordance with this agreement.

[55] See Lewis Cass to Buchanan, December 12, 1860, draft of letter from Buchanan to Cass, December 17, 1860, draft of letter from Buchanan to Governor Francis W. Pickens, December 20, 1860, memorandum of conversation with Daniel Hamilton by Buchanan, December 20, 1860, and Robert W. Barnwell, James Adams, and James L. Orr to Buchanan, December 28, 1860, all in James Buchanan Papers, PaHS. In his reply to Cass's letter of resignation, the President explained, "believing as I do that no present necessity exists for a resort to force for the protection of the public property, it was impossible for me to have risked a collission [sic] of arms in the harbor of Charleston, and thereby defeated the reasonable hopes which I cherish of the final triumph of the Constitution and the Union."

from newspapers, from private correspondence, and from communications with the highest levels of the national government persuaded the people of South Carolina that there would be no coercion so long as aggression by the state was avoided. "Civil War," as Mrs. Gilman wrote, "was *foreign to the original plan.*"[56]

In any popular movement there are, of course, those who crave the thrilling release of violence. South Carolinians were hardly an exception to this. Many of her most rabid secessionists had been eager for the catharsis of bloodshed for decades. But most of the state's citizens, however enraged they were over the apparent threat to their physical and social security posed by the Republican party, sought not to destroy their Northern countrymen, but to get away from them, and to do so without unnecessary conflict.[57] Some Carolina leaders recognized the possibility that the North would ignore the state's rights logic of secession, and would forcibly resist it. Those who opposed disunion, or even separate state action, harped on the potential for war in their vain effort to divert the revolution. Other men seemed reconciled to conflict, believing a short war and the establishment of a Southern nation preferable to no war and no security.[58]

[56] Caroline Gilman to her daughters, December 16, 1860, Caroline Howard Gilman Papers, SCHS. Reiteration of this confidence may be seen in the Edmund Ruffin MS Diary, LC, November 10, 1860; Columbia *Tri-Weekly Southern Guardian,* November 29, 1860; Chesley D. Evans to his wife, December 28, 1860, Chesley D. Evans Papers, SHC; Mary W. Milling to J. S. Milling, January 18, 1861, J. S. Milling Papers, SHC; Thomas Green Clemson to Henry Gourdin, January 20, 1861, and William Henry Trescot to W. P. Miles, February 6, and March 3, 1861, in Miles Papers, SHC; and Emma Holmes MS Journal, SHC, February 13, 1861.

[57] There were few references to secession in the last weeks which did not stress the need for prudence to avoid a clash with the Federal Government. The caution stemmed from the desire to execute disunion in a calm, "constitutional" manner, to retain the sympathy of Northerners and especially Buchanan, to make secession as attractive as possible for the other slave states, and, of course, to prevent a needless war. See, for example, Thomas Green Clemson to J. H. Hammond, November 21, 1860, Hammond Papers, LC; Henry Gourdin to T. G. Clemson, November 22, 1860, Thomas G. Clemson Papers, Clemson; and Louis G. Young to Robert N. Gourdin, November 27, 1860, Gourdin-Young Papers, Emory.

[58] Jane to Charles Pettigrew, November 20, 1860, Pettigrew Family Papers, SHC; William Capers to Louis Manigault, October 31, 1860, Louis Manigault Papers, DU. The state was certainly preparing for possible war; the militia companies which had been forming since midsummer were not al-

Secessionists, however, could not permit the fear of civil war to take hold. The thought of war would trouble any sane group of men. For a slaveholding society it was truly frightening. The farm journal of David Harris gives an illustration of the meaning of war even in his up-country district. Harris was a slaveholder who operated a modest farm in Spartanburg. He had welcomed the secession of his state and spurned any suggestion of coercion. Finally, by late February 1861, he began to see the "probability of war," and his reaction, though belated, was typical. "I fear that we will have a long Civil, Bloody war—and perhaps an inserections [sic] among the slaves—" he wrote, "The Lord save us from such a horrid war.[59] Because such fears had currency in South Carolina as the time of secession approached, and could have broken down the essential appearance of unity, the question of coercion became part of the propaganda campaign. In 1863 Unionist William John Grayson bitterly recalled how this aspect of the radical persuasion had operated.

> To induce the simple people to plunge into the volcanic fires of revolution and war, they were told that the act of dissolution would produce no opposition of a serious nature; that not a drop of blood would be spilled; that no man's flocks, or herds, or negroes, or houses, or lands would be plundered or destroyed; that unbroken prosperity would follow the ordinance of secession; that cotton would control all Europe, and secure open ports and boundless commerce with the whole world for the Southern States.[60]

together inspired by politics or racial fears. "As to whether the dissolution will be peaceable," Isaac Hayne wrote on December 10, "there is a great difference of opinion; the Southern States think the chances of war such as to make them prepare for it and they are all consequently arming." Three days after secession, the clouds had darkened, and Hayne confessed that war was a "probable contingency." Letters to Charles Cotesworth Pinckney, III, December 10 and 23, 1860, Charles C. Pinckney, III, Papers, USC.
[59] David Golightly Harris MS Farm Journal, SHC, February 22, 1861. Civil War could also bring the ultimate catastrophe. "Secession will not be a peaceable measure," a Carolina Unionist exclaimed, "it will mean war, and war will mean the emancipation of our slaves." A. Toomer Porter, *Led On! Step by Step. Scenes from Clerical, Military, Educational, and Plantation Life in the South, 1828–1898* (New York, 1898), pp. 115–16.
[60] William John Grayson, *James Louis Petigru. A Biographical Sketch* (New York, 1866), pp. 146–47.

— 6 —

The secession of South Carolina was an affair of passion. The revolution could not have succeeded, and it certainly would not have instilled the astounding degree of unanimity in all classes and all sections that it did, were this not so.[61] The emotional momentum was a function of the intensity of the fear which drove the revolution forward. Divisions, doubts about the wisdom or efficacy of secession were met, or overturned. The ostensible leaders of the movement could not agree on whether they had created this tempest, or had themselves been picked up and carried along by it. Barnwell politician Alfred Aldrich described events in terms which Rhett, and many others could appreciate.

> I do not believe the common people understand it, in fact, I know that they do not understand it; but whoever waited for the common people when a great move was to be made. We must make the move & force them to follow. This is the way of all revolutions & all great achievements, & he who waits until the mind of every body is made up will wait forever & never do any thing.[62]

But there were many of Aldrich's associates who strongly disagreed with this description. Poet William Gilmore Simms drew endless pictures of the "landsturm," his romantic image of the essentially popular nature of the movement for secession. Alfred Huger, with his accustomed anxiety warned his friend Joseph

[61] There were innumerable remarks upon this striking unity. A good sample is this description by a visitor to Charleston. "I have taken pains to ascertain the prevailing sentiment of all classes, and have yet to find a single Southerner who does not prefer disunion before submission to the incoming administration. The young men ardently desire disunion. So do old men, and wise men. The tradespeople wish it, entertaining a consciousness of its disastrous entailment upon their business. The clergy add their counsels on the same side. Reliable men are freely offering their property to maintain secession." J. W. Claxton to "My dear Mr. Jones," November 10, 1860, Bonham Papers, USC. See also the Columbia *Tri-Weekly Southern Guardian*, November 26, 1860; and the Yorkville *Enquirer*, November 29, 1860.

[62] Alfred P. Aldrich to Hammond, November 25, 1860, Hammond Papers, LC.

Holt that "this revolution is beyond the reach of human power. . . . We have no leaders of any prominence," Huger lamented, "the masses are in the front-rank and cannot be restrained."[63] Such a state of affairs did not frighten everyone. Augustus Baldwin Longstreet, then president of South Carolina College in Columbia, wrote to the editor of the Richmond *Enquirer* on December 6 to refute charges that the secession movement in Carolina had been "gotten up" by the politicians for their own selfish purposes.

> Never was there a greater mistake. It is the result of one universal outburst of indignation on the part of the people at Lincoln's election—the unanimous and almost spontaneous resolve, from the mountains to the sea-board, that they never should come under Black Republican rule. . . . You might as well attempt to control a tornado as to attempt to stop them from secession. They drive politicians before them like sheep.[64]

Where was the truth in the kaleidoscope of power? Which way did the lines of action-reaction go, and who ruled whom? Textbook truths usually lie "somewhere in the middle." The answer to this riddle of authority and response probably rested in a like balance. Much has been written to show the deep division of the Southern people, including South Carolinians, on the question of secession. It nearly failed, it is said. More to the point is the fact that it was at last consummated. Against the twin forces of Unionism and fear of secession the revolution carried the day. Analyzing political feeling in the state, all who supported the movement were, of course, prosecessionists, and many of those who opposed

[63] *Simms Letters*, IV, 260–62, 267–70; Alfred Huger to Joseph Holt, November 27, 1860, Joseph Holt Papers, LC.
[64] A. B. Longstreet to Editor, Richmond *Enquirer*, December 6, 1860, quoted in Spartanburg *Spartan*, December 20, 1860. On November 27 Christopher Memminger wrote Virginia politician John Rutherfoord that "it would be impossible" to delay secession. "Our people are so warm, that it would be vain to attempt to retard their movement. In my opinion it is not desirable to do so. Any hesitancy or faltering would harm our deliverance and throw back the States from the position of resistance . . . our great point is to move the other Southern States, before there is any recoil." Memminger to Rutherfoord, November 27, 1860, John Rutherfoord Papers, DU.

immediate action were disunionists as well. Of those who resisted separate secession many may certainly be described as either timid men, men who wanted security, saw it in Southern nationalism, but also feared the unknowable changes that a revolution might bring; men who wanted secession to come, but only as a cooperative venture by a sizable portion of the slave states; or men who believed disunion to be inevitable, if not desirable, but craved some "overt act" of aggression by Lincoln to cite for their consciences and the eye of history. That immediate secession triumphed over these sentiments is the remarkable phenomenon, not the fact that there was still a voice of conservatism in the lower South. Secession has been castigated as a usurpation because a majority allegedly did not support it wholeheartedly; yet these same historians applaud the glories of the American Revolution when all agree that barely one-third favored independence.

The Secession Convention which came together in Columbia on December 17, and in Charleston three days later signed the declaration creating the independent republic of South Carolina, was as representative as it was distinguished.[65] The wealthy, the powerful, the famous were there, as were many unassuming figures from districts across the state. Some had been elected as the traditional leaders in their home districts and parishes. Others perhaps gained the vote of their neighbors at the election on December 6 because of their ardent work for the revolution; one of the representatives from Williamsburg District had gained fame in his association with the Kingstree *Star* during its campaign against abolitionist influences in the region.[66] The people

[65] The December 6 election of delegates was sparsely attended because the action of the convention was a foregone conclusion. The moderate Anderson *Intelligencer* noted that only about one-half of the registered voters in that district had cast their ballots for the uniformly secessionist candidates, but at least half of those not voting were for disunion in some form, and perhaps most of the remainder as well. Anderson *Intelligencer*, December 13, 1860.

[66] The frantic atmosphere which prevailed at the nomination of delegates to the convention is described in the Newberry *Rising Sun*, November 21, 1860. On the average, the convention was composed of much older men than the legislature which had created it. Its membership was composed of most of the leading politicians in the state, including Barnwell Rhett and Memminger, U.S. Senator Chesnut and Congressmen Miles and Orr, five governors, U.S. Judge Andrew Magrath, as well as clergymen, railroad pres-

had indeed responded to Lincoln's election with a ferocious roar; but that in part had been planned and hoped for by men such as Aldrich. Still, once those potent fears of secession which so damaged the plans of disunionists elsewhere were mollified or quelled in South Carolina, the movement for secession *was* a popular revolution, Simms's "landsturm." Shortly after the consummation of secession, Isaac Hayne wrote Charles Cotesworth Pinckney, Jr., to tell him the good news. The feeling in favor of the step throughout the state was so strong, Hayne wrote, that no one, not even the old gadflies Perry and Orr, had "dared to oppose the onward current." When the signed ordinance of secession was held up in crowded Institute Hall a thunderous shout filled the large chamber, and Hayne, "who put but little faith in the shout of the mob, felt at last that in *this*, the people were in earnest."[67] Affairs had been put into such shape by the leaders as to compel a decision for secession. The people did not hesitate to endorse the compulsion. Plebiscitory democracy triumphed in South Carolina.

---

idents, bankers, and many influential planters, merchants and lawyers. [Franklin J. Moses, Jr.], "How South Carolina Seceded, by the Private Secretary of Gov. Pickens of South Carolina." *The Nickell Magazine*, (December 1897), p. 349. See also Ralph A. Wooster, *The Secession Conventions of the South* (Princeton, 1962), pp. 11–25.

[67] Hayne to Pinckney, December 23, 1860, Charles Cotesworth Pinckney, Jr., Papers, USC.

CHAPTER NINE

The Crisis

Secession was the product of logical reasoning within a framework of irrational perception. The party of Abraham Lincoln was inextricably identified with the spirit represented by John Brown, William Lloyd Garrison, and the furtive incendiary conceived to be lurking even then in the midst of the slaves. The election of Lincoln was at once the expression of the will of the Northern people to destroy slavery, and the key to that destruction. The constitutional election of a president seemed to many, North and South, an unjustifiable basis for secession. But it was believed that that election had signalled an acceptance of the antislavery dogmas by a clear majority of Northerners, and their intention to create the means to abolish slavery in America. Lincoln was elected, according to South Carolinians, on the platform of an "irrepressible conflict." This, as James Hammond believed, was "no mere political or ethical conflict, but a social conflict in which there is to be a war of races, to be waged at midnight with the torch, the knife & poison."[1] Submission to the rule of the Repub-

[1] James Hammond, draft of letter to South Carolina legislature, n.d. [November 1860], Hammond Papers, USC. See also James Hammond to Alfred Aldrich, et al., November 6, 1860, James Hammond Papers, LC; Samuel Philson to Jeremiah S. Black, December 12, 1860, Jeremiah S. Black Papers, LC.

licans would be more than a dishonor. It would be an invitation to self-destruction. Implementing the power of the Presidency, and in time the rest of the Federal machinery, slavery would be legally abolished in time. What would that bring? Baptist minister James Furman thought he knew.

> Then every negro in South Carolina and every other Southern State will be his own master; nay, more than that, will be the equal of every one of you. If you are tame enough to submit, Abolition preachers will be at hand to consummate the marriage of your daughters to black husbands.[2]

South Carolinians were repeatedly called on to explain the reasons for secession to their uncomprehending Northern friends and relatives. The description these Northerners received of the dominant new party—and of themselves—must have shocked them. "Who are these Black Republicans?" Sue Keitt, wife of the congressman, wrote to a woman in Philadelphia. "A motley throng of Sans culottes and Dames des Halles, Infidels and freelovers, interspersed by Bloomer women, fugitive slaves, and," worst of all, "amalgamationists."[3] The Republican party was the incarnation of all the strange and frightening social and philosophical doctrines which were flourishing in free Northern society, doctrines which were not only alien but potentially disruptive to the allegedly more harmonious and conservative culture of the slave South. It has been suggested that slavery was merely a handle seized upon by extremists in both sections to wage a battle founded in far deeper antagonism. The election of 1860 proclaimed to the South that it must accept a new order of consolidation, industrialization, and democratization. According to this in-

---

[2] Letter to the Citizens of South Carolina from James Furman, et al., Spartanburg *Spartan*, November 22, 1860, quoting the Greenville *Patriot and Mountaineer*.

[3] Susan Sparks Keitt to Mrs. Frederick Brown, March 4, 1861, Lawrence M. Keitt Papers, DU. "It was apparently impossible for the antislavery advocates to surmise all the implications, to a slavery minded person, that might grow out of the aggression of the abolitionists under the leadership of Lincoln." Gilbert Graffenreid Glover, *Immediate Pre-Civil War Compromise Efforts* (Nashville, 1934), p. 21.

terpretation, secession spelled the rejection of these terms for the preservation of the Union by the old ruling classes.[4]

There is no doubt that those who dominated political life in South Carolina feared the nature of the new social order rising in the North, and feared the party that stood for this order. "The concentration of absolute power in the hands of the North," Lawrence Keitt predicted, "will develop the wildest democracy ever seen on this earth—unless it shall have been matched in Paris in 1789—What of conservatism?—What of order?—What of social security or financial prosperity?"[5] Many Carolinians believed that two separate and distinct civilizations existed in America in 1860, one marked by "the calculating coolness and narrow minded prejudices of the Puritans of New England in conflict with the high and generous impulses of the cavalier of Virginia and the Carolinas."[6] By pecuniary choice and racial compulsion the South had "opted" for slavery and out of that decision had arisen a superstructure of social attitudes and institutions which marked the uniqueness of the slaveholding South.

Moreover, just as Northerners failed to comprehend the Southern view of the world, many Carolinians refused to admit that

[4] Avery O. Craven, *Civil War in the Making, 1815–1860* (Baton Rouge, 1959), p. 35, *ff*. South Carolina planter, poet, and sometime Unionist leader William John Grayson, gave contemporary credence to this idea in his autobiography just before his death in 1863.

> "There are men, South as well as North, who used Slavery as a trumpet to excite sedition, who desired a dissolution of the Union and found Slavery as the readiest means to bring it about, who sought a cement for a party Union and found the negro the strongest within their reach. In both sections of the Union, were short sighted men striving to avoid slight or imaginary evils by rushing into others of incalculable magnitude. In both, were heated shallow partizans scoffing at dangers because their limited faculties were unable to perceive them. . . . They were eager to sever the Union because they saw nothing more in the act than their own personal advantage."

"The Autobiography of William John Grayson," edited by Samuel Gaillard Stoney, *The South Carolina Historical and Genealogical Magazine,* LI (1950), 32. It has even been suggested that abolition was not an issue in the election of 1860. See Mary Scrugham, *The Peaceable Americans of 1860–1861; A Study in Public Opinion* (New York, 1921), p. 58, *et passim*.
[5] Lawrence M. Keitt to Miles, October 3, 1860, William Porcher Miles Papers, SHC.
[6] Speech of E. McIver Law, in Yorkville *Enquirer,* July 5, 1860.

there was, or could be, any moral or idealistic quality in the anti-slavery pillar of the Republican party. Hammond affirmed that if the Republicans could have been defeated at the polls in 1860 and 1864, abolitionism would have been abandoned, for "no great party question can retain its vitality in this country that cannot make a President."[7] A number of his fellow citizens declared that they too rejected the "mock humanity" of the Republicans. The issue was one of political power, they said, of controlling the national government, of party spoils. There was an almost pathetic element in this refusal to admit, and inability to see, the sincerity of the moral quality of abolitionism. Nevertheless, particularly in the private correspondence of unassuming soldiers and farmers, one can see frequent references to resistance to the threat of Northern despotism, to the need to protect certain vaguely understood "rights and privileges," often guaranteed by the Constitution.[8] "I care nothing for the 'Peculiar institution'" claimed one former Unionist, "but I cant stand the idea of being domineered over by a set of Hypocritical scoundrels such as Sumner, Seward, Wilson, Hale, etc. etc."[9]

Still, the conclusion is inescapable that the multiplicity of fears revolving around the maintenance of race controls for the Negro was not simply the prime concern of the people of South Carolina in their revolution, but was so very vast and frightening that it literally consumed the mass of lesser "causes" of secession which have inspired historians. James Hammond recognized the question of economic exploitation, and the fact that Southerners believed in Northern financial and commercial domination is clear. Nonetheless, the issue went virtually unnoticed in private exchanges throughout the year. Some leaders denounced what they

[7] Draft of letter to the South Carolina Legislature, n.d. [November 1860], Hammond Papers, USC.
[8] John Cheves Haskell to his father, Charles Thomson Haskell, August 30, [1861], Haskell Family Papers, SHC; [John Cheves Haskell], *The Haskell Memoirs*, edited by Gilbert E. Govan and James W. Livingood (New York, 1960), p. vi; Franklin Gaillard to Maria Porcher, April 25, 1861, Franklin Gaillard Papers, SHC; John R. Shurley MS Diary, SHC, January 9, 1862; Lawrence M. Keitt to Sue Sparks Keitt, February 11, 1864, L. M. Keitt Papers, DU.
[9] R. N. Hemphill to William R. Hemphill, December 14, 1860, Hemphill Family Papers, DU.

thought was the injustice of the colonial status of the economic South, but this did not touch the hearts of the people, great and low. Attempts to organize such devices as direct steamship trade with Europe, use of homespun cloth, and conventions to promote Southern economic self-sufficiency were, like the more transparent plans for commercial non-intercourse, aimed at wielding the economic power of the region to gain political ends, specifically an end to agitation of the slavery question.[10]

The glorious potential of an independent Southern nation held great emotional appeal for many, but no one was prepared to enter into the perilous business of nation building without some more basic incentive. South Carolina's spokesmen revelled in the contemplation of the political, economic, and social power of the South. They were eager to prove to the North and to the entire world that the South could establish a great nation in her own right.[11] Yet who could fail to see that this was in part a rationalization for the strong desire to escape the moral obloquy heaped upon slaveholders by the North for so many years past;[12] in part an element in the pro-slavery argument, which held a civilization based upon the peculiar institution to be the highest possible culture; and in part a function of the secession persuasion designed to attract and calm adherents to the cause.

As for the "dry prattle" about the constitution, the rights of minorities, and the like, there never was any confusion in the minds of most contemporaries that such arguments were masks for more fundamental emotional issues. Trescot welcomed the speeches of William Seward because they eschewed textual interpretations of the Constitution, and frankly posed the only true and relevant question: "Do the wants of this great Anglo Saxon race, the need of our glorious and progressing free white civiliza-

---

[10] James H. Hammond MS Diary, USC, November 7, 1860. There was also the fact of general prosperity.

[11] William Porcher Miles to Howell Cobb, January 14, 1861, in *The Correspondence of Robert Toombs, Alexander H. Stephens, and Howell Cobb,* edited by Ulrich Bonnell Phillips, American Historical Association, *Annual Report for the Year 1911,* 2 volumes (Washington, 1913), II, 528–29; Hammond to Francis Lieber, April 19, 1860, in Thomas Sergeant Perry, *The Life and Letters of Francis Lieber* (Boston, 1882), pp. 310–11.

[12] Louise Porcher to Jane Pettigrew, January 7, 1861, Pettigrew Family Papers, SHC.

tion require the abolition of negro slavery?" Charles Hutson, son of William F. Hutson, a Beaufort rice planter and a signer of the secession ordinance, phrased the matter more directly. Writing from an army camp near Mt. Vernon, Virginia, in September 1861, Hutson commented on a sermon which described the cause of secession as the defense of the noble right of self-government. "It is insulting to the English common sense of the race which governs here," the young soldier retorted, "to tell them they are battling for an abstract right common to all humanity. Every reflecting child will glance at the darkey who waits on him & laugh at the idea of such an abstract right." And when the family of planter John Berkeley Grimball was torn apart by the secession crisis, his son Louis bitterly denounced his sister for charging that South Carolina had willfully destroyed the Union. "What are you writing?" he gasped. "You speak as if we are the aggressors, and would dissolve the union in Blood shed upon a *mere abstract principle*, when the fact is we are oppressed and are contending for all that we hold most dear—our Property—our institutions—our Honor—Aye and our very lives!" To understand what the revolution was all about, he advised his sister to return home from the North, and become a slaveholder herself. So, writing on a broader canvass, Arthur Perroneau Hayne assured President Buchanan that his acquiescence in secession was a noble act of humanity to the white people of the South.

> Slavery with us is no abstraction—but a *great* and *vital fact.* Without it our every comfort would be taken from us. Our wives, our children, made unhappy—education, the light of knowledge—all *all* lost and our *people ruined for ever.* Nothing short of separation from the Union can save us.[13]

[13] Trescot to Hammond, April 15, 1860, Hammond Papers, LC; Charles W. Hutson to his brother, September 14, 1861, Charles W. Hutson Papers, SHC; Louis M. Grimball to Elizabeth, November 27, 1860, John Berkeley Grimball Papers, SHC; A. P. Hayne to James Buchanan, December 22, 1860, James Buchanan Papers, PaHS. The dispute over Christopher Memminger's "Declaration of the Immediate Causes Which Induce and Justify the Secession of South Carolina from the Federal Union," and Robert Barnwell Rhett's "Address to the Slaveholding States," both drafted in the Secession Convention in December, provides a good illustration of the urge to frame in abstract constitutional terms what were essentially issues of great emotion. See Cauthen, *South Carolina Goes to War,* pp. 73–74.

The people of 1860 were usually frank in their language and clear in their thinking about the reasons for disunion. After the war, for many reasons men came forward to clothe the traumatic failure of the movement in the misty garments of high constitutional rights and sacred honor. Nevertheless, there were two "abstract rights" which were integral to secession, state sovereignty and property rights. No historian could surpass the discussion of these questions by wartime governor Andrew Gordon Magrath. From the fastness of his imprisonment in Fort Pulaski in 1865 Magrath looked back upon the cause of secession with a detachment which had not yet been colored by the sterilization and obfuscation of the post-war remembrance. There were tangential reasons for the revolution, Magrath allowed, but the central "motive power" was the belief that the ascendancy of the Republican party threatened to disturb their "right of property in slaves." To his credit, Magrath did see the rich variety of implications enmeshed in this property right. For those who did not own a slave, Lincoln's election implied that they might never be able to purchase that essential key to social and economic elevation. In addition, the former jurist understood that the people of the antebellum South conceived slavery to be the basis of stability for their social order, the foundation of their economy, and the source of their moral and cultural superiority. State sovereignty was an issue only because the retreat to the inviolability of state's rights had always been a refuge for those fearful of a challenge to their property.[14] Certainly, the "right of property in slaves" is closer to the heart of the problem than "fear of the antislavery movement,"[15] or similar propositions which raise more questions than they answer.

Mid-nineteenth century Americans lived in an age of romanticism. Men had fought for lesser glories than independence and Southern nationalism; and once the terrible momentum was begun, who could say for certain what myths, compulsions, and

[14] Andrew Gordon Magrath to ———, November 20, 1865, Andrew Gordon Magrath Papers, USC. The letter is extensively quoted in Cauthen, *South Carolina Goes to War*, pp. 71–72.
[15] Harold S. Schultz, *Nationalism and Sectionalism in South Carolina, 1852–1860; A Study of the Movement for Southern Independence* (Durham, 1950) p. x.

desires drove men on into revolution and civil war. But somewhere in the intellectual hiatus of the war the clear and concrete understanding of the cause of it all, an understanding shared by those who joined to tear away from the Union, was lost. For the people of South Carolina perpetuation of the Union beyond 1860 meant the steady and irresistible destruction of slavery, which was the first and last principle of life in that society, the only conceivable pattern of essential race control. Perpetuation of the Union, according to Senator Hammond, meant servile insurrection, and ultimately abolition. "We dissolve the Union to prevent it," he told a Northerner in 1861, "and [we] believe, I believe it will do it." Secession was a revolution of passion, and the passion was fear.

> Here we have in charge the solution of the greatest problem of the ages. We are here two races—white and black—now both equally American, holding each other in the closest embrace and utterly unable to extricate ourselves from it. A problem so difficult, so complicated, and so momentous never was placed in charge of any portion of Mankind. And on its solution rests our all.[16]

The nation was led into war in 1861 by the secession of the lower South, not by the desire of the Northern people either to end slavery or bring equality to the Negro. Subsequent generations of Americans came to condemn the racist fears and logic which had motivated that secession, yet the experience of our own time painfully suggests that it was easy to censure racism, but more difficult to obliterate it. If the history of race relations in the United States is an accurate measure, we can assume that there will not and perhaps cannot be a genuine reconciliation between the races, that white and black will never achieve equality because of the fears of the one, and their oppression of the other. But human experience also indicates the possibility of transcending history, for history is neither a lawgiver nor an impenetrable obstacle. As Hammond could not foresee, the solution must and will go on.

[16] Hammond to F. A. Allen, February 2, 1861, Hammond Papers, LC.

Bibliography

I. PRIMARY SOURCES

A. Manuscripts

Alabama State Department of Archives and History, Montgomery
    Benjamin F. Perry Papers
    Executive Papers, Governor Albert B. Moore
Calhoun County Historical Commission, St. Mathews, S. C.
    O. M. Dantzler Papers
University of Chicago Library
    Stephen A. Douglas Papers
Clemson University Library, Clemson, S. C.
    Thomas Green Clemson Papers
Duke University Library, Durham, N. C.
    Iveson Lewis Brookes Papers
    Armistead Burt Papers
    John Caldwell Calhoun Papers
    David Campbell Papers
    Clement Claiborne Clay Papers
    James Dunwoody Brownson DeBow Papers
    George Wymberley Jones DeRenne Papers
    Stephen A. Douglas Papers
    John Fox Papers
    George A. Gordon Papers
    Robert Newman Gourdin Papers
    James Henry Hammond Papers

Hemphill Family Papers
Edward Thomas Heriot Papers
Alfred Huger Papers
David Flavel Jamison Papers
Samuel T. Jones Papers
Daniel W. Jordan Papers
Lawrence Masillon Keitt Papers
Francis Lieber Papers
Vardry McBee Papers
Louis Manigault Papers
Samuel Finley Patterson Papers
Lalla Pelot Papers
Francis Wilkinson Pickens Papers
William W. Renwick Papers
John Rutherfoord Papers
Richard Singleton Papers
South Carolina County Papers, Charleston
Isabella A. R. Woodruff Papers
Benjamin Cudworth Yancey Papers
Emory University Library
Gourdin-Young Papers
Library of Congress, Manuscripts Division
Thomas Francis Bayard Papers
Jeremiah Sullivan Black Papers
Samuel Downing Papers
Lewis R. Gibbes Papers
Henry Gourdin Papers
James Henry Hammond Papers
Joseph Holt Papers
McCarter MS Journal
Manton Marble Papers
Christopher G. Memminger Papers
James Louis Petigru Papers
Pickens-Bonham Papers
Edmund Ruffin Diary
John Tyler Papers
National Archives
Attorney General Papers
Muster Rolls, South Carolina Confederate Organizations
New York Historical Society, New York, N. Y.
James Buchanan Papers
Howell Cobb Papers
Thomas Caute Reynolds Papers

North Carolina Department of Archives and History, Raleigh
    Pettigrew Family Papers
The Historical Society of Pennsylvania, Philadelphia
    James Buchanan Papers
    Claude W. Unger Collection
South Carolina Department of Archives and History, Columbia
    Grand Jury Presentments,
        Charleston District, January 1860
        Kershaw District, December 1860
        Richland District, December 1860
        Spartanburg District, November 1860
        York District, Spring Term, 1859
South Carolina Historical Society, Charleston
    Robert Francis Withers Allston Papers
    Bacot-Huger Papers
    Chesnut-Miller-Manning Papers
    Cheves Family Papers
    Caroline Howard Gilman Papers
    Jacob Sass Schirmer Diary
South Caroliniana Library, University of South Carolina, Columbia
    George Adams Papers
    William Aiken Papers
    Mary Bates Papers
    William Blanding Papers
    Milledge Luke Bonham Papers
    Branchville Vigilant Association Journal
    Iveson Lewis Brookes Papers
    Democratic Party Papers, 1860
    Wilmot N. DeSaussure Papers
    Henry Laurens Garlington Papers
    William Henry Gist Papers
    James Henry Hammond Papers
    James Henry Hammond Diary
    James Henry Hammond Plantation Journal
    Sally Baxter Hampton Papers
    Mary Hort Journal
    John Jenkins Papers
    Kershaw County, Grand Jury Papers, 1805
    Francis Lieber Papers
    Samuel McGowan Papers
    Andrew Gordon Magrath Papers
    Minute Men Association Paper
    James Louis Petigru Papers

Francis Wilkinson Pickens Papers
Charles Cotesworth Pinckney Papers
Charles Cotesworth Pinckney, III, Papers
Joel Roberts Poinsett Papers
William Campbell Preston Papers
Henry William Ravenel Journal
William W. Renwick Papers
John S. Ryan Papers
David Thomson Papers
William Henry Trescot Papers
Williams-Chesnut-Manning Papers
Southern Historical Collection, University of North Carolina at Chapel
    Hill
Daniel Moreau Barringer Papers
Botany Department, University of North Carolina Papers
Iveson Lewis Brookes Papers
John Hamilton Cornish Diary
Elliott-Gonzales Papers
Chesley D. Evans Papers
John Edwin Fripp Plantation Journal
James M. Gage Papers
Franklin Gaillard Papers
David Gavin Diary
John Berkeley Grimball Papers
David Golightly Harris Farm Journal
Haskell Family Papers
William P. Hill Diary
Charles Woodward Hutson Papers
Mitchell King Papers
E. M. Law Papers (microfilm)
Christopher G. Memminger Papers
Nathaniel R. Middleton Papers
William Porcher Miles Papers
James S. Milling Papers
Rosina Mix Papers
Orr-Patterson Papers
Benjamin Franklin Perry Papers (photostats)
Benjamin Franklin Perry Diary
Pettigrew Family Papers
Isaac DuBose Porcher Diary, Stoney-Porcher Papers (microfilm)
Robert Barnwell Rhett Papers
William A. Round Diary, Louis Round Wilson Papers
Edmund Ruffin Papers (microfilm)

Archibald Rutledge Papers
John R. Shurley Diary (microfilm)
James Simons Papers
Singleton Family Papers
Clement L. Vallandigham Papers (typescript)
Benjamin Cudworth Yancey Papers
Virginia Historical Society, Richmond
William Chisolm Papers (typescript)
Virginia State Library, Richmond
Executive Papers, Governor John Letcher

B. OFFICIAL RECORDS AND DOCUMENTS

1. Publications of the South Carolina State Government

Declaration of the Immediate Causes Which Induce and Justify the Secession of South Carolina from the Federal Union and the Ordinance of Secession. Charleston: Evans & Cogswell, 1860.

Journal of the House of Representatives of the State of South Carolina: Being the Session of 1859. Columbia: R. W. Gibbes, 1859.

Journal of the Senate of the State of South Carolina: Being the Session of 1859. Columbia: R. W. Gibbes, 1859.

The Militia and Patrol Laws of South Carolina, December 1841. Published by order of the General Assembly. Columbia: R. W. Gibbes, 1842.

Proceedings of the Democratic State Convention of South Carolina, held at Columbia on the 16th and 17th of April, 1860 for the purpose of electing delegates to the Democratic National Convention, to meet in Charleston 23d April. Columbia: R. W. Gibbes, 1860.

Proceedings of the State Democratic Convention held at Columbia, S. C., May 30–31, 1860. Columbia: Southern Guardian Steam Press, 1860.

South Carolina Reports and Resolutions for the Year 1859. Columbia: R. W. Gibbes, 1859.

2. Other Publications

Annals of Congress, 1789–1824. 24 volumes. Washington: Gales and Seaton, 1834–1856.

The Congressional Globe. Containing the Debates and Proceedings of the First Session of the Thirty-Sixth Congress. Washington: John C. Rives, 1860.

Official Proceedings of the Democratic National Convention held in 1860, at Charleston and Baltimore. Cleveland: Plain Dealer Job Office, 1860.

The Public Laws of the State of South Carolina, from its First Establishment as a British Province down to the Year 1790, inclusive. . . . Edited by John Faucheraud Grimké. Philadelphia: R. Aitkin & Son, 1790.

C. Newspapers

Anderson *Intelligencer,* 1860.
Camden *Weekly Journal,* 1860
Charleston *Daily Courier,* 1859–1860
Charleston *Mercury,* 1859–1860
Columbia *Tri-Weekly Southern Guardian,* 1860
Edgefield *Advertiser,* 1859–1860
Frankfort (Kentucky) *Argus of Western America,* June 20, 1824
Laurens *Herald,* 1860
Newberry *Rising Sun,* 1860
New York *Herald,* 1859, 1860
Pickens *Keowee Courier,* 1860
Spartanburg *Express,* 1860
Spartanburg *Spartan,* 1859–1860
Yorkville *Enquirer,* 1860

D. Published Sources

The Papers of James A. Bayard, 1796–1815. Edited by Elizabeth Donnan. American Historical Association. *Annual Report for the Year 1913.* 2 volumes. Washington: Government Printing Office, 1915, II.

Childs, Arney R. (ed.). *Planters and Business Men. The Guignard Family of South Carolina, 1795–1930.* Columbia: University of South Carolina Press, 1957.

Letters of General James Conner. Edited by Mary Moffet Conner. Columbia: R. L. Bryan Company, 1950.

The Letters of Stephen A. Douglas. Edited by Robert W. Johannsen. Urbana: University of Illinois Press, 1961.

Dumond, Dwight Lowell (ed.). *Southern Editorials on Secession.* New York: The Century Company, 1931.

"The Autobiography of William John Grayson," edited by Samuel

Gaillard Stoney, *The South Carolina Historical and Genealogical Magazine*, XLVIII (1947), 125–33, 189–97; XLIX (1948), 23–40, 88–103, 163–69, 216–44; L (1949), 19–28, 77–90, 131–43, 209–15; LI (1950), 29–44, 103–17.

The Papers of Alexander Hamilton. Edited by Harold C. Syrett and Jacob E. Cooke. (15 volumes.) New York: Columbia University Press, 1961– (1969).

The [John Cheves] *Haskell Memoirs*. Edited by Gilbert Govan and James W. Livingood. New York: G. P. Putnam's Sons, 1960.

Correspondence of Robert M. T. Hunter, 1826–1876. Edited by Charles Henry Ambler. American Historical Association. *Annual Report for the Year 1916*. 2 volumes. Washington: Government Printing Office, 1918. II.

The Writings of Thomas Jefferson. Edited by Albert Ellery Bergh. 20 volumes. Washington: Thomas Jefferson Memorial Association of the United States, 1907.

The Collected Works of Abraham Lincoln. Edited by Roy P. Basler. 8 volumes. New Brunswick: Rutgers University Press, 1953–1955.

"Some Papers of Franklin Pierce, 1852–1862," *American Historical Review*, X (January 1905), 350–70.

Ruchames, Louis (ed.). *A John Brown Reader. The Story of John Brown in His Own Words, In the Words of Those who Knew Him, and in the Poetry and Prose of the Literary Heritage*. Edited and with Introduction and Commentary by Louis Ruchames. New York: Abelard-Schuman, 1959.

The Letters of William Gilmore Simms. Edited by Mary C. Simms Oliphant, Alfred Taylor Odell, and T. C. Duncan Eaves. 5 volumes. Columbia: University of South Carolina Press, 1952–1958.

Mason Smith Family Letters, 1860–1868. Edited by Daniel E. Huger Smith, Alice R. Smith and Arney R. Childs. Columbia: University of South Carolina Press, 1950.

Taylor, Rosser Howard (ed.). "Letters Dealing with the Secession Movement in South Carolina," *Furman University Faculty Studies Bulletin*, XVI (December 1934), 3–12.

The Correspondence of Robert Toombs, Alexander H. Stephens and Howell Cobb. Edited by Ulrich Bonnell Phillips. American Historical Association. *Annual Report for the Year 1911*. 2 volumes. Washington: Government Printing Office, 1913. II.

The Record of the Hon. C. L. Vallandigham on Abolition, the Union, and the Civil War. 3rd edition. Columbus, Ohio: J. Walker & Co., 1863.

E. Articles, Books, Memoirs, and Miscellaneous Writings

Adger, John Bailey. *My Life and Times, 1810–1899.* Richmond: The Presbyterian Committee of Publication, 1899.

Bascom, H. *Methodism and Slavery: with other matters in Controversy between the North and South; being a Review of the Manifesto of the Majority, in reply to the Protest of the Minority, of the Late General Conference of the Methodist E. Church, in the Case of Bishop Andrew.* Frankfort, Kentucky: Hodges, Todd, & Pruett, 1845.

[Brookes, Iveson Lewis]. *A Defence of Southern Slavery. Against the Attacks of Henry Clay and Alexander Campbell. In which much of the False Philosophy and Mawkish Sentimentalism of the Abolitionists is met and refuted. In which it is moreover shown that the Association of the White and Black Races in the relation of Master and Slave is the Appointed Order of God, as set forth in the Bible, and constitutes the best social condition of both races, and the only true principle of republicanism.* By a Southern Clergyman. Hamburg, South Carolina: Robinson & Carlisle, 1851.

[DeBow, James Dunwoody Brownson]. *The Interest in Slavery of the Southern Non-Slaveholder.* Charleston: Evans & Cogswell, 1860.

DeLeon, Edwin. *Thirty Years of My Life on Three Continents.* . . . 2 volumes. London: Ward & Downey, 1890.

[Drayton, William] *The South Vindicated from the Treason and Fanaticism of the Northern Abolitionists.* Philadelphia: H. Manly, 1836.

Elliott, William, *The Letters of Agricola.* . . . Greenville, Office of the Southern Patriot, 1852.

Grayson, William John. *James Louis Petigru. A Biographical Sketch.* New York: Harper and Brothers, 1866.

Great Union Meeting. Philadelphia. December 7, 1859. Philadelphia: Crissy & Markley, 1859.

Grier, R. C. "Public Communication by [Rev.] R. C. Grier, Due West, October 1, 1850," Southern Broadsides Collection, Duke University Library.

Halstead, M[urat]. *Caucuses of 1860. A History of the National Political Conventions of the Current Presidential Campaign.* . . . Columbus, Ohio: Follett, Foster and Company, 1860.

Hammond, James Henry. *Speech . . . Delivered at Barnwell C[ourt] H[ouse], October 29, 1858.* Charleston: n.p., 1858.

Memminger, Christopher Gustavus, *Address of the Hon. C. G. Mem-*

minger, *Special Commissioner from the State of South Carolina, before the Assembled Authorities of the State of Virginia, January 19, 1860.* Richmond: n.d., [1860].

[Miles, James Warley]. *The Relation Between the Races at the South.* Charleston: Evans & Cogswell, 1861.

[Moses, Franklin J., Jr.]. "How South Carolina Seceded, by the Private Secretary of Gov. Pickens of South Carolina," *The Nickell Magazine* (December 1897), 345–51.

Official Report of the Great Union Meeting held at the Academy of Music in the City of New York, December 19, 1859. Published by Order of the Committee of Arrangements. New York: Davie & Kent, 1859.

Paulding, James Kirke. *Slavery in the United States.* New York: Harper and Brothers, 1836.

Perry, Benjamin Franklin. *Biographical Sketches of Eminent American Statesmen; with Speeches, Addresses, and Letters.* Philadelphia: The Free Press, 1887.

———. *Reminiscences of Public Men.* Philadelphia: John D. Avil & Company, 1883.

[Pettigrew, James Johnston]. "The Militia System of South Carolina," *Russell's Magazine,* VI (March 1860), 529–40.

[Porcher, Frederick Adolphus]. "Matters and Things in General," *Russell's Magazine,* VI, (February 1860), 436–45.

Porter, A. Toomer. *Led On! Step by Step. Scenes from Clerical, Military, Educational, and Plantation Life in the South, 1828–1898.* New York: G. P. Putnam's Sons, 1898.

[Pringle, Edward J.]. *Slavery in the Southern States. By a South Carolinian.* Cambridge: J. Bartlett, 1852.

The Pro-Slavery Argument; as maintained by the most distinguished Writers of the Southern States, containing the several Essays on the Subject, of Chancellor Harper, Governor Hammond, Dr. Simms, and Professor Dew. Charleston: Walker, Richards & Company, 1852.

Ruffin, Edmund. *The Political Economy of Slavery; or, The Institution Considered in Regard to its Influence on Public Wealth and the General Welfare.* Washington: Lemuel Towers, 1853.

[Simms, William Gilmore]. *Slavery in America. Being a Brief Review of Miss Martineau on that Subject. By a South Carolinian.* Richmond: White, 1838.

Simons, Thomas Y. *Speech in Favor of South Carolina being Represented in the Democratic Convention, delivered at a Meeting of the Citizens of Charleston, held in Hibernian Hall, February 26, 1860.* Charleston: A. J. Burke, 1860.

Taylor, Richard. *Destruction and Reconstruction: Personal Experiences of the Late War.* New York: D. Appleton & Co., 1879.

Thornwell, James Henley. *The State of the Country: an article republished from the Southern Presbyterian Review.* Columbia: Southern Guardian Press, 1861.

de Tocqueville, Alexis. *Democracy in America.* Edited by Phillips Bradley. 2 volumes. New York: Alfred A. Knopf, 1945.

Townsend, John. *The Doom of Slavery in the Union: Its Safety Out of It; An Address to the Edisto Island Vigilant Association, October 29th, 1860.* Charleston: Evans & Cogswell, 1860.

————. *The South Alone, Should Govern the South, And African Slavery should be Controlled by those only who are Friendly to It.* Charleston. Evans & Cogswell, 1860.

Trescot, William Henry. *Memorial of the Life of J. Johnston Pettigrew.* Charleston: John Russell, 1870.

II. SECONDARY SOURCES

Alden, John Richard. *The South in the Revolution, 1763–1789.* Volume III of Wendell Holmes Stephenson and E. Merton Coulter, editors, *A History of the South.* Baton Rouge: Louisiana State University Press, 1957.

Bernstein, Barton J. "Southern Politics and Attempts to Reopen the African Slave Trade," *Journal of Negro History,* LI (January 1966), 16–35.

Boney, F. N. *John Letcher of Virginia: The Story of Virginia's Civil War Governor.* University, Ala.: The University of Alabama Press, 1966.

Bonner, Thomas N. "Horace Greeley and the Secession Movement," *Mississippi Valley Historical Review,* XXXVIII (December 1952), 425–44.

Boucher, Chauncey S. "The Secession and Co-operation Movements in South Carolina, 1848–1852," *Washington University Studies,* V, (1918).

————. "South Carolina and the South on the Eve of Secession, 1852 to 1860," *Washington University Studies,* VI (1918).

Brent, Joseph L., III. "The Ante-Bellum Origins of Southern Totalitarianism." Paper presented at a session of the Southern Historical Association, Atlanta, Georgia, November 10, 1967.

Brown, William Garrott. *The Lower South in American History.* New York: The Macmillan Company, 1903.

Capers, Henry D. *The Life and Times of C. G. Memminger*. Richmond: Everett Waddey Company, 1893.

Cash, Wilbur J. *The Mind of the South*. New York: Alfred A. Knopf, 1941.

Cauthen, Charles E. *South Carolina Goes to War, 1860–1865*. Chapel Hill: The University of North Carolina Press, 1950.

Craven, Avery Odelle. *Civil War in the Making, 1815–1860*. Baton Rouge: Louisiana State University Press, 1959.

———. *The Coming of the Civil War*. New York: Charles Scribner's Sons, 1942.

———. *The Growth of Southern Nationalism, 1848–1861*. Volume VI of Wendell Holmes Stephenson and E. Merton Coulter, editors, *A History of the South*. Baton Rouge: Louisiana State University Press, 1953.

Crenshaw, Ollinger, "C. G. Memminger's Mission to Virginia in 1860," *Journal of Southern History*, VIII (August 1942), 334–50.

———. *The Slave States in the Presidential Election of 1860*. Baltimore: The Johns Hopkins Press, 1945.

———. "The Speakership Contest of 1859–1860. John Sherman's Election a Cause of Disruption," *Mississippi Valley Historical Review*, XXIX (December 1942), 323–38.

Davis, Robert R., Jr. "James Buchanan and the Suppression of the Slave Trade, 1859–1861," *Pennsylvania History*, XXXIII (October 1966), 446–59.

Denman, Clarence Phillips. *The Secession Movement in Alabama*. Montgomery: Alabama State Department of Archives and History, 1933.

Dubay, Robert W. "Mississippi and the Proposed Atlanta Convention of 1860," *Southern Quarterly*, V (April 1967), 347–62.

DuBose, John Witherspoon. *The Life and Times of William Lowndes Yancey*. 2 volumes. New York: Peter Smith, 1942.

Dumond, Dwight Lowell. *The Secession Movement, 1860–1861*. The Macmillan Company, 1931.

Ellen, John Calhoun. "The Public Life of Richard Yeadon." Unpublished master's thesis, University of South Carolina, 1953.

Fite, Emerson D. *The Presidential Campaign of 1860*. New York: The Macmillan Company, 1911.

Foner, Philip S. *Business and Slavery. The New York Merchants and the Irrepressible Conflict*. Chapel Hill: University of North Carolina Press, 1941.

Franklin, John Hope. *The Militant South*. Cambridge: Harvard University Press, 1956.

Freehling, William W. *Prelude to Civil War: The Nullification Controversy in South Carolina, 1816–1836.* New York: Harper & Row, 1966.

Gettys, James Wylie. "Mobilization for Secession in Greenville District." Unpublished master's thesis, University of South Carolina, 1967.

Glover, Gilbert Graffenreid. *Immediate Pre-Civil War Compromise Efforts.* Nashville: George Peabody College for Teachers, 1934.

Graebner, Norman A. (ed.). *Politics and the Crisis of 1860.* Urbana: University of Illinois Press, 1961.

Hamer, Philip M. *The Secession Movement in South Carolina, 1847–1852.* Allentown, Pennsylvania: H. Ray Haas & Company, 1918.

Heck, Frank H. "John C. Breckinridge in the Crisis of 1860–1861," *Journal of Southern History,* XXI (August 1955), 316–46.

Henry, Howell Meadoes. *The Police Control of the Slave in South Carolina.* Emory, Virginia: n.p., 1914.

Herd, Elmer Don, Jr. "Chapters from the Life of a Southern Chevalier: Lawrence Masillon Keitt's Congressional Years, 1853–1860." Unpublished master's thesis, University of South Carolina, 1958.

Hesseltine, William B. "Some New Aspects of the Pro-Slavery Argument," *Journal of Negro History,* XXI (January 1936), 1–14.

Jordan, Winthrop D. *White Over Black: American Attitudes Toward the Negro, 1550–1812.* Chapel Hill: University of North Carolina Press, 1968.

Kibler, Lillian Adele. *Benjamin F. Perry, South Carolina Unionist.* Durham: Duke University Press, 1946.

———. "Unionist Sentiment in South Carolina in 1860," *Journal of Southern History,* IV (August 1938), 346–66.

Klein, Herbert S. *Slavery in the Americas; A Comparative Study of Virginia and Cuba.* Chicago: University of Chicago Press, 1967.

Klein, Philip Shriver. *President James Buchanan, A Biography.* University Park, Pa.: The Pennsylvania State University Press, 1962.

Knoles, George Harmon (ed.). *The Crisis of the Union, 1860–1861.* Baton Rouge: Louisiana State University Press, 1965.

Lipset, Seymour Martin. *Political Man, The Social Bases of Politics.* New York: Anchor Books, 1963.

Lofton, John. *Insurrection in South Carolina: The Turbulent World of Denmark Vesey.* Yellow Springs, Ohio: The Antioch Press, 1964.

Lowrey, Lawrence Tyndale. "Northern Opinion of Approaching Secession, October, 1859–November, 1860," *Smith College Studies in History,* III (July 1918), 191–257.

MacArthur, William Joseph. "Antebellum Politics in an Up Country

County: National, State and Local Issues in Spartanburg County, South Carolina, 1850–1860." Unpublished master's thesis, University of South Carolina, 1966.

May, John Amasa, and Faunt, Joan Reynolds. *South Carolina Secedes. . . . With biographical sketches of members of South Carolina's Secession Convention. . . .* Columbia: University of South Carolina Press, 1960.

Merritt, Elizabeth. *James Henry Hammond, 1807–1864.* Baltimore: The Johns Hopkins Press, 1923.

Morrison, Chaplain W. *Democratic Politics and Sectionalism. The Wilmot Proviso Controversy.* Chapel Hill: University of North Carolina Press, 1967.

Nevins, Allan. *The Emergence of Lincoln.* 2 volumes. New York: Charles Scribner's Sons, 1950.

Nichols, Roy Franklin. *The Disruption of American Democracy.* New York: Collier Books, 1962.

Nicolay, John G., and Hay, John. *Abraham Lincoln. A History.* 10 volumes. New York: The Century Company, 1890.

Nixon, John T. "The Circumstances Attending the Election of William Pennington . . . as Speaker," New Jersey Historical Society *Proceedings,* 2nd ser., II (1872), 205–20.

O'Connor, Mary Doline. *The Life and Letters of M. P. O'Connor.* New York: Dempsey & Carroll, 1893.

O'Connor, Thomas H. *Lords of the Loom. The Cotton Whigs and the Coming of the Civil War.* New York: Charles Scribner's Sons, 1968.

Olsberg, Robert Nicholas. "William Henry Trescot: The Crisis of 1860." Unpublished master's thesis, University of South Carolina, 1967.

Perry, Thomas Sergeant. *The Life and Letters of Francis Lieber.* Boston: James R. Osgood and Company, 1882.

Potter, David M. "Horace Greeley and Peaceable Secession," *Journal of Southern History,* VII (May 1941), 145–59.

Rainwater, Percy Lee. *Mississippi, Storm Center of Secession, 1856–1861.* Baton Rouge: Louisiana State University Press, 1938.

Rogers, Tommy W. "The Great Population Exodus from South Carolina, 1850–1860," *The South Carolina Historical Magazine,* LXVIII (January 1968), 14–21.

Schultz, Harold S. *Nationalism and Sectionalism in South Carolina, 1852–1860. A Study of the Movement for Southern Independence.* Durham: Duke University Press, 1950.

Scrugham, Mary. *The Peaceable Americans of 1860–1861; A Study in*

Public Opinion. New York: Columbia University Press, 1921.

Sellers, Charles Grier, Jr. *The Southerner as American.* Chapel Hill: University of North Carolina Press, 1960.

Shanks, Henry T. *The Secession Movement in Virginia, 1847–1861.* Richmond: Garrett and Massie, 1934.

Speare, Susan Teague. "The Law of Self-Preservation: The Negro Seaman Acts, 1822–1856." Unpublished master's thesis, University of North Carolina, 1964.

Takaki, Ronald. "The Movement to Reopen the African Slave Trade in South Carolina," *South Carolina Historical Magazine,* LXVI (January 1965), 38–54.

———. "A Pro-Slavery Crusade: The Movement to Reopen the African Slave Trade." Unpublished doctoral dissertation, University of California, Berkeley, 1967.

Taylor, Rosser Howard. "The Gentry of Ante-Bellum South Carolina," *North Carolina Historical Review,* XVII (April 1940), 114–31.

Treudley, Mary, "The United States and Santo Domingo, 1789–1866," *Journal of Race Development,* VII (July 1916), 83–145 (October 1916), 220–74.

Vallandigham, James L. *A Life of Clement L. Vallandigham.* Baltimore: Turnbull Brothers, 1872.

Van Deusen, James G. *Economic Bases of Disunion in South Carolina.* New York: Columbia University Press, 1928.

Venable, Austin L. "The Conflict Between the Douglas and Yancey Forces in the Charleston Convention," *Journal of Southern History,* VII (May 1942), 226–41.

Von Holst, Hermann. *John Brown.* Edited by Frank Preston Stearns. Boston: Cupples and Hurd, 1889.

Wade, Richard C. *Slavery in the Cities; The South, 1820–1860.* New York: Oxford University Press, 1964.

Wells, Tom Henderson. *The Slave Ship Wanderer.* Athens: University of Georgia Press, 1967.

White, Laura A. "The National Democrats in South Carolina, 1852 to 1860," *The South Atlantic Quarterly,* XXVIII (October 1929), 370–89.

———. *Robert Barnwell Rhett: Father of Secession.* New York: The Century Company, 1931.

Woodward, C. Vann. *The Burden of Southern History.* New York: Vintage Books, 1960.

Wooster, Ralph Ancil. *The Secession Conventions of the South.* Princeton: Princeton University Press, 1962.

Index